ALEXANDER HERZEN AND THE ROLE OF THE INTELLECTUAL REVOLUTIONARY

Alexander Herzen

Alexander Herzen and the role of the intellectual revolutionary

EDWARD ACTON

Lecturer in Modern History, University of Liverpool

CAMBRIDGE UNIVERSITY PRESS

CAMBRIDGE

LONDON · NEW YORK · MELBOURNE

Published by the Syndics of the Cambridge University Press
The Pitt Building, Trumpington Street, Cambridge CB2 1RP
Bentley House, 200 Euston Road, London NW1 2DB
32 East 57th Street, New York, NY 10022, USA
296 Beaconsfield Parade, Middle Park, Melbourne 3206, Australia

First published 1979

Printed in Great Britain by
Cox & Wyman Ltd., London, Fakenham and Reading

Library of Congress Cataloguing in Publication Data
Acton, Edward.
Alexander Herzen and the role of the intellectual revolutionary.
Bibliography: p.
Includes index.
1. Hertzen, Aleksandr Ivanovich, 1812–1870.
2. Intellectuals – Russia – Biography. I. Title. DK209.6.H4A64 947′.07′0924
[B] 78–56747
ISBN 0 521 22166 8

TO STELLA

CONTENTS

PREFACE

Alexander Herzen has been the subject of innumerable studies in the Soviet Union and of considerable attention in the west. He was one of the most gifted and attractive figures of nineteenth-century Europe and occupies a key position in the history of the Russian revolutionary movement. His ideas were the most important product of the initial contact between western and Russian socialist thought. They represented a synthesis between the rival philosophies of the Westerners and the Slavophiles. They formed the main bridge between the men of the forties and the men of the sixties, between the gentry and the populist phases of the revolutionary movement. Herzen's work provides one of the central points of reference around which any interpretation of the development of Russian political thought must be formulated. His social philosophy, his political activity, his private life and his literary achievements have been analysed in detail. Much of this work, however, would benefit from being related to a unified picture of his development. For it was of the essence of Herzen that the different aspects of his life and thought were inextricably intertwined: the interaction between private and public life is a central feature of his own portrayal of his experience – the classic autobiography the pattern and scope of which foreshadow Tolstoy's *War and Peace*. My aim in this book has been to evoke such a picture during the central years of his career, by tracing the impact of public events and private tragedy upon his political thought and activity.

The focus is on the years between 1847 and 1863. This period, embracing the abortive western revolutions of 1848 and the Emancipation of 1861, saw the most dramatic and complex changes in his outlook. I have sought to analyse the process of disillusionment through which he passed between 1847 and 1852 and to establish the vantage point from which he laid the foundations of his 'Russian Socialism'. The reappraisal involved provides the background against which the rise and fall of his subsequent career on the Russian political scene may be viewed. It brings to light the impact which the disillusionment he suffered in the west had upon his 'Russian Socialist' vision, and the part this played in forging his pragmatic approach to Russia's problems during the 1850s. And it helps to explain the ambivalent attitude towards revolution he developed in these years – that mixture of respect for the people and disbelief in their political maturity which lay behind his failure to find a politically viable role in the face of government reaction after Emancipation.

I would like to acknowledge the permission of Chatto & Windus and Alfred A. Knopf Inc. to quote extracts from their edition of Herzen's *My Past and Thoughts*, translated by Constance Garnett, revised by Humphrey Higgens.

Among the many friends and relations to whom I am indebted for help in writing this book, I would like particularly to thank: Professor E. Lampert for encouraging my early interest in Herzen and for the stimulus of his knowledge of Herzen and of the period; Professor E. H. Carr for his sympathetic supervision of my doctoral thesis on Herzen; the Master and Fellows of St Edmund's House, Cambridge for assistance during my research and for financing a visit to Russia; and Chris Ryan and Roy Davison for their invaluable advice and criticism. I am also grateful to Mrs Norah Coventry for the combination of care and speed with which she prepared the typescript. Finally, I would like to thank both my parents for all they have done to enable me to study history.

E. D. J. L. D. A.
The University of Liverpool

1

Introduction

In 1847 Alexander Herzen left Russia for western Europe, never to return. 'I found everything I sought – yes, and more,' he would write later, after his first five years abroad, 'ruin, the loss of every blessing and every hope, blows from behind my back, sly treachery, desecration . . . and moral corruption of which you can have no conception' (VIII, 398).[1] Although the west did not give Herzen what he wanted, it did provide the richest personal and political contrast and drama. The product of auto-cratic, serf-ridden, agricultural Russia, he was to spend the rest of his life in the west, witnessing revolution, parliamentary government and indus-trialisation. Born into a cosmopolitan generation he was to confront the growing nationalist current in Europe. Having developed, under the influence of the romantics, an overweening self-confidence, he was to undergo the most devastating blows to his ego. And maturing with the euphoric expectations of utopian socialism, he was to suffer the shock of 1848 and live his most productive years in the calm of Victorian England. He stood at a central crossroad of mid-nineteenth century European history. And he had the attributes to make him an unusually sensitive barometer of the period. He had the intellectual power and insight to form a coherent world-view on which the developments he witnessed made a definite and measurable impact. He had the ability – and the capital – to create an important journalistic role for himself on the political scene in Russia. He had the personality to develop a full private life which played an integral part in what he saw as the series of dis-illusionments he underwent in the west.

[1] This form will be used throughout for reference to A. I. Gertsen, *Sobranie sochinenii* (30 vols., Moscow, 1954–65).

What set his experience apart, in terms both of interest and of complexity, was the sheer range of new events and ideas which impinged upon him, and his responsiveness to them. Political, social and ideological developments in Russia, France, Italy and England, as well as the dramatic events in his own life, affected him intimately. And he was ready, while retaining the same values, to reappraise his assumptions and his role when experience seemed to challenge them. Moreover, the different facets of his life – his political philosophy, his practical activity and his private life – conditioned each other directly. Changes in one facet had immediate repercussions on the others. The development of each facet cannot, in fact, be explained satisfactorily in isolation. And it is only in studying their interaction that something of the man himself may be recaptured.

The nodal point from which their interaction may best be seen is that of Herzen's changing concept of his role. What role did he wish to play and how did his view of that role change and develop? It is a question that might lead to a better understanding of many historical figures: in the case of the author of *My Past and Thoughts* it is crucial. He was led by both temperament and social and intellectual environment to a remarkably self-conscious approach towards the events of his day – as was demonstrated by his life-long penchant for autobiography skilfully woven into the social and political background.[2] Well aware that he was an outstandingly gifted man within a minute elite, he felt himself born to a role on the grand historical scene. And this role demanded that he be fully in tune with the times, with change – 'In history,' he wrote, 'the worst crime is to be uncontemporary' (XIV, 104). From early youth he understood this role in terms of protest against oppression and commitment to an approaching socialist millennium. The content of his socialism was not precisely spelt out when he left Russia, but it involved every aspect of life. He sought to be the personification of the future society. For him this meant both to work for the socialist utopia and to affirm in his own private life the values he hoped to see embodied socially. It was therefore here, in his view of his role, that his experiences, public and private, were most clearly registered. The changes involved were striking. From preoccupation with interpreting the direction of contemporary history, he was led by the triumph of reaction in 1848 to primary emphasis on a private life true to the ideals he now feared he

[2] It was in his mid-twenties that Herzen made his first attempt at an autobiography.

might never see generalised; personal catastrophe drove him from this to the desire for immediate involvement in practical political affairs. And the combination of personal and political disillusionment transformed the historico-philosophical assumptions in terms of which he saw his role.

To understand Herzen's experience in the west in the period from the 1840s to the 1860s, it is necessary first to establish his stance when he left Russia in 1847. This requires an outline of the social context from which he sprang, and of his development within it. Herzen was born into the wealthy ranks of the Russian landowning class. Peter the Great had moulded this class into a nobility, formalised by the Table of Ranks, to serve the state. The army and bureaucracy were to draw on western experience, and the nobility were accordingly forcibly westernised in dress, custom, language and culture. This process cut them off from the illiterate and enserfed mass of the Russian peasantry. And the demands of state service prevented them establishing firm provincial ties of the sort that integrated the contemporary British landowning classes into the society around them.[3] The humiliation of the Church by Peter weakened the ideological hold of Orthodoxy on the better educated and more reflective members of the nobility. And at the same time the insensitive bureaucratic machine which evolved from Peter's initiative destroyed for many the sense of personal loyalty and duty to the Tsar. When, in the course of the latter part of the eighteenth century, the compulsory nature of their state service was gradually eroded, a number of noblemen became professionally as well as ideologically cut off from the Russian state. It was among these elements that radical criticisms of the establishment took root, and that European ideas and the European tour exercised their chief attraction. Catherine II herself enjoyed the attention and stimulation of the *philosophes*, and though she took fright at the implications of the French Revolution, she could not prevent Russia from being drawn into the ensuing war. The march to Paris at the end of the Napoleonic Wars stimulated the hopes and imagination of a broad section of the nobility still within the fold of state service. Six hundred men, some from the very highest families, went on trial for the Decembrist rising of 1825 – the rising which was to provide a sense of revolutionary heritage and a source of inspiration for Herzen throughout his life.

[3] On the eighteenth-century background, see M. Raeff, *Origins of the Russian Intelligentsia* (New York, 1966).

It was to the less heroic majority of the Decembrist generation that Herzen's father belonged. He had enjoyed the European tour, brought back Herzen's German mother, preferred French to Russian and owned a thoroughly western library. An unhappy figure, he personified the political and intellectual impasse created for his kind by a Russia still dominated by autocracy and Orthodoxy. Without himself going beyond cynicism, Iakovlev nevertheless bequeathed a rationalist irony to his son which could be put to more radical purposes.

Herzen was born in 1812, the year in which Alexander I dismissed his reforming minister, Speransky, and faced Napoleon's invasion. The political atmosphere in which he matured was one of almost unrelieved gloom. The ruthless Arakcheev dominated the last years of Alexander's reign, and Nicholas's ascent to the throne in 1825, ushered in with the suppression of the Decembrists, was characterised by an even more stagnant, unimaginative conservatism. The Third Section of His Majesty's Personal Chancellery, the proliferating secret police, epitomised the regime that took as its slogan 'Orthodoxy, Autocracy and Nationality' – the last merely implying the natural loyalty of Russians to the former concepts. Independent thought and initiative were in effect discouraged by a government which adopted the military approach towards every sphere of national life. As a result, those who began to find fault with the Russian *status quo* were provoked to more and more revulsion. Herzen's generation were even more responsive to progressive political and humanitarian principles than his father's most enterprising contemporaries. They were further estranged from the Russian state. Where the Decembrists had for the most part been officers in the Tsar's army, the men of the forties were outside the army and the bureaucracy, and those who had the option – which by no means all the 'gentry' generation of intelligentsia did – rejected the role of serf-owning farmers. Frustrated by an environment which in relative terms was becoming more and more backward socially, politically and economically, they were driven to intransigent denial. Moreover, they had the Decembrist example before them. To some extent they could draw progressive ideas from Russian poets and writers. And their political impotence, borne in upon them by the hopeless failure of the Decembrists, attracted them to an approach towards political and social progress which stressed ideas and philosophy at the expense of more tangible levers of change. Both the intensity and the nature of Herzen's approach must be seen in this context.

The particular features of Herzen's outlook derived from his personal experience of Russia. At home he was the emotional focus of his father, his mother, and to some extent the household serfs. Quick and attractive, he aroused near adulation as a child. At university he was a centre of attention and he was the acknowledged heart of his circle of friends in the thirties and forties. He developed an enormous, ebullient ego. In the poet Ogarev he found, while they were still boys, a kindred spirit with a similarly romantic though less egocentric view of life. The friendship they developed seemed to Herzen the épitome of what life could offer. Perhaps most important of all was his relationship with Natalie, which evolved from cousinly affection to the most intense romance. Natalie's devotion played a vital part in heightening his self-esteem, and in creating the exalted view of life with which he came to the west. For while in exile in the provincial town of Vyatka (1835–8) he underwent a crisis of confidence which shook him deeply. Cut off from his university friends, and bored by his job in the local administration, he felt corrupted by the 'vulgar remarks, dirty people, mean ideas and coarse feelings' which surrounded him (*Past*, 232).[4] He was humiliated in his own eyes by his petty interests and above all by what he saw as a sordid affair with a woman whom he felt he deceived since he had no desire to marry her. His dishonourable intentions were clearly exposed by the untimely death of her husband. Natalie appeared as his Beatrice leading him back to the heights his ego demanded. Their courtship was carried on in the most heady, romantic correspondence of the period. Encouraged by his fiancée and A. L. Vitberg, the mystical Russian architect with whom he was living at the time, Herzen passed through a religious period during which he saw their relationship as symbolic of the regenerative power that love would soon exercise over the world. [5] Although the religious mood would fade, and their marriage (1838) would suffer some strain during the forties, Natalie's devotion remained a cornerstone of his self-esteem. When he came to write his memoirs it was his early married life which evoked his most lyrical and self-confident lines. 'There was not

[4] This form will be used throughout for reference to *My Past and Thoughts. The Memoirs of Alexander Herzen*, translated by Constance Garnett, revised by Humphrey Higgens (4 vols., New York, 1968). I have used this translation for the 4 volumes of Herzen's works covered except when I have preferred my own translation, where reference is made to A. I. Gertsen, *Sobranie sochinenii* (30 vols., Moscow, 1954–65).

[5] On Herzen's ordeal in the 1830s, see F. F. Seeley, 'Herzen's "Dantean" Period', *Slavonic and East European Review*, XXXIII (1954), 44–74.

the shadow of a sad memory, not the faintest dark foreboding; it was all youth, friendship, love, exuberant strength, energy, health and an endless road before us' (*Past*, 392). His romantic image of their love, their relationship and his consciousness of the envy of others for their idyllic home cast a glow over his whole view of life. He developed and left Russia with what he called 'an overweening confidence in life' (*Past*, 1859). His ego, his extraordinarily gifted and vibrant personality gave him a sense of the richness and beauty of life unusual among his contemporaries and reminiscent rather of the receding age of Pushkin. It would be tested by experience, but when he emigrated, this sense, this sheer *joie de vivre* inspired an intense personal aspiration to lead the full life.

Herzen's lofty image of what life could be chafed against the interference of authority to produce a sweeping denial of the real in the name of the ideal. The oppressive cossetting of a morose and hypochondriac father served as a foretaste of political constrictions to follow.[6] He recalled identifying with his father's oppressed serfs and believed that the sight of their treatment sparked off his lifelong commitment to liberty. His discovery that in the eyes of the Russian state he was illegitimate, since his father had not married his mother in the Orthodox Church, gave Herzen a sense of independence and defiance of that state. The young Ogarev developed a similar protest against the *status quo*. They shared a heady view of their own historical mission in the name of this protest. They identified with the heroes of December 1825. The romantic, idealistic atmosphere they breathed is captured by the scene of their famous vow, on the Sparrow Hills overlooking Moscow, to dedicate themselves to the struggle for freedom. 'Flushed and breathless we stood there mopping our faces,' recalled Herzen. 'The sun was setting, the cupolas glittered, beneath the hill the city extended farther than the eye could reach; a fresh breeze blew on our faces, we stood leaning against each other and, suddenly embracing, vowed in the sight of all Moscow to sacrifice our lives to the struggle we had chosen. This scene may strike others as very affected and theatrical, and yet twenty-six years afterwards I am moved to tears as I recall it; there was a sacred sincerity in it' (*Past*, 69). Their feeling of isolation, both now and in the circles of the

---

[6] The view that his home life was a crucial factor provoking Herzen's rebellion against authority has been argued in detail by M. Malia, *Alexander Herzen and the Birth of Russian Socialism, 1812—1855* (Cambridge, Mass., 1961), pp. 13–24.

thirties and forties, increased their sense of their own historical im-portance.[7] Political opposition never seemed more noble and glamorous than in the Russia of the 'remarkable decade'. The articulate opposi-tion was so small, the odds so overwhelming, the future promise so great.

The point is not to imply an element of posturing, of insincerity in Herzen's social and political crusade: the everpresent offence of serfdom, on which he knew his own privileged opportunities had depended, guaranteed against that. In any case, as a young man he felt the direct impact of government interference in his own life. He was accused of sedition, imprisoned and suffered two intensely frustrating periods in provincial exile (II, 212–13). Political conditions in Russia made it impossible for him to separate his private life from political questions, even if such separation had been theoretically possible. Herzen in fact did not see it as possible even in theory. In his view, sheer lack of social involvement was the cause of Natalie's tendency to morbid intro-spection, which at times seemed to mar their married life. And the example of his father's generation convinced him that, without social and political commitment, the 'superfluous man's' life is bound to be aimless and distorted. Both his novels, *Who is to Blame?* and *Duty before All* (the latter written after he emigrated) illustrated how one-sided characters were destroyed by the narrowness of their purely personal interests. The point that must be made is, rather, that the socio-political crusade in the name of freedom for all, for the mass of the peasantry, was not set over against but was part of his aspiration to the full life. His literary heroes, such as Schiller's Karl Moor, 'did not cut themselves off by love from general interests of citizenship, art, science; on the contrary, they brought all its animation, all its ardour into these spheres, and, on the other hand, they carried the breadth and scale of these worlds into their love' (II, 68).

Herzen's personal experience of Russia under Nicholas moulded the three central features of his outlook in the forties. In the first place, he saw the overriding problem facing contemporary thinkers and society as the reconciliation of the individual and the community. The free

[7] See I. Berlin, 'A Marvellous Decade, 1838–1848', *Encounter* (June 1955), 34–5, and P. Shashko, 'Unity and Dissent among the Russian Westerners' (Ph.D. Dissertation, University of Michigan, 1969), Chapters I–VI, on the atmosphere of the circles. M. Perkal', *Gertsen v Peterburge* (Leningrad, 1971), brings out Herzen's personal acquaintance with major establishment figures in Russian society, which doubtless increased this sense of importance.

individual and the just and cohesive society were his supreme ideals. And
his conception of man as inherently social and political, his view that a
satisfying private life implies involvement in 'general interests', not only
removed any fundamental contradiction between the two, but made
them complementary. The second point is that his outlook was imbued
with optimism. He confidently expected the 'future reformation' which
would resolve the problem. Finally, the balanced and rich individual life
was not merely the end product of this socialist regeneration: he aspired
to it himself. Even if the political dimension of his life was to be lived in
working towards utopia and not enjoying it, even if appalling social
injustice and oppression of the individual continued, he wanted the full
life himself, now. It is in terms of these three points that the controversial
question of his attitude to western thought and society in the forties may
best be understood.

Herzen was brought up on thoroughly western intellectual fare. He
was given private lessons in history and language by western tutors. Like
many of his peers he was at ease in French and German. Lonely and
intelligent, as a boy he enjoyed reading and made full use of his father's
library. He tasted Pushkin and Ryleev, but his childhood favourites were
Schiller, Voltaire and Rousseau;[8] he greatly admired Shakespeare and
Goethe; as a young man he encountered many of the ideas of Schelling
and soon after leaving university he discovered the Saint-Simonists;
during the thirties and forties he read Blanc, Fourier, Proudhon, Sand
and Considérant, among other French authors of the left;[9] he was
delighted by Feuerbach and made a close study of Hegel.[10] He was in a
position from his earliest youth to draw on the western classics and on the
great romantics, socialists and philosophical idealists of the period. That
they interacted with his environmentally shaped preoccupations and
figured in his thought and work throughout his life was readily acknowl-

---

[8] Malia, *Alexander Herzen*, and R. Labry, *Alexandre Ivanovic Herzen* (Paris,
  1928), give detailed treatment of Herzen's early intellectual mentors. Labry
  provides a table of the works read by Herzen between 1842 and 1845, pp.
  307–11. On Schiller's influence, see also M. Malia, 'Schiller and the Early
  Russian Left', in H. McLean, M. Malia, G. Fischer eds., *Russian Thought
  and Politics* (The Hague, 1957), pp. 169–200.
[9] On Proudhon's influence, see R. Labry, *Herzen et Proudhon* (Paris, 1928),
  and M. Mervaud, 'Herzen et Proudhon', *Cahiers du Monde Russe et
  Soviétique*, XII (1971), nos. 1–2, 110–88, which includes their
  correspondence.
[10] On Hegel's influence, see M. Mervaud, 'Herzen et la Pensée Allemande',
  Cahiers du Monde Russe et Soviétique, V (1964), 32–73.

edged by Herzen himself. He paid particular tribute to Schiller, Saint-Simon, Proudhon and Hegel. Their ideas offered positive attraction as well as compensation for the frustrations of Russian life. Yet it does not follow that his ideas were a mere reflection of western thought. The Russian intelligentsia as a whole would draw from foreign thinkers those elements which helped them to solve their own problems. When they were enamoured of a whole body of ideas, they interpreted them in accordance with their own predilections. The particular impact on Herzen of western philosophical idealism and western socialism must be seen in this light.[11]

He was fully involved in the philosophical debates which characterised the first half of the nineteenth century in Russia. The outlook with which he came to the west was informed by his reading in pure philosophy, and he always considered a knowledge of Hegelianism, 'the algebra of revolution', essential for a man to be 'modern' (*Past*, 402–3). But concentration on pure philosophy was engendered by political impotence and censorship, and in Herzen's case at any rate, once out of this rarefied atmosphere, his primary social and personal interests asserted themselves explicitly. 'An exclusively speculative tendency,' he later remarked, 'is utterly opposed to the Russian temperament' (*Past*, 397). The story of his development after his emigration to the west in 1847 did not involve any shift in his basic philosophical values, and the changes in his concept of his role did not follow from purely philosophical insights.[12] However, in 1840 when he returned from exile to Moscow, he found Hegel in vogue. He had not abandoned his sense of being more concerned with real life and social problems than the Stankevich and early Slavophile circles, but since the German philosopher dominated

---

[11] Recently there has been a reaction against the view, epitomised by Malia, that Herzen's generation of intellectuals were 'alienated' from Russian society, and that this is the basic explanation for their political ideals. V. C. Nahirny, 'The Russian Intelligentsia: from Men of Ideas to Men of Convictions', *Comparative Studies in Society and History*, IV (1962), no. 4, 403–35; J. L. Scherer, 'The Myth of the "Alienated" Russian Intellectuals' (Ph.D. Dissertation, Indiana University, 1968). While Herzen later certainly exaggerated his reaction to his environment before 1842, he did withdraw, emigrate, engage in revolutionary activity and become estranged from most of his Russian friends. However inherently attractive the intellectual currents from the west, the source and nature of his receptivity to them lay in a growing reaction against his Russian environment.

[12] See E. Lampert, *Studies in Rebellion* (London, 1957), on Herzen's philosophical development. Lampert concludes that his philosophical views were fully formed by the time he left Russia, p. 198.

the field of intellectual debate, he now plunged into the study of his thought.

In 'Dilettantism in Science' (1842–3) and 'Letters on the Study of Nature' (1845) he made the most important critique of Hegel from the Russian left. His approach to Hegel has generally been seen as a search for philosophical guarantees of the socialist utopia for which he yearned.[13] The philosophy of history, an interpretation of history which would bolster their rejection of the Russian *status quo*, was a primary concern of both Westerners and Slavophiles. And in so far as he accepted Hegel's system, he did see in the dialectic an explanation for the vicissitudes of an historical process which could be seen to be moving forward – and forward far beyond the realm of ideas and the contemporary Prussian state into a utopian future uniting thought and action, the individual and society. He could enthuse over the prospect of the Ideal realising itself (III, 64–88). But Hegel did not create his optimism, and even in the mid-forties his system could provide only qualified support for it in Herzen's eyes. For Herzen questioned the pantheist implications of Hegel's philosophy. Rather than agonising over the rival claims of materialism and idealism, he rejected an Absolute dominating human development because of his prior affirmation of the individual.[14] Moreover, personal experience made him question any rational principle at all in history: the uphill work of restoring Natalie's morale was destroyed by sheer ill-fortune – their son Sasha's illness (II, 316–17). An alarming storm made him ponder, in his diary, the helplessness of man amidst 'the terrible vortex of chance' (II, 370). The discovery that individual men are subject to chance and guaranteed nothing, whatever capacities they may feel in themselves, led him to question any purpose, any definite direction, in history in general. It is comforting 'to think that the fate of man, for example, is secretly preordained, to try to unravel this mystery, to grasp something', but in reality 'there is no concealed secret about the life of each man' (II, 286). He was struck by the earth's dependence on arbitrary developments in the solar system: the whole world, animals, plants, and man could be instantly destroyed – 'It is a terrible thing, but undeniable' (II, 369). He warned against relying on 'a dream about the future which will never be realised

[13] See, for example, A. I. Volodin, *V poiskakh revoliutsionnoi teorii (A. I. Gertsen)* (Moscow, 1962), Chapter 2.

[14] Herzen did not settle in his own mind the dispute between materialism and idealism. See Lampert, *Studies in Rebellion*, pp. 198–205; Volodin, *V poiskakh revoliutsionnoi teorii*, pp. 31–43.

in line with our thought' (II, 346). This scepticism prevented Herzen
from imbibing deeply a rationally constructed philosophy of history
which saw an idea being inevitably realised – and by 1847 he had rejected
Hegel's system. But his optimism was intact. Its source lay deeper than
any logical justification drawn from western philosophy – it lay primarily
in the conjuncture of his personality and Russian reality. Only political
and personal blows could undermine what was essentially an emotional
assumption.

If Herzen rejected the structure of Hegelian idealism while deriving a
certain encouragement from it, his debt to western socialist thought was
of a rather similar kind. As with Hegel, however, he was at first very
impressionable. The Saint-Simonists, Blanc, Fourier and Proudhon, he
believed, were working on the same problem as he was. They were not
isolated malcontents nor impotent speculators, but confident prophets
and analysts of an impending reformation. He approached their work
with the question 'how will it be?' rather than 'will it be?' or 'how can we
help to bring it about?' Indeed during the early forties he seemed at times
to adopt wholesale their prescriptions for the future. He was attracted by
their critique of the political and economic domination of the
bourgeoisie, and was excited by their vision of total transformation,
economic equality, true republican freedom, feminine emancipation and
the overthrow of religion. 'In the future epoch,' he would write with
enthusiasm after reading George Sand, 'there will be no marriage, the
wife will be free from slavery . . . Free relationships of the sexes, public
education of children and the organisation of property. Morality, conscience and not the police or public opinion will determine the details of
relationships' (II, 290). And in 1843 he recorded the general impression
he had formed: 'Events will show the form, the flesh, the strength of the
reformation. But its general sense is clear: the public control of property
and capital, communal living, the organisation of labour and of wages
and the right to private property placed on different foundations' (II,
266).

Western authors and his view of western society thus reinforced his
concern for social solidarity, but now for the sake of the masses rather
than for the individual personality, for economic rather than primarily
aesthetic reasons. From the books and articles of men of industrialising
countries he learned of the sense of social dissolution particularly acute in
France after the Napoleonic wars. He was made conscious of the injustice
and wretched poverty which characterised early capitalism, and of the

unbridled individualism to which it might be attributed. For a period
this western concern increased his consciousness of the claims of the
Russian peasant masses *as opposed* to those of individuals like himself.
And this led him to see on the 'banner' of the coming epoch, 'not the
individual but the commune, not liberty but fraternity, not abstract
equality but the organic division of labour' (II, 336). It is symptomatic of
the broad spectrum of concern for social cohesion in the west which
affected Herzen that it should have been a conservative baron from
Germany who drew his attention to the Russian peasant commune as a
possible answer to the problem. Both socialist and conservative protests
were initially very similar in the west, seeking a replacement for communal religion and liberal optimism as a foundation for social solidarity.[15] The sympathy between Herzen and the Slavophiles over the
commune reflected a similarly widespread concern within Russia to
avoid western atomisation. At any rate, for a while Herzen did toy with
the commune as the solution. But while still in Russia he rejected it. Both
his prior commitment to the free flowering of the individual, and his
optimism limited the influence that western anxiety could bring to bear
upon him. In the later forties his aspiration to the full life was at its most
intense. And he could not overcome his sense that the commune
absorbed, limited, constricted the individual.[16] During his final two
years in Russia he left little comment on the commune and the whole
thrust of his thought was towards a total reconciliation for which it was
inadequate. His optimism led him to seek a higher ideal: the individual
and the community, freedom and fraternity were compatible to the very
full.

On reflection Herzen was inclined to modify radically the predictions
he had at first taken almost uncritically from western authorities – he
quickly came to see the forced removal of children from their mothers as
barbaric. In part his more critical attitude reflected growing independence of judgement. But basically the influence of western socialists
on the content of his socialism was not more positive because their
preoccupations and approach were not the same as his. In common with
other members of the intelligentisa, he showed a remarkable lack of
interest in the economic and industrial aspects of their thought, con-

---

[15] See G. Lichtheim, *Marxism* (London, 1971), on the consciousness of this
problem in mid-nineteenth-century Europe, pp. 25–6.

[16] Herzen expressed these criticisms even during 1844, the year in which he
took the commune most seriously while still in Russia (II, 334).

sidering how central these were to western socialists.[17] He did not see economic inequality as the greatest evil, and economic forces played a subsidiary role to that of ideas among his interests and in his understanding of the development of social and political life. The rigid conservatism of the Russian state ensured that his vision soared not only beyond such mundane steps as the abolition of serfdom but beyond the concrete organisation of a socialist society. Whether it was their failure to integrate philosophy into their analyses, or the constriction on the individual that he detected in their programmes, he found something lacking in all western socialists.

To depict Herzen's outlook as the passive creation of western ideas, is, then, clearly false. Yet his interest in and debt to western thinkers and western society was extremely deep. The point that must be made in placing him on the Westerner–Slavophile spectrum is not that he was intellectually uncritically receptive, but that he was emotionally involved. He identified with western strivings, and specifically with those of France. This is in no way to deny that his first love was Russia, that his pride in her had been nourished since boyhood by tales of Borodino, the defeat of Napoleon and the march to Paris. He could enthuse over the potential in the Russian peasant (II, 217) and speculate on the possibility of the Slavs solving the problem of contemporary man (II, 336). To see socialism realised in Russia would be for him the highest reward. Nor is it to deny his early interest in the commune, and his emphasis that the Slavophiles were exaggerating the hope rather than inventing the possibility.[18] But in the mid-forties he rejected the commune, and for all his love of Russia he could not overlook the unfavourable contrast with Europe in terms of past achievements and imminent prospects of progress towards freedom. It was because of this that he became so caught up in the future of the west. The twin ideals which lay at the root of his

---

[17] Analysing Herzen's political thought before he left Russia is of course complicated by the restrictions of censorship, though such works as his novel *Who is to Blame?* (1844) expressed clearly enough his hostility to the existing social and political structure, his sympathy for the peasantry, and his frustration at the helplessness of men of his own stamp. But in fact even in the privacy of his diary his properly political and economic analyses did not go beyond the kind of brief formula quoted above.

[18] 'Our Slavophiles talk about the communal basis, about how we have no proletariat, about the sharing of the land – these are all good germs ... but they forget, on the other side, the absence of any respect for self, the stupid endurance of every oppression, in a word, the [im]possibility of living in such conditions' (II, 288).

outlook – his socialism and his personal aspiration to the full life – not
only permitted but made necessary a profoundly cosmopolitan approach
rather than preoccupation with Russia's claims. For the conditions of
Russia, the oppressive sense of stagnation, the smallness, helplessness
and isolation of his 'circle', the evident strength of the regime and the
passivity of the masses presented an overwhelming denial of these ideals.
And Herzen often voiced the deep gloom this could induce: 'Our position
is hopeless,' he would write in his diary, 'because it is false, because
historical logic shows that we are outside the needs of the people and
our fate is desperate suffering' (II, 278). The fact that he did not despair
but, more than any of his contemporaries, maintained a sweeping
optimism about the 'future regeneration' and a determination himself
to find 'a wide arena' must be seen in the context of the European
dimension.

The west, and above all France, was the home of revolution; it was
there that concrete steps had been taken in the past, it was there that the
best work was being done on the approaching millennium, and it was
France which offered the greatest hope of an imminent sequel in the
direction of socialism. From boyhood he had identified with the heroes of
1789 and 1793. He was fully involved in the hopes and disappointments
of 1830. His diary of the 1840s reflects his cosmopolitanism, his delight at
events infinitely distant from Russia. He was thrilled by the release, in
the face of the wishes of the British establishment, of the Irish nationalist
O'Connell. 'This event is universal,' he wrote in 1844, 'its importance is
incalculable ... the poor petty Slavophiles! ... The soil of Europe is
holy, blessings on it, blessings!' (II, 380–1). Progress towards liberty in
Europe provided his utopian hopes with support at a level incomparably
deeper than the logical constructs of Hegel. Victory there was his victory
– both his own and Natalie's reactions to the events of 1848 would prove
the point. And even before the great transformation began, while the
bourgeoisie still dominated the west, he saw there the relative freedom
which could enable him to lead an integrated public and private life
himself. He did not wish to accept the fate of a victim of Russia's
backwardness: his order of priorities was not such that he would be a
stoical martyr for Russia's future. He wanted to take part in the vibrant
intellectual and social search he saw in the west. Long before the opportunity to emigrate arose, he yearned to take Natalie there to begin a free
and rich life (II, 211). And when the chance at last arrived, he seized
upon it, took no trouble to keep the road home open, and quickly

adopted western customs and friends. To overlook this emotional cosmopolitanism, to see his development in terms of a dominant nationalism
which took precedence over his humanist ideal and personal aspiration to
the full life would be to distort his outlook and make his subsequent
experience incomprehensible.[19]

His yearning to believe in an approaching millennium, then,
interacted with the evidence and hope which Europe seemed to offer.
Without building up too detailed a picture of the structure and operation
of socialist society, he was able to associate the tone, the extremism of
western schemes with his own far more psychological approach to the
changes required. Annenkov has left a slightly jaundiced but useful
first-hand account of the socialism of Herzen and his friends during the
forties. It consisted in 'more or less fortuitously combined and coor-
dinated collections of startling, stupefying and imperious aphorisms'.
Citing several examples, including those of Proudhon and Weitling, he
concluded that 'The strength of these thunder-bearing postulations lay
not in their logical inevitability but in the fact that they heralded some
new order of things and seemed to throw beams of light into the dark
vista of the future, making discovery there of unknown and felicitous
domains of work and pleasure about which each person judged according
to the impressions he received in the brief instant of one or another such
flash of light'.[20] The irony is excessive, at any rate where Herzen's
knowledge of the works of socialist thinkers is concerned. But even he
did not gain a concrete and consistent picture of socialist society but
rather an insubstantial vision and a strong sense of movement into which
he could project his own preoccupations.

In the forties Herzen equated his role with that of socialist writers in
the west. Like them he would analyse the basis of the change society must
and will undergo. This was the role in 'general affairs' with which he
began his European adventure. But the terms in which he approached
the central problem of reconciling the free individual with social cohesion
reflected the Russian socio-political air he breathed. Ideas were the most
visible area of exhilarating change, and it was to ideas rather than to
economics or institutions, that he looked for the dynamics of change. He

---

[19] The point entails a basic corrective to the widespread interpretation which
portrays Herzen in terms of a life-long messianic and revolutionary
nationalism. A. Koyré, *Études sur l'histoire de la pensée philosophique en Russie*
(Paris, 1950); Malia, *Alexander Herzen*.

[20] P. V. Annenkov, *The Extraordinary Decade*, translated by I. R. Titunik
(Michigan, 1968), p. 141.

sought a psychological liberty not to be enjoyed in splendid isolation but as the basis for social transformation. It was from this viewpoint that he would analyse western society when he emigrated. And during the forties it was friction over this approach which constituted a central cause of the rift in his circle – the rift which finally precipitated his emigration. Both he and Natalie felt themselves driven to confrontation with their friends by the conviction that they had 'with great labour worked out for themselves an inward liberty', and by frustration that the others should refuse to see the light. Their friends objected because, as Natalie reported N. M. Satin's opinion, they found her 'cold, hard and completely under the influence of Alexander, who was spreading a theory of false self-sufficiency and egoism' (*Past*, 1007).[21]

What Satin called a theory was not in fact something external to Herzen, a mere thing to be juggled with. It informed the very structure of his thought and derived from his most basic assumptions. The point of departure was his profoundly optimistic view of human nature. 'The egoism of the developed, thinking man,' he believed, 'is noble' (II, 97). His contemporaries were struck by this straightforward faith.

> As if to restore some equilibrium in his moral make-up, Nature had taken measures to implant in his soul one indomitable belief, one invincible proclivity: Herzen believed in the noble *instincts* of the human heart; his analysis would fade away and stand in awe before the instinctive promptings of the moral organism, as before the single, indubitable truth of existence.[22]

In fact, one source of the tension in his later work was that he was led to question precisely this. But when he left Russia, this faith was crucial to his approach. His early romantic and idealist reading and his relationships with Ogarev and Natalie, the warmth of friendship that characterised his close-knit, isolated circle, and his intuitive faith in the simple nobleness of the peasants, which was derived in part from pity, may be cited as contributing to this confidence. A lofty evaluation of his own nature and instincts – and, despite the proportions of his self-

---

[21] In her memoirs T. A. Astrakova, another member of the circle, recalled finding Herzen spoilt and wanting adulation. *Literaturnoe nasledstvo*, 63 (1956), 547–54.

[22] Annenkov, *The Extraordinary Decade*, p. 87. It was the whole moral organism, reason and conscience as well as passion and instinct, in which Herzen placed such faith.

esteem, he does appear to have been a warm, generous and self-controlled man – was probably central. He was himself the prototype of what men could and, unfettered, would be. Boldly and clearly he declared his faith in the potential harmonious, free and uncoerced cohesion of men:

> To be humane in a human society is certainly not a
> burdensome obligation, but the simple development of an
> internal need; no one would say that a bee has a bounden duty
> to make honey; it makes it because it is a bee ... To do
> nothing anti-human is natural to every human nature, for this
> not even much intelligence is necessary; I don't give anyone the
> right to demand from me heroism, lyrical poetry etc., but
> everyone has the right to demand that I do not insult him and
> that I don't insult him by insulting others. (II, 94)

Does this faith in man, asked Herzen rhetorically, imply that 'all passions, debauchery, gluttony are fully justified?' Not at all. Only 'a degraded man has degraded desires ... The more developed a man, the purer his breast becomes and the harder it becomes for him to believe that white is black, that everything natural is a crime, that everything giving real pleasure must be shunned.' Passions regarded as base are not base in themselves – 'in themselves they are good, but debased by repression' (II, 395).

It was this repression, perpetuated by laziness and habit, which Herzen blamed for the fact that man had never achieved the desirable state he believed to be natural. And the source of this repression he saw not in economic 'alienation' or political oppression, but in the internal, psychological state of man. Man repressed his own yearnings because he imbibed ideas which made him distrust his passion, his instincts, his conscience, his reason, ideas, in short, which humiliated him. Religion had been a prime source of this humiliation, preaching dualism, the divorce of body and soul, the struggle between instincts and conscience, man's duty to crush his evil urges. In the Middle Ages,

> man was ashamed of his thoughts and feelings, and afraid of
> them ... of course he abandoned himself to joys and pleasures
> even then, but he did so with the feeling with which a Moslem
> drinks wine, yielding to an indulgence which he had
> renounced. Giving way to his yearnings, he felt humiliated
> because he could not resist a desire which he could not deem
> just. (III, 241)

Ashamed, men accepted the authority of external rules and directives from the church. It is only because they are deceived and humiliated in their own eyes that men's moral perception becomes distorted, and it is only because it is distorted that they accept external guidance, external domination. There is one escape from this vicious circle – developed egoism. Man must trust his unfettered nature, he must believe in his natural goodness, and thereby he will free himself from the 'slanders' which he has accepted and which perpetuate his subservience.

Herzen saw definite political implications in this analysis. If only they could respect their true nature men would at once see they had no need of external constraint, religious or secular, and would reject it. He saw an historical development towards this liberation. When man became conscious, he inevitably developed 'the need to save *something of his own* from the vortex of chance', to attach supreme value to something (II, 154). But 'they always respect something outside themselves – father and mother, superstitions of their family, the morals of their country, science and ideas, before which they are completely effaced . . . It never enters their heads that inside them is something worthy of respect which, without blushing, bears comparison with everything they do respect' (II, 93). In his essay 'Some Observations on the Historical Development of Honour', he gave an account of the various idols which have been accepted as of superior value and wisdom to that of the individual – family, tribe, custom, tradition, one man's god against his neighbour's. But there had been progress. Before the classical period there was no concept at all of individual dignity. In Greece and Rome men were at least respected as citizens, though not as individuals and not for their inherent nature. Christianity revealed man's dignity to himself, and the collapse of the Roman state opened the way to a higher concept than that of the citizen. The feudal knights, in fact, provided, in a one-sided form, the prototype of the future universal transformation. They developed 'an unlimited self-assurance in the dignity of their personality, and of course the personalities of their neighbours, acknowledged as equal according to the feudal concept' (II, 162). Respecting themselves they acquired dignity and automatically respected their equals, not because they were ordered to do so, but because this was the inherent consequence of their own respect for themselves. Within the 'Gothic brotherhood', the result was a fusion of individual freedom and social cohesion. But the knights were no more than a prototype. 'A great step had been taken since the ancient world – what was honoured, inviolable, holy was understood to be inside one's breast, and not in the city; but for the full development of the human personality, moral independence was lacking' (II, 167). The knight's respect for himself was based on a one-sided, physical concept of his honour, and not simply on his human nature. This made possible on the one hand, the oppression of the vast mass of the population, excluded from a brotherhood which still did not respect man as such. On the other, knights shook from fear before moral injunctions since they still did not have faith in their own instincts and judgement. The feudal world was therefore corrupted. The modern revolution, Herzen believed, started from the premise of the inviolability of the personality, but in fact elevated the republic above the personality, removed its rights for the good of the republic, and thus again placed an idol above the human individual. 'The dignity of a man is measured by his part in the *res publica*, his significance is purely as a citizen in the ancient sense. The revolution demanded selflessness, self-sacrifice to the one and indivisible republic' (II, 174).[23] Once again men accepted their inferiority. The escape from this continual sacrifice and humiliation was for Herzen the key to the social problem. A man who has thrown aside moral and social idols and attained full consciousness of his own inherent dignity will act 'humanely, because for him to act thus is natural, easy, automatic, pleasant, reasonable' (II, 94). Inwardly liberated men would combine in the social context they needed – but it would be a fully free society.

The links between these two processes – the inward liberation of respect for self and the external political, social and economic liberation – were left undefined. His expectation of a creative, purifying 'revolution' was as near as Herzen came, in 1846, to bridging the gap between the two. The practical elaboration was not his role in the forties. His role was to grasp the underlying basis of the impending transformation. And he approached this in psychological terms. He believed man cannot be liberated more in his outward, social life than he is liberated within. In 'New Variations on an Old Theme' (1846), in which he expressed this

[23] Malia cites this paragraph to demonstrate Herzen's approval of involvement in the *res publica* being the measure of a man's worth (*Alexander Herzen*, p. 317). Herzen's *disapproval* of such a standard, of the implied superiority of the *res publica* over the individual, of any external and not intrinsic value-measurement of man, is central to his argument in the essay, and important in understanding his rejection of the commune in this period precisely because it committed a similar crime against the individual.

outlook, he explicitly stated that he was talking 'not at all about external constraints, but about the timorous, theoretical consciences of people, about constraints of the interior, of the free will, of the warmth within one's own breast, of fear before the consequences, of fear before the truth'. When he asserted that 'authority [is] based on self-contempt, on the annihilation of one's dignity', he was not using 'Aesopian' symbols to incite the few sympathetic readers among the minute Russian educated elite to stage an armed uprising. He was attacking this 'self-contempt' for creating the vacuum into which authority had stepped. 'The responsibility of independence frightens people,' he wrote. 'External authority is far more comfortable' (II, 90–3).

This then was what Satin called Herzen's 'theory of false self-sufficiency and egoism'. And it was in large measure over this that his dispute with his circle developed. Where Herzen was intrigued and excited by the heralded upheaval of socialism in Europe, and equated it with his own view of liberation, the others were less positive and the spectre of destructive revolution appalled one of his closest friends, the historian Granovsky. Granovsky's studies in history may have encouraged a moderation which stressed the difficulty of constructing conditions of freedom – precisely the kind of doubt and scepticism in man to which Herzen was objecting. Annenkov believed that explicit differences between the two men over western socialism and the significance of the bourgeoisie played the central role in the rift, but other ramifications of Herzen's 'egoism' played a comparable part. Soon after his emigration, he gave his Moscow friends his extremely hostile account of the French bourgeoisie. Granovsky replied that he had no inclination to discuss the real meaning of the bourgeoisie – 'I say enough about that in the lecture theatre' – and that what he treasured were his personal relationships. He was offended that in Herzen's letters 'There is a kind of secret reproach . . . an unfriendly *arrière pensée* that threatens every moment to make its way into the open' (*Past*, 1784–5). The condemnation of the bourgeoisie was hardly an '*arrière pensée*', and this may have referred to the fact that Herzen's critique of the bourgeoisie was cast in exactly the same mould as his earlier criticisms of his Moscow friends.

The demands he made of the French, and his analysis of their shortcomings in terms of dualism and contempt for human nature, echoed his previous strictures on his friends. It was in fact a metaphysical dispute which Herzen recalls bringing the rift into the open. One of the most pernicious sources of 'self-contempt' was in Herzen's view, as we have seen, a religious concept of man which divided him into a soul and body locked in moral conflict. He recalls Granovsky emotionally denying the implications. 'I shall never accept your dry, cold idea of the unity of soul and body, for with it the immortality of the soul disappears. You may not need it, but I have buried too many [friends] to give up this belief' (IX, 209). It has been argued that Herzen's account, written between 1856 and 1857, was distorted and that he wanted to gloss over the painful memory that Granovsky defended the bourgeoisie.[24] There may be some truth in this, though Granovsky was as disgusted as Herzen by the bourgeois reaction of 1848, and in the summer of 1849 told Herzen, 'If we could meet now, probably, we would no longer differ in ideas.'[25] Natalie, writing in her diary at the time of the dispute, cited their friends' refusal to abandon 'prejudices' such as belief in an after-life as a cause of the estrangement (*Past*, 1007–8).

For Herzen, of course, not only were there no supernatural truths which would – as he saw it – impose limits on the grandeur and moral autonomy of man, but ideally there should be no subservience to any external value which would stultify the full expression of each individual's being. People 'do not understand,' he insisted, 'that if a man, while despising himself, respects anything else, he surely reduces himself to dust before the object, becomes its slave' (II, 93). But whereas in his view this 'egoism' was compatible with, was in fact the necessary corollary of social harmony, freedom and mutual respect and equality, the idea struck many of his friends as self-indulgent and irresponsible. These early Russian intellectuals were not morbidly guilt-stricken;[26] the champagne flowed freely enough during their philosophical feasts, and their concern was with truth and thought rather than external political action. But their sense of historical mission easily turned into an obligation for self-sacrifice, and during Herzen's last years in Russia this became the vogue. They nurtured a profound sense of duty, of being the conscious part of the nation and therefore bound to sacrifice themselves to Russia and the Russian people. In his memoirs Annenkov recalled the pervading atmosphere among Herzen's friends before he emigrated. 'Control of oneself, relinquishment of certain impulses of heart and nature as of some pernicious element, constant practice of the same ritual of duty, responsibilities and lofty ideals – all this resembled a kind of strict

[24] See Ia. Z. Cherniak's essay in *Literaturnoe nasledstvo*, 62 (1955), 86–92.
[25] *Ibid*. 94.
[26] See Berlin, *Encounter* (June 1955) 27–39.

monastic initiation.'[27] The portrait may be too colourfully drawn; the
manifestations of this sacrifice were largely verbal or negative – the
refusal to work for and cooperate with the regime. But there is no reason
to doubt the sincerity and intensity of the feeling of constraint evoked in
both Herzens. For Natalie the circle may have been partly the scapegoat
for her frustrated longing for the romantic euphoria which had surrounded her courtship and early married life.[28] But doubtless she and
Alexander discussed the constriction they felt, and Annenkov recalls
Natalie on arrival in Paris emotionally condemning 'the eternal
glorification of the sacrifices, labours and voluntary deprivations which
were constantly borne before her eyes to the altars of various more or less
honourable Molochs which went, in her opinion, under the name of
ideas'.[29] Herzen had repeatedly expressed in his diary his rebellion
against self-sacrifice. Though he felt himself committed to social transformation, he rejected the sacrifice of the present, of himself, to a utopian
vision of the future. 'If one looks deeply into life, indeed,' he wrote in
June 1842, 'one sees that the highest good is existence itself, whatever the
external circumstances may be. When people understand this they will
understand that there is nothing stupider than to ignore the present in
favour of the future. The present is the real sphere of existence ... the
aim of life – is life' (II, 217). It was his own experience of personal
happiness which brought out his greatest cascades of enthusiasm and his
most impassioned protest. Just before Christmas, 1844, Natalie bore him
a girl. He was sure the baby would live, Natalie was happy, he was
ecstatic. 'Such days, periods in a man's life must be cherished; our cursed
lack of attention to the present makes us only able to remember what we
have lost ... Everything beautiful is delicate ... life in its highest
manifestations is weak ... Such are the blessings of love – one must revel
in them, give oneself up to them, live in them, seize and cherish every

[27] Annenkov, *The Extraordinary Decade*, p. 188. The picture Herzen left of
what perhaps had been the atmosphere in his circle in the earlier forties, has
been too readily accepted for the whole decade. 'Feasting,' he said, 'goes
with fullness of life; ascetic people are usually dry and egoistical ... We were
not like the emaciated monks of Zurbaran; we did not weep over the sins of
the world – we only sympathised with its suffering, and were ready with a
smile for anything, and not depressed by a foretaste of our sacrifices to come'
(*Past*, 491). The reaction of both Herzen and Natalie against a vogue of
self-sacrifice later in the forties was an important factor in their attitude to
their escape abroad.
[28] See E. H. Carr, *The Romantic Exiles* (London, 1968), pp. 22–4.
[29] Annenkov, *The Extraordinary Decade*, p. 190.

moment.' For him the ideal was 'To grasp the present, to activate in oneself all the possibilities for bliss – by this I mean both general activity, and the bliss of knowledge, as well as the bliss of friendship, of love, of family feeling' (II, 393–5).

For Herzen, apart from emigration itself, the obvious practical manifestation of this full, 'egotistical' life, was the fortune he inherited from his father shortly before the rift. There is evidence that some members of the circle felt uneasy amidst this new degree of affluence, and that Herzen was annoyed by what he took for envy. Herzen saw the injustice of wealth amidst abject poverty, but he was not plagued by guilt. He would yield to none in his compassion for the impoverished peasantry. But central to his view of his role was the affirmation of the full life, balancing love and poetry with social and political involvement – that life which was itself at once the means and purpose of social transformation. And financial independence made this affirmation possible.[30]

The friction in the circle was in part due to causes which were petty and are now untraceable. Natalie was at odds with almost all the women. And Herzen was later conscious that he might have argued with conceit, intolerance and sarcasm. But his own account of the intense emotion aroused by differences on specific ideas rings true. When Herzen and Ogarev insisted that belief in immortality was an escapist 'fairy-tale', Granovsky, 'turning pale and assuming the air of a disinterested outsider', replied:

> 'You will truly oblige me if you never speak to me on these subjects again; there are plenty of interesting things to talk about with far more profit and pleasure.'
>
> 'Certainly. With the greatest pleasure,' I said, feeling a chill on my face. Ogarev said nothing; we all looked at one another and that glance was quite enough; we all loved one another too much not to gauge to the full by our expressions what had happened ... Ogarev and I had expected that we should come to an agreement ... We were as sad as though someone near and dear had died. (*Past*, 586–7)

---

[30] Later Herzen also justified his inheritance as the means for more concrete political action: 'Money is independence, power, a weapon; and no-one flings away a weapon in time of war, though it may have come from the enemy and even be rusty' (*Past*, 757). Apart from financing the Free Russian Press during the fifties and sixties, he subsidised many political refugees.

Herzen's commitment to his convictions was too deep to leave personal friendships unaffected.[31]

During 1846 his relationship with Granovsky, Korsh, Ketscher and the others was strained and for a while even cold. Ogarev was himself restless and Belinsky was away in St Petersburg. At the same time his frustration with censorship and with the improbability of any tangible political progress in Russia intensified throughout the forties. Unsuccessful arguments within a small group of men utterly divorced from power and cramped by a hostile and, for the foreseeable future, unshakeable regime felt increasingly limited. He yearned for the full life the west seemed to promise. His friends' strictures on his 'egoism' only made more urgent his desire to use his inheritance 'to go away, far away, for a long time' (*Past*, 589).

[31] See Nahirny, 'The Russian Intelligentsia', for a very different interpretation. Nahirny draws a sharp line between Belinsky, as the prototype of those Russians totally and intensely committed to ideas, on the one hand, and Granovsky, Herzen and the others as too cultured and independent to be absorbed by an 'ism' or to allow differences of opinion to affect friendship. Whatever the merits of the argument generally, it is misleading in regard to Herzen. His commitment was to a vision rather than to an 'ism', but it was none the less the guiding principle of his life. And though he was a more gregarious, less thorny character than Belinsky, his description of his break with Granovsky precisely over differences of opinion could not be more poignant.

2

To the west: 1847

Herzen left Russia with relief and looked forward to his journey with excitement. 'I was beckoned by another life, length, breadth, open struggle and free speech,' he later recalled. 'My restless spirit sought an arena and independence; I wished to try my strength in freedom' (*Past*, 1859). It was to the west, and above all to France, that he looked for revolution and the inauguration of socialism. But he was well aware that the dawn had not begun, and he had no precise idea of how soon the revolution would take place. His expectations were in a sense more personal than political. Apart from gaining first-hand knowledge of western society and enhancing his reputation among his Moscow friends, he would experience relative freedom of speech and discussion and have direct contact with the broader circles of western thinkers. His role would be to contribute to the ideological work of this *avant-garde*, to deepen his understanding of contemporary society and of 'the future reformation'. This would constitute that vigorous involvement in 'general affairs' which he yearned for as the complement to the full private and family life.

In his first years abroad he composed a series of letters in which he described his broadest historical and political judgements – above all his condemnation of the bourgeoisie and his admiration for the working people of the west. Addressed at first to his Russian friends and later to a western audience as well, these letters were written in the most vivacious, direct, autobiographical style. Like his essays and memoirs they benefit, just as his fiction suffers, from the sheer strength of his personality intruding into what he describes. A century later the boldness of his generalisations, his sweeping judgements made without a shred of

statistical evidence, are breath-taking. But they live. And they reflect his
confident approach to knowledge and not, as has been argued, ten-
dentious polemic inspired by nationalist dislike for European society and
propped up on flimsy examples.[1] Years of politico-philosophical debate
and reading shaped the categories into which he marshalled his first-hand
information, and his admiration for socialist authorities brought him to
the west with definite preconceptions. He would not like the bourgeoisie
and he would sympathise with the working classes. But the basis on
which he analysed society reflected his remarkably independent
approach. His romantic and idealistic background led him to accept the
most subjective impressions and chance experiences as reliable evidence
of general truths. He could pontificate on societies and great events
because he was there, breathing the atmosphere, hearing immediate local
reactions, reading the newspapers, going to the theatre, strolling about
the streets. The evidence he cited to support his judgements was to
Herzen and many of his contemporaries not symbolic but the very stuff
of social analysis – Annenkov called these letters 'the first attempts at
applying the sociological way of apprehending and discussing things in
Russian writing'.[2] And the terms in which he praised and condemned
bore the authentic stamp of his singular approach to social and political
questions. His castigation of the bourgeoisie, indeed his definition of the
bourgeoisie, was not primarily economic or even political but psychological and aesthetic; he approved of the working people not merely
as the victims of injustice but as morally superior. These first letters
provide clear illustration of Herzen's method throughout these years.
The first four, 'The Letters from the Avenue Marigny', describing his
initial impressions of Germany, Brussels, and Paris, were tailored to
satisfy the Russian censor. But despite 'Aesopian' elements, comparison
with his later, uncensored letters suggests that his ideas were not
seriously distorted. His attitude towards social injustice and his insistence on radical economic redistribution are easily discernible. And he
had no detailed economic or political theory to conceal.

Initially his tone is light and cheerful. He speculates on the connection
between the abysmal quality of German cuisine, and the yawning dis-
crepancy between occasional flashes of German artistic genius and their
general mediocrity. His remarks are those of the aristocrat reacting
against impersonal, jostling, uncomfortable travel among a crowd of

[1] Malia, *Alexander Herzen*, pp. 335–68.
[2] Annenkov, *The Extraordinary Decade*, p. 174.

anonymous social inferiors. He disdains the vulgar and orderly life, the merchants absorbed in their dreary day-to-day business activities. His judgements are much affected by the personal treatment and friendliness he found among his neighbours in the trains, other guests in the hotels, porters and ticket-collectors. Warmth and response from a few individuals soon rouse his enthusiasm. He is led to the pleasing conclusion that Germans understand and esteem 'the breadth of our nature' when it is expressed energetically (XXIII, 14). Although he found the architectural evidence of centuries of 'unbroken' history mildly claustrophobic, he was also impressed. Europe was too dominated by the past – or perhaps that was only one aspect of Europe. His delight at Königsberg was frank: 'The Russian traveller meets Europe for the first time at Königsberg; this is not a memorial of a past life, but a home for the present, here memorials and reminiscences mingle with young life' (V, 26). He was 'simply in love with Cologne', and he found the grace of Brussels 'excels all description' (XXIII, 14).

But Herzen restrained his enthusiasm. His friends believed this was because he did not wish to appear a naïve, impressionable tourist. Some commentators play down his initial caution, accept completely his own recollection that at first he was utterly delighted by Europe, and see his quick reaction against life in Paris purely as the result of a penetrating analysis.[3] Malia, on the other hand, goes to the opposite extreme and concludes that 'before he ever left Russia ... Herzen had made up his mind that he would not find Granovsky's Europe to his liking'.[4] Herzen's commentary on the west was essentially a function of his 'amorphous yet deep nationalism'.[5] Quite apart from the controversy over the subject, Herzen's encounter with Europe merits attention as a fascinating example of a westernised representative of a backward country being forced to define himself and his country in relation to this foreign home of

[3] See, for example, Richard Hare, *Pioneers of Russian Social Thought* (Oxford, 1951), pp. 234–5; V. A. Putintsev, *Gertsen – pisatel'* (Moscow, 1963), pp. 128–30.

[4] Malia, *Alexander Herzen*, p. 341.

[5] *Ibid.* p. 337. Malia sees Herzen arriving in the west the victim of nationalistic messianism, and portrays this as a dominant motif in the subsequent evolution of his ideas. The distortion involved in this picture is in need of correction, especially since Malia's major work is exerting such a strong influence on the interpretation of Herzen accepted by western historians. See, for example, K. W. Swart, *The Sense of Decadence in Nineteenth-century France* (The Hague, 1964), p. 223; M. Cadot, *La Russie dans la vie intellectuelle française (1839–1856)* (Paris, 1967), pp. 39–43.

his culture. Such encounters by elites from outside Europe – from Asia and Africa – have tended to produce basically defensive responses. The nature of the defence has depended on individual characters and on broader factors such as the degree of backwardness of their own country, or the threat of political domination by the west. Despite the paradox created by their own westernisation, the elite's reaction has sometimes been manifested not only in political and social nationalism, but also in religious, customary and even cultural nationalism.[6] On the other hand, elites who have been more thoroughly assimilated by the west, or who have felt more secure, have defended only the right of their nation to express its particular genius through the admittedly superior western means. This has been made easier when they have seen Europe's ascendancy as a step in the universal progress in which their nation may in turn take the lead. It is instructive to place Herzen on this spectrum, a spectrum coinciding with aspects of the Slavophile–Westerner divergence, at the moment of his contact with the west.

Though Europe may be experienced and venerable, he argues, Russia has the advantage of youth and freshness. He contrasts the primitive parochialism of some Russian peasants with the 'layer upon layer' of history in the west. The encouragement he took from idealist notions – from the idea that each nation sooner or later makes a contribution to mankind and that backwardness therefore holds promise of future greatness – would be drawn upon by later generations of Russian intellectuals.[7] But the argument depended upon evidence that Russia could renounce 'Asian stagnation' and utilise her 'virginity'. Herzen finds this evidence in Peter the Great's *western* innovations. The ability to imitate and learn is a valuable quality, enabling Russia to enter the mainstream of history. He declares that the adoption of western skills, techniques and culture, far from depriving a nation of its character, facilitates the expression 'of all that seethes within its mind and spirit' (V, 25). The literary and intellectual vitality of his own circle provides ample proof

[6] Nineteenth-century West African reaction to British imperialism illustrates this particularly well because of the articulate reflections of such differing members of the elite as Africanus Horton and E. Blyden.
[7] For some interesting remarks on the changing view of Russia's backwardness taken by the intelligentsia, see A. Gerschenkron, 'The Problem of Economic Development in Russian Intellectual History in the Nineteenth Century', in E. J. Simmons, ed., *Continuity and Change in Russian and Soviet Thought* (Cambridge, Mass., 1955), 37–88. Herzen was by no means the first Russian to see advantages in backwardness but he was influential in popularising the idea among radicals.

that Russia has preserved her character. It is with the enlightened few and their chance of realising their ideals in mind that he remarks: 'We begin where he [the European] leaves off' (V, 21). It is these who, by obeying Peter and producing Pushkin, have shown the potential in Russia and the promise of her future. Herzen's own self-confidence, as well as his genuine pride in Russia's literary achievements, helped to deflect the pressure which would have led to a very defensive, nationalist reaction. But the prime error in attributing a dominant nationalist motif to his reactions is that it seriously underrates the sincerity and depth of his humanist idealism. It was this idealism which was the crucial factor in his reaction to Europe. It suggested to him that Europe herself was in transition to a higher social order. She was therefore not oppressively superior, but rather an aspirant like Russia, the acknowledged source and probable pioneer, though not necessarily the greatest product, of the socialist era. His cosmopolitan socialism enabled him to identify with her problems and her progress.

Herzen arrived in Paris at the end of March. Describing his emotions fifteen months later, he recalled: 'The name of this city is bound up with all the loftiest aspirations, with all the greatest hopes of contemporary man – I entered it with a trembling heart, with reverence, as men used to enter Jerusalem and Rome' (V, 317). He was excited; he hurried to look at the historic sights of the revolutionary capital, quickly adopted Parisian dress and custom, and according to Annenkov, who was well placed to observe him, showed 'feverish haste to place himself in the centre of his new life . . . The Herzen house became a sort of Dionysius' "Ear" where all the noise of Paris, the least movement and perturbation playing over the surface of its street and intellectual life was clear echoed.'[8] What survives of Herzen's private correspondence gives the impression that if he was so sociable, he found few of his new companions really congenial. But he was certainly quickly caught up in analysis of French society – Bakunin and Sazonov, plays and lectures and a heavy diet of Parisian newspapers stimulated the involvement he had eagerly awaited.

What he found in Paris confirmed the impression, drawn largely from Louis Blanc, which he had recorded in his diary as long ago as 1843: 'The timid, cowardly, self-interested and vacillating bourgeoisie seized everything [in 1830] . . . and in its centre . . . was Louis Phillipe, . . . King in the name of and for mediocrity' (II, 284). The need for social revolution had become obvious and 'the enemies of development, like Guizot,

[8] Annenkov, *The Extraordinary Decade*, pp. 164, 185.

understand and tremble' (II, 289). Recording his own first-hand impressions, he saw two sections of Parisian society: the bourgeoisie, who tended to be the richer, enfranchised, governing class, but who were distinguished by their taste and values rather than as a socio-economic caste; and the poorer, voteless lower classes. During his first few months the chief source for his analysis was the theatre – since plays are financed by the bourgeoisie, they must reflect its taste.[9] His criticisms were at first aesthetic but developed into forthright moral condemnation. The bourgeois proclaims a code of morals but acts in direct conflict with it. For all his talk of freedom, he is a despot in his own home. For all his philanthropy he lives happily side by side with wretched poverty, which he calls laziness. Instead of a frank enjoyment of natural instincts, open appreciation of feminine beauty, he believes these desires to be evil, yet he yields to them with secret and ashamed visits to a salacious vaudeville. As with the Middle Ages, so with the contemporary French bourgeoisie, Herzen saw this duplicity as the consequence of contempt for human nature. The bourgeois distrusts the human heart and conscience, his own self. This leads him to make virtue obligatory, to turn love into duty – so that if a woman wishes to live fully, to love and enjoy life, she must refuse to be a wife. Scribe's plays demonstrated to Herzen bourgeois horror at caprice, passion, enthusiasm in a woman. The bourgeois does not respect in man his nature – his emotions, his love, his intellect, his beauty, his enjoyment, his natural morality – he respects his productivity and income. Economics is the nearest thing to philosophy that the bourgeois has. It is money that is the object of his respect – it is money that provides the most powerful external idol, the most perverting imperative. Where Romans bowed down to the *civitas*, and feudal knights to the Church, the bourgeois humiliates himself before Money. This is the point of Herzen's famous contrast between the two faces of Beaumarchais's Figaro. The original bourgeois, the artful Figaro, exploited his livery at one remove from his dignity. Whereas 'under the livery of the old Figaro, a man was visible, under the dark coat of the new Figaro appears livery, and, worst of all, he cannot throw it off like his predecessor, it has grown to him so that it is impossible to remove it without his skin as well' (V, 33). Submitting to the external authority of money, he has become accustomed to blatant hypocrisy, has perverted his instincts and destroyed the natural harmony between value and action. Exploitation of the masses

---

[9] For a discussion of the great importance Herzen attached to the theatre, see Putintsev, *Gertsen – pisatel'*, pp. 128–32.

was to Herzen the worst facet of the basic bourgeois crime, contempt for themselves, for the dignity of their own nature.

This stands in sharp contrast with his assessment of the French lower classes. He was struck in the first instance by the domestic servants he encountered. That they are servants at all is explained by the fact that like every sane man they like, they need money. But, unlike the bourgeoisie, they are not prepared to sell everything, their comfort, their right to argue, their *point d'honneur*, in order to acquire it. They make no pretence that they serve willingly, and the very correctness of their manners conveys that their service is no more than form, that in fact they are fully equal to their employers. (Herzen goes so far as to recommend to his Moscow friends the actual *practice* of doing without servants, and merely sharing a porter available to a whole block of apartments for specific errands – it is so convenient, healthy and liberating to do without them. V, 41.) But the typical 'proletarian'[10] is the *ouvrier*, who may lack the external polish of the servant but is in fact more developed. Protected from the corruption of bourgeois ideas and values by their fathers and grandfathers, participants in the great French Revolution, this younger generation is polite and even gentle provided it is not interfered with. Their parties are gay and happy but modest. They are vivacious and yet have all the self-control and mutual harmony which flows from a true appreciation of their human dignity. The evidence Herzen cites to demonstrate this throws light on his own character, and on his method. A child is taken to watch an open-air play, but is too small to see. Immediately a *bluznik* lifts him on to his shoulders, and those nearby automatically take a turn when the first is tired. There is no need to ask or organise, the help is voluntary, spontaneous. Children playing on a pavement block the way – rather than break up their game in the name of adult precedence and haste, a hundred passers-by walk all the way round to leave them in peace. A small boy carries a bag of silver down the street, the bag bursts open, the money scatters and the boy begins to cry. He is quickly surrounded by helpful workers who pick up, count and re-pack the money, and then return it to him.

Herzen elaborated his description of the lower classes after seeing a play by Pyat, *The Parisian Vagrant*. All his sympathy was roused by the innocent suffering and yet warm heart of the heroine. She is a penniless girl, hard-working and yet at the point of despair until a bourgeois villain happens to abandon an unwanted child with her. Despite her misery she

[10] Herzen did not limit the word to the *urban* working class.

is so moved by the child's helplessness that she forgets her own suffering. Herzen was even more struck by the hero of the play, the orphan-to-beggar vagrant who 'had no family – he was too poor to have a family; one is not allowed to love in that condition'. He was delighted by the virtue and subtlety of the pauper in defending the innocent girl against the ruthlessness of the rich bourgeoisie. 'He is a philosopher, a sage, but above all a character' (V, 47). And praising French feminine beauty he sees such care for their appearance as the product of 'an old civilisation and respect for self, a feeling of their dignity and, consequently, a concept of the personality; of course I don't mean an abstract concept of the personality and its citizen's rights, but that instinctive appreciation which is so evident in the very lowest classes of the European states, quite independent of their political structure' (V, 54). It was their superior dignity and charm which he stressed in the first three of his 'Letters from the Avenue Marigny'. They had preserved their natural instincts from the corruption, hypocrisy, deceit and contempt for human nature which disfigured the bourgeoisie. 'The poorer a man is here, the further he is on the good side from the petty bourgeoisie' (XXIII, 21).

Now, given his faith in the natural goodness of human nature, it was the bourgeoisie and not the people who deviated from the norm. Certainly their victimisation and impoverishment contributed to his sympathy for the lower classes. But so far as their moral purity was concerned, it did not require explanation, economic or otherwise, since it was natural. So far as the bourgeoisie were concerned, he did iden-tify them broadly with the richer, property-owning classes, but he specifically denied that they were 'an Indian caste ... A bourgeois is a man who knows he is one, who hates the aristocrat on the one hand and despises the people on the other' (V, 240). They were an integral part of this unjust society, but he made no attempt to spell out which was cause and which effect, how their different economic condition could have *caused* their corruption. They stood condemned as the modern mani-festation of the tendency in men 'eternally [to] respect something outside themselves ... before which they are completely effaced' (II, 93).

Between June and September, when he wrote the fourth and last of this first cycle of letters, his analysis did take on a broader dimension. He became more closely acquainted with the journalistic criticisms of France and his comments became more directly political and economic. He endorsed the common view that material interests now dominated all others, and attributed this to a reaction against the excessively abstract nature of the great revolution of the eighteenth century. Disdain for economic questions is absurd: they form a crucial part of the social fabric, and in any case the people will no longer be moved by abstractions devoid of economic content. The future revolution he envisaged would involve the transformation of the unjust conditions on which the bourgeoisie prospered. But Herzen believed that political thinkers had now gone to the other extreme. Their ideas were too intellectual for the people – and too one-sided for Herzen. Having conceded the importance of economics, he was concerned to emphasise that taken on their own, economics are barren. He rejected a reduction of contemporary problems to a function of economics, a treatment of man as a machine, society as a factory, and the state as a market. Few of these modern thinkers knew how to raise the question of political economy 'into that sphere of general interests in which it has its rights and outside which it has no real meaning'. Moreover, the new obsession with economics treated man not as a human being but as 'a sort of pitiful creature whom they freed from poverty or unjust money-grubbing only to lose him in the commune'. Herzen concluded that the *avant-garde* was still confronted with the problem of reconciling the individual with society. 'To understand the personality of man, to understand all the sanctity, all the breadth of the real rights of the person – this is the most difficult task, and, apart from details and exceptions, it has never been achieved by any previous historical form; for it great maturity is necessary and man has not reached it' (V, 237–8). What he sought was a synthesis of economic realism and his own emphasis on psychological liberation and the freedom of the full personality.

As Herzen prepared to leave France and visit Italy, he assured his Moscow friends that the slightest acquaintance with France, a morning in a café, a glance at a newspaper full of the latest political scandal, was enough to see her 'black and sordid side'. But he insisted that the present state of affairs must be seen in relation to the past, and that 'Then you will see much that is confused, much that is difficult, much that is bad, but at the same time you will see that there is nothing hopeless or desperate and that France can still recover without drastic means.' He rejected the Slavophile slur that 'earthquake, heavenly fire, [or] deluge' are necessary. Yet for all this ultimate optimism, he had not seen the way forward, either politically or ideologically. Paris had disappointed him. This cannot be explained by his disgust with the bourgeoisie, intense though that was, since he had known he would not like them before he arrived.

He was disappointed more by the firmness of their grip on government, property and the army. He damned them as a transitory phenomenon with neither past nor future, and he saw in the poor the foundation for the future reformation. But as time passed he could see no evidence that the process of transformation, that 'revolution' whose mechanics he had never analysed, was imminent. The parliamentary opposition and its allied newspapers called for petty palliatives. And apart from Proudhon, the communist and socialist thinkers seemed to him people 'with distant ideals, barely visible in the future'. Oppressed by these thoughts, and perhaps under the influence of western revolutionaries' preoccupation with economic redistribution, he even concluded that 'The mob will remain a mob until it has created leisure for itself, the necessary condition for development' (V, 233–4). These pessimistic reflections were against his instinct; he would renounce them amidst the hope and excitement of the upheavals of the following year.

But during the last months of 1847 the revolution seemed depressingly far off, the process of creating socialism painfully slow. France would recover, the old world would eventually be replaced, but meanwhile his attention focused on the position of individuals like himself who rejected the bourgeois present but might never live to see it replaced, and might in any case find the immediate replacement unsatisfactory. He wrote his first analysis of his own predicament and role in the west. Travelling south, Herzen left France and spent some time in Nice, where Natalie was ill.[11] Here he met an old friend and minor member of the Moscow circle, I. P. Galakhov. Conversations with him inspired Herzen to write what he called 'an analysis of the contemporary scene', later entitled 'Before the Storm'.[12] The dialogue form it took was perfectly suited to Herzen's purpose. Several of his preoccupations could be woven together, without the need to taper his ideas into a systematic form.[13] The protagonist, generally expressing Herzen's point of view, dominates the

[11] Nice was ceded to France in 1860.

[12] See VI, 324–40 for the earliest known version of this work. Quotations are taken from this version. The work was published in France in 1850 and became the first chapter of *From the Other Shore*, published in German in 1850 and in Russian in 1855.

[13] For an analysis of some literary aspects of *From the Other Shore*, see Francis B. Randall, 'Herzen's *From the Other Shore*', *Slavic Review*, XXVII (1968), 91–101. A useful discussion of some of the problems involved in interpreting these dialogues is provided by L. Ia. Ginzburg, '*C togo berega* Gertsena', *Izvestiia Akademii nauk SSSR. Otdelenie literatury i iazyka*, XXI (1962), 112–24.

discussion but his companion's objections enable him to show his sympathy for the positions both of his Moscow friends and of his new acquaintances in the west. He dedicated the work to Granovsky, and undoubtedly the ideas and character of the companion are in part drawn from Galakhov. But in fact the companion has more affinity with those involved in the west, with Bakunin, Sazonov and their western friends – and in the original version he was cast as an Italian educated in Germany. This complicated ancestry, and the irrelevance of specific national references to the argument, underlines the cosmopolitan nature of Herzen's approach to the contemporary world.

The dialogue establishes a contrast between an impatient zeal, noble but misguided, and the calmness derived from experience and deep reflection. Herzen had assumed this tone of stoical serenity before – in 1843 he called it 'the grey, clear but cold sun of real understanding' (II, 272) – and the pain of an idea was inclined to pass in his mind as a token of its validity. But, as he later realised, the 'realism' of the essay reflected only a brief foretaste of the deeper disillusionment to come. The exhilarating events in Italy and France in the weeks after he completed 'Before the Storm' quickly demonstrated that his own hopes and impatience were far less under control than he imagined.

Herzen addresses to his companion a more sophisticated version of the same reproach he had made to Granovsky and his Moscow friends before leaving Russia, and in more virulent form to the Parisian bourgeoisie. 'We believe in everything but we do not believe in ourselves' (VI, 330). Whether by family life, 'wine, numismatics, cards, botany, hunting, story-telling', or retreat into mysticism, men take infinite pains not to be left alone with themselves, not to come to terms with their own nature, to accept themselves (VI, 325). This is the result of generations of distorted indoctrination. 'How long ago was it that, intimidated and downtrodden, we ceased to suppress with horror the most innocent desires; how many of us have yet understood that in its right place, pride is no crime; that without egoism there is no love; that in some cases to be humble is base; that to want pleasure is completely just?' (VI, 327–8). Distrust in human morality creates external authorities which humiliate man and perpetuate the individual's conviction that he is indeed insignificant and too irresponsible for freedom. It is this which leads men to bind themselves to some 'greater' cause, idol, aim than the individual. They accept the fallacious concept of duty. Duty, the demand for sacrifice and

suppression in the name of some superior 'Moloch' is both disagreeable
and profoundly confusing to the moral sense. *Duty Before All*, the novel
Herzen planned and began that same autumn, was concerned with
precisely this problem. As he said later, Anatole, the hero, was 'to
represent a man full of strength, energy, nobleness and readiness for
action, whose life is empty, painful and cheerless because he is continually struggling *with duty*. This man grows stronger and succeeds in
reconciling his rebellious will with what he takes to be his duty – and all
his strength is lost in the struggle' (VI, 410). He respects his father from
duty, he marries from duty, he helps to quell the Polish rising with which
he sympathises from duty, emigrates and serves a church he does not
believe in from duty.[14] The result is the destruction of an individual who
would have been capable of a full and rich life. In 'Before the Storm',
Herzen tells his companion: 'You are looking for a banner, I am trying to
lose one; you want a book of rules, but I think that when one reaches a
certain age one ought to be ashamed of using one' (VI, 330). Religion,
money, patriotism – all may provide an idol which imposes self-effacing
reverence and duty: but it was the idol of progress, the worship of some
future utopia, that Herzen became particularly concerned with at the end
of 1847. It was this ideal which threatened to distort the role of the
intellectual revolutionary.

For his companion, it is progress towards a social ideal which provides
the purpose and consolation of his life. It is the young man's fundamental
assumption that 'We who have run ahead [are] like surveyors fixing the
landmarks of the new world . . . [and] some time long after our death, the
house for which we cleared the ground will be built, and it will be
comfortable and pleasant for others.' Herzen questions this assumption:
'There is no reason to think that the new world will be built according to
our plan,' for 'what are the necessities in virtue of which the future must
play the role we have devised for it?' (VI, 330–1). Progress is not assured;
history has no 'itinerary'; 'the future does not exist' (VI, 334). Herzen
had it both ways. He retained a fundamental, emotional assumption of
progress, of the victory of socialism. But philosophically, logically he
denied this inevitability, he explicitly overthrew Hegelian guarantees.
And hence he could elevate the present and the creative role of man in
history.

---

[14] The novel, which Herzen planned on a grand scale but did not complete,
     included vigorous social criticism of serf-based Russian society, as well as this
     central personal theme.

Since the path forward now seemed slow and difficult, he wanted to place the emphasis on the present. He advises his young companion to leave the 'old world', which may yet linger for years, and undertake an 'internal emigration' (VI, 332). He deliberately rejects a geographical emigration – there is no hidden nationalist implication. The point is rather to convince revolutionaries that *they* are individuals, that *they* must not efface themselves before the future. Their preoccupation with the future induces neglect of the richness of life, of human experience in the present. The idea is embodied in one of Herzen's most brilliant passages:

> If progress is the aim, then for whom are we working? Who is this Moloch who, as the toilers approach him, instead of rewarding them, draws back, and as consolation to the exhausted, doomed multitude crying, *'Morituri te salutant'*, can only reply 'After your death it will be beautiful on earth'? Do you really wish to condemn people to the sad role of caryatids, supporting the floor on which others will dance . . . or of wretched labourers, up to their knees in mud, dragging a barge filled with some mysterious treasure and with the humble inscription *'Progress* in the future' on its flag? Those who are exhausted fall in their tracks, others, with fresh strength, take up the ropes, but the path remains just as long as it was at the beginning. Progress is infinite. This alone should serve as a warning to people; an aim which is infinitely remote is not an aim but, if you like, a brilliant trick; an aim must be more immediate – it ought to be, at the very least, the labourer's wage, or pleasure in the work done. Each age, each generation, each life had and has its own fullness. (VI, 336)

Consciousness and appreciation of this fullness can remove both the sense of duty and the melancholy of unrealised ideals. When the young companion disdains serenity and claims that life is a mockery if all the efforts, all the 'grain upon grain', come tumbling down, Herzen rebukes him:

> To look at the end and not at the action itself is the greatest error. Of what use to the plant is its bright, glorious flower, its intoxicating scent – none at all . . . And what is the aim of the song that the singer sings? . . . Sounds, the sounds that burst from her throat, the melody that dies as soon as it has sounded. If you look beyond your pleasure in them for something else, for some other aim, you will find that the singer has stopped

singing, and then you will have only memories and regrets that
instead of listening you waited for something else.
By demanding of life something it does not grant, all its blessings and
grandeur are wasted. 'I prefer to think of life, and therefore of history, as
an end attained rather than as a means to something else.' And in reply to
his companion's horrified question – 'You mean, in short, that the aim of
nature and of history is just – you and me?' – Herzen lets his imagination
soar to conjure up all that is rich and beautiful but taken for granted and
neglected in life:

> Partly, *plus* the present state of everything existing; everything
> is included in this: the legacy of past efforts, the inspired work
> of the actor, the energy of citizens' feats, the rapture of art,
> and the delight of the youth who, at this very moment,
> somewhere or other, is stealing his way to some secret arbour
> where his shy love awaits him, trembling at every rustle . . .
> and the pleasure of a fish splashing in the moonlight . . . and
> the harmony of the entire solar system. (VI, 333–5)

In a sense, Herzen was endorsing at a more politico-philosophical level
Natalie's frustration at their Moscow circle's 'eternal glorification of
sacrifices, labours and voluntary deprivations'.[15] He had found a similar
mood of utopian dedication among his new acquaintances. Against this
he defended the rights of the living, of this generation, of himself to the
fullness of life. The revolutionary intellectual must affirm the value of life
and the individual even amidst bourgeois injustice.[16] For philosophically, and ultimately politically, he saw in the noblest utopianism a threat
to the value of the individual. An absorbing faith in progress and devotion to the future could inspire the sacrifice of these priceless moments,
lives, generations. It could provide the very moral imperatives and
disrespect for human beings that he abhorred. It is a striking characteristic of the dialogue that the two disputants share the same ultimate
wishes for society; the dispute is not about the merits of a socialist system
or immediate political upheaval. Indeed, if political implications are
drawn superficially from 'Before the Storm', it seems the most gross
product of aristocratic complacency about the deprivation, mental and

---

[15] Annenkov, *The Extraordinary Decade*, p. 190.
[16] Ginzburg's article, '*C togo berega* Gertsena', is marred by overlooking this
affirmation of the present as such in *From the Other Shore*. The point is vital
in understanding the role of Herzen's family tragedy in his evolution from
the position adopted in the final chapter of the book – '*Omnia Mea Mecum
Porto*'. See below, Chapters 3–6.

physical, of millions in the mid-nineteenth century. This was the risk Herzen took in trying to contain the tension between his intense, vibrant appreciation of life 'whatever the circumstances', and his most intransigent social idealism. The tension was, of course, most acute in periods like this when the social ideal receded into the distant future. His attention was turned to the question of the enlightened few, their values, priorities and lives. For Herzen, this emphasis on the present was neither quietist nor conservative, but profoundly revolutionary. He sought to make the young zealot, his readers, contemporary revolutionaries, free themselves by this 'internal emigration' before trying to free others. His method was to inspire that respect for human nature which he saw as vital for the creation of a free and just society. To do this he questioned the existence, let alone the beauty, of the future; he objected to the humiliating idea that men were mere 'cogs in a wheel', helpless puppets. Above all, he tried to engender this respect by a highly artistic expression of his own consciousness of the physical, intellectual and emotional beauty and power of man. He saw in this consciousness the crucial but untapped source of enjoyment, psychological purification, and hence social and political harmony. When men believe in themselves, in their own reason, instincts and conscience, they can be free. In this sense, 'Before the Storm' was as political in purpose as his more obvious polemics about tyranny, the bourgeoisie, and freedom of the individual.

3

1848

Herzen arrived in Italy in November 1847 and spent nearly six months there. From the start the visit was a success. He was delighted by the climate, the countryside, the cities. He was full of praise for the Italian people. From his point of view he could not have arrived at a more invigorating moment. It was in Italy that the revolutions of 1848 began, and he was there to witness them. The whole country was as alive, as colourful, as happy, it seemed to him, as a village on holiday. If at first he had reacted against Rome, soon the art, the magnificent ruins and above all the *Risorgimento* convinced him that she not only had a great past but also a future whose promise and vitality were being borne out before his eyes. He saw popular demonstrations induce government concessions all over the country. He witnessed the vacillation of Pope Pius IX, and the public bow to the people made by King Ferdinand of Naples. His 'Letters from the *Via del Corso*', vividly conveyed his enthusiasm for the spontaneity and courage of the Italian crowds. As so often, his personal reception played a great part in forming his impressions. Five years later he recalled a March evening in Rome, with the Corso filled with people demanding to join the war for the liberation of Lombardy from Austria:

'Fall in, fall in with us,' shout dozens of voices.
'We are foreigners.'
'All the better; *Santo Dio*, you are our guests.'
We joined the ranks.
'The front place for the guests, the front place for the ladies, *le donne forestiere!*'

And with passionate shouts of approval the crowd parted to
make way . . .
Ciceruacchio was on the balcony in the glaring light of
torches and candelabra, and beside him under the Italian flag
stood four young women, all four Russians – was it not
strange? . . . The aristocratic proletariat, the descendants of
Marius and the ancient tribunes, gave us a warm and genuine
welcome. We were received by them into the European
struggle. (*Past*, 655–6)

Recounting his first experience of these popular movements, Herzen
told his Moscow friends only two months after arriving in Italy, that
'These memories are holy for me; with them is linked my moral recovery'
(V, 252). The essence of that 'recovery' was that he was taken out of
himself by the evidence of social movement. There was no need for
'internal emigration' when the whole society around him was manifesting
the same urge forward. He assured Granovsky that they had both under-
rated Italy and turned his energies to grasping the spirit of what was in
progress (XXIII, 56–7).

Just as in France he had enthused over the strength and incor-
ruptibility of the repressed people, so in Italy he idealised the national
spirit which had survived centuries of foreign domination. In spite of the
foreign yoke, their spirit was never broken – though they had forfeited
most of their rights, they had, like the original Figaro and the Parisian
servants, retained an inner dignity. Sheer diversity, an instinctive yearning for independence, the distance kept between themselves and the
government, 'elusive disorder', had saved the Italians. Their respect for
the individual personality preserved them from identifying their whole
existence with the state, from 'belittling' the individual person.[1] Only
Russians and Italians were so little marked by poverty and work. 'Such
people have a secret thought or, to express it better, that principle of
independence, a principle not understood by themselves, as yet, which
gives them the power to preserve themselves, and passive protection
against which, as from rocks, everything threatening to destroy their
independence rebounds' (V, 271). He had not forgotten his initial
enthusiasm for the French lower classes, but his delight with the Italians

---

[1] 'Among the Italians,' wrote Herzen in the version of 'Letters from the *Via del
Corso*' revised for publication in Germany in 1850, 'respect for self, for the
personality is remarkably developed; they don't *construct* democracy, like the
French, it is in their *mores*' (V, 76).

was even more intense. He did not see them overshadowed by a dominant bourgeoisie, and, above all, there were outward, political signs of this undestroyed inner dignity.

The Italian experience encouraged him to draw out more concrete political corollaries of the personal, psychological approach he took towards social analysis. What impressed him about Italian political life was its decentralisation and the vigour of independent municipal life. He saw in this institutional defence against foreign oppression and humiliation a manifestation of the independence and variety of the Italian personality. Suppressed in one town, the Italian spirit sprang up in another. Similarly, he saw Italians as inherently hostile to uniforms, to the depersonalised and regimented life of an army. They preferred the freedom of individual, guerrilla resistance. 'A government demanding the absorption of towns, an army demanding the absorption of personalities, are anathema to Italians' (V, 269). For the first time, Herzen spelled out the condemnation of centralised government which his emphasis on the nonsubordination of the individual had always implied.[2]

However, his description of Italy during these months confirms the impression that he was still far from formulating a socialist programme: there was still notably little explicit economic content in his ideas. Nor were the demands of these popular movements clear in his mind – the details, elementary civil and political liberties comparable perhaps to those of contemporary England, would not have begun to approach his utopian vision. But he was exhilarated by the atmosphere pervading the crowds of Rome and Naples, the sense of cooperation and movement, of spontaneous and irrepressible initiative from the people. Vagueness about the details enabled him to associate the upheavals with the total revolution in men's minds as well as in society which he had hoped to find the west approaching.

While he was in the grip of this euphoria, news came of the revolution of 24 February in Paris. The question of how he reacted to this has been the subject of controversy. The point is important since on it turns the question of the impact made upon him by the failure of the revolutions. The established view that he was delighted by the French upheaval has been challenged, and instead it has been argued that he was cool to the news and dilatory about returning to France either because of jealous

---

[2] This impact of Herzen's Italian experience has often been noted. See, for example, Labry, *Alexandre Ivanovic Herzen*, pp. 328–30.

nationalism[3] or because of indifference to constitutional and political phenomena.[4] It has been argued that the notes of doubt in his letters derived not from prescience but from dislike for French success, and that it was for the same reason that he denounced the Provisional Government so soon after arriving in France.[5] In fact his reaction was of half-disbelieving delight. He was certain to hear conflicting reports, but as the rumours were confirmed, his spirits rose still higher: 'I never believed more in life than now,' he wrote, 'strength and hope . . . to-day the sky is blue, warm, broad – welcome life!' (XXIII, 69). The dual personal and political sense of this enthusiasm was clear to his Russian correspondents, even if not to the Russian censor. He had left France disappointed and predicted a long and slow recovery; his critical reputation might suffer if she was indeed so suddenly to create a true republic. But the thrill of Paris, the mecca of revolution, coming to life, especially now when he could witness it himself, was more powerful than his scepticism. Shortly before leaving Rome, he added a revealing footnote to his first letters from Italy. After debating whether or not to send them at all since they were written in December 1847 and February 1848 – which 'means 200 years ago' – he decided he would because 'They have gained an historic interest, in them is preserved the memory of a time which has suddenly been separated from us; so far separated that it is scarcely any longer visible; we begin to forget the lines of old France and adolescent Italy, since the moment one gave up its spirit to God and the other reached manhood' (V, 245). Euphoria seems to have had the upper hand in the Herzen household during those dramatic months. 'Every moment embraced a century,' wrote Natalie, 'there began a broad, full life – everything personal, family, domestic ceased to be trivial and exclusive and took on a universal character, it seemed as if property and separate motherlands no longer existed – but a sea that was unanimous and free! And with hope we surrendered ourselves to its waves.'[6] If their infatuation with Italy delayed their return, by the end of April they had

---

[3] Malia, *Alexander Herzen*, pp. 369–74.

[4] A. McConnell, 'Against all Idols: Alexander Herzen and the Revolutions of 1848. A Chapter in the History of Tragic Liberalism' (Ph.D. Dissertation, Columbia University, 1954), Chapter 7.

[5] Malia's judgement is that Herzen 'was not completely displeased . . . by the fiasco of France's efforts to liberate herself' (*Alexander Herzen*, p. 346).

[6] *Literaturnoe nasledstvo*, 63, (1956), 371. To invoke Natalie's record of their euphoria, made at the time, seems useful, since Herzen's own account has given rise to conflicting interpretations.

set off, and both had the impression that, as Natalie wrote, 'we flew to
Paris'.[7] Herzen may have been less sanguine than Natalie but he shared
her cosmopolitan delight and sense of involvement.

Herzen was tremendously excited to see the words *'République Française'* stamped on his papers when he entered France again. As they
travelled towards Paris, he saw evidence of the mixed reception the
revolution had received. He did not record his immediate impressions,
and we have to rely upon the account he gave towards the end of June
when the euphoria had worn off most revolutionaries. But at the beginning of May he was thrilled to be addressed *'citoyen'*, to hear the *Marse-
illaise* sung beneath his window, to see the true republicanism of the
workers of Lyon. Reaching Paris on 5 May, he found it much changed.
The streets were lively, cheerful; and, despite the political and expected
social upheaval, the boulevards were perfectly safe at night. Freedom did
not mean the breakdown of social harmony! The revolution, the historical leap he had begun to despair of seeing, appeared to be taking
place. His hopes soared: he would later recall the pride and excitement he
shared during those days: 'We were so openly duped by the February
revolution, we went so proudly and so freely, with our heads high, along
the streets of the republican capital' (XXIII, 94). The Italian dream had
warmed him towards western crowds and this cemented the
identification he felt with the insurgents: he was taking part in a European thrust to freedom.

But just ten days after arriving in Paris, Herzen heard a worker
describe how Lamartine, the head of the Provisional Government, had
raised the tricolour and spurned the red flag. It was 15 May. The worker
told Herzen that he threw away his weapon and went home to tell his wife
'We have been fooled again' (XXIII, 84). In retrospect he always looked
back upon this as the fateful moment for the revolution. Two weeks later,
in the series 'Again in Paris', he began his analysis of the revolution. The
doubts he had expressed about the French 'mob' at the end of 1847 were
swept away. The revolution and the proclamation of a republic convinced him that Guizot had fallen not at the hands of the moderate
reformists or the intellectual and journalistic opposition, but at the hands
of the workers. The credit was due to 'the party of socialists and com-
munists', the heirs of Babeuf, nourished by the ideas of Saint-Simon and
Fourier, the very group who so recently he had described as people 'with
ideals barely visible in the future'. And the party consisted essentially of

[7] *Ibid.* 372.

workers – 'all the conscious and reasoning workers were socialists'. These were the 'new Nazarenes'. 'These persecuted people who conserve so much fresh strength, such deep feeling for human dignity, took up arms on 23 February – and appeared in all the greatness of the French people; as soon as the worker [*bluznik*] stood at his full height, everything disappeared before him, like stars before the sun' (V, 314–15). The dignity and humanity he had seen among them in 1847 had indeed turned out to be the hallmark of socialism; their respect for human nature really was revolutionary. The ideological skeleton of his understanding of the future reformation had taken on social flesh. And although 15 May had checked the revolution, he now saw the country clearly divided in political terms between those two worlds he had described in aesthetic terms in 1847. There were two camps, 'open struggle between the people and the bourgeoisie before our eyes – it is the beginning of a terrible social war. It is impossible to avoid' (V, 321).

The June Days had an effect on Herzen that was little short of traumatic. Having clearly identified the Parisian workers as the physical power of the socialist future, he was intensely involved in their fate.[8] The violence and blood, sheer horror at the massacre of men and women he considered courageous martyrs, as well as his own maltreatment and arrest provoked the extremism of his reaction.[9] 'After the Storm', dated 29 July, brilliantly expressed his sympathy with and admiration for the defeated insurgents, and his disgust with the triumphant bourgeoisie. He abominated not only them, but the blind *littérateurs* and the ignorant peasants. 'Moments like this make one hate for a whole decade, seek revenge all one's life. *Woe to those who forgive such moments!*' (VI, 43).[10]

[8] It was precisely because of his cosmopolitan hope and involvement in the French drama that Herzen reacted so passionately. Malia's view that Herzen's attitude to Europe was completely dominated by nationalism makes 'After the Storm' inexplicable.

[9] Describing his arrest, Herzen recalled that while being marched away by soldiers he came across Tocqueville, who was a representative in the National Assembly. 'I addressed myself to him and told him what had happened: it was not a joking matter; they kept people in prison without any sort of trial, threw them into the cellars of the Tuileries, and shot them. Tocqueville did not even ask who we were; he very politely bowed himself off, delivering himself of the following banality: "The legislative authority has no right to interfere with the executive." How could he have helped being a minister under Napoleon III!' (*Past*, 658). The encounter aptly symbolises the different attitudes of these two major commentators on 1848.

[10] This famous quotation is drawn from the German edition of 1850, and not from the earliest known version of 'After the Storm', but it captures the spirit of the original.

His analysis remained primarily ideological, he still insisted that it is not until 'everything religious has been turned into something human, simple, open to criticism and denial' that there can be freedom (VI, 344). But the slavery before 'canonised truth' now related to immediate political issues. He was specifically warning his Russian friends against simplistic reverence for the French achievement, and indeed reproaching himself and all revolutionaries for the concrete political error of undue respect for 'the Republic' and universal suffrage. His tone was not of despair but of outrage and impatience. Morally and intellectually bankrupt, the victors were the representatives of a dying but stubborn order. The executioners, the citizens of the new world were already in the streets, cold and hungry. Owing nothing to the established order, they had no pity for the old civilisation. They were the leaders of an international revolution, embracing the Chartists of Britain and the people of Russia. Addressing his Moscow friends, he said, 'We can hold out a hand to them, because they know how to answer sympathetically. They, like us, have none of that stifling narrowness which strikes one in the educated European' (VI, 346).

The heroism of the workers during the June Days shifted his criticism from their failure to choose their own leaders to the conduct of the Provisional Government. He had tasted the flavour of revolution, its suddenness and euphoria, and his indignation at the wasted opportunity was intense. He stressed the magnificence of the opportunity the workers of Paris had given to the government to educate and liberate France. French centralisation made it possible for Paris to lead the backward provinces. He saw the masses, the peasants, those lower classes not already at the forefront of the revolutionary movement as potential socialist converts. The government was in a position to develop 'the strong though unripe nature of the French people' (V, 352). But from the moment it proclaimed universal suffrage, the government had revealed a faint-hearted approach in its handling of the entire issue. Herzen claimed that had elections been held either immediately or after a considerable period, the representatives returned might have been true democrats. But the government had done neither one thing nor the other.[11] And during the unsatisfactory delay, Ledru-Rollin alone among the ministers had perceived the need for government explanation, for exhortation and propaganda, and had composed a suitable circular for the provinces.

[11] After the revolution of 24 February, elections were held on 23 April. Radicals and socialists won only 100 out of 876 seats.

But when the conservative press denounced this as interference in free elections, Lamartine yielded. The revolutionary case went by default. Indeed the government positively alienated the peasants with a provocative tax levy which could only be evaded by a humiliating plea of destitution. Without preparation or education, completely under the influence of rich landowners and urban bourgeoisie, who could the peasants choose with their first vote except enemies of the revolution? 'How could the government refrain from interfering in the vote at a time when it was necessary to reconstruct the whole social edifice?' (V, 354).

The same inability to live up to the demands of the occasion was, as Herzen saw it, reflected throughout the government's policies. It not only enlarged the National Guard quite unnecessarily, but it also retained the old discipline and uniform, thereby separating it from the people and subjecting new recruits to the old, purely reformist and anti-revolutionary values of the Guard. The National Workshops amounted to little: the government virtually shelved the question of creating jobs, which was a matter of vital importance to the workers. It failed to replace reactionary prefects, let alone junior personnel. It neither deported nor rendered harmless known enemies of the revolution. The same sheer waste of opportunity was reflected in its pusillanimous reaction to the welcome and demand for leadership it received from all over Europe. Lamartine sought a republic in name but a monarchy in fact.

Herzen saw the Provisional Government blessed with a brilliant chance to realise his ideals. So tangible did the chance seem that for a moment he even considered a temporary dictatorship would have been justified. But he took a very optimistic view of the kind of regime that would have been necessary. For success 'it would have been necessary to have had the faith and energy of the Committee of Public Safety, and, notice, only its faith and dedication; circumstances were such that the Provisional Government would not at all have had to condemn itself to a strict, punitive role' (V, 352). And at the very moment he seemed willing to condone this gentle form of dictatorship, he spelled out with unprecedented clarity the political implications of an idealism that had reached the point of anarchism.[12] He did this in the third and greatest letter in the

---

[12] Soviet authors are inclined to seize on Herzen's justification of a brief dictatorship as a permanent element in his thought, demonstrating his 'revolutionary democratism'. Z. V. Smirnova, *Sotsial'naia filosofiia A. I. Gertsena* (Moscow, 1973), pp. 104–5; B. P. Koz'min, *Iz istorii revoliutsionnoi mysli v Rossii: izbrannye trudy* (Moscow, 1961), p. 587. In fact, as we shall

cycle 'Again in Paris', completed on 18 September 1848.[13]

Herzen contrasted the true republic with monarchy, or a monarchic republic. Monarchy is hierarchical, however hard it may try to disguise the rulers as representatives of the people. It is based on submission. It rests on 'dualism', on the idea that man is fallen and the government divine, that man is not to be trusted with liberty and must therefore submit himself to the direction of the government. Laws are decreed from on high, regardless of the true interests of the people. Obedience is prescribed by a church which perpetuates illiberality by its fundamentally humiliating attitude towards man. Alien courts and uniformed police, set over and apart from the people, enforce 'order' designed not for them but against them. Herzen's most scathing contempt is poured upon the shopkeeper who claims to be on neither side, but only for order. He is the most helpless, unconscious victim of monarchic indoctrination. The republic is completely different. There the people direct themselves. The typical unit of the republic is the *artel* of workers, with its own managers but no proprietors. On a national scale the republic is made up of voluntarily coalescing municipalities, individual, self-governing, varied. Unlike monarchy the republic 'leads to atheism and anarchy'.[14] Yet 'anarchy does not mean disorder, but non-

---

see, he quickly dropped this justification, and it was precisely because his basic protest in the name of liberty prevented him advocating any such capture of state power even for a progressive dictatorship that he would fail to find a new role among the revolutionary intelligentsia after 1861. See below, Chapter 8.

[13] The anarchist elements in Herzen's thought, given most clear expression in this letter, have led to close analysis of the possibility that Proudhon exercised a major influence on his development. Labry, *Herzen et Proudhon*; Mervaud, 'Herzen et Proudhon'. Mervaud has demonstrated that even when Herzen most admired Proudhon, during the negotiations over their joint newspaper, *Voix du Peuple*, their differences were deep. From their different standpoints, both Labry and Mervaud conclude that Herzen's anarchist elements developed independently.

[14] See E. S. Vilenskaia, *Revoliutsionnoe podpol'e v Rossii (60-e gody XIX v.)* (Moscow, 1965), pp. 58–66, for a useful review of this period in relation to Herzen's approach in *The Bell*. Her analysis differs from mine in that she equates his indifference at the end of the forties to the relative merits of monarchy and monarchic or 'political' republic with his subsequent willingness to cooperate with the Tsar. As will emerge below, Chapters 7 and 8, his attitude towards political power and the Tsar at the end of the fifties was related to the same protest against all use of authority which inspired him in *From the Other Shore*. But it was only as a result of a profound crisis in 1851–2 that he moved from a sweeping rejection of all government

government, self-government – the impudent hand of government is replaced by clear knowledge of necessary compromises, laws flow from the living conditions of contemporary reality, of nationality, of circumstances, they not only are not eternal but are continually changed, repudiated.' In so far as there is a government, a central administration, it is truly the servant of the people, and they in no way respect it as something superior to themselves. Whereas in a monarchy, government pressure is necessary to keep the people together, in the republic love and unity, flowing from common interests, culture, and history which form nationality, are sufficient. 'The republic demands only one thing from people – that they be people; it is based on faith in man, it is natural and therefore does not impose bonds.' Herzen made quite explicit the basis of his optimism and his indignation.

> One must not forget that social life for man is natural and therefore easy. Look how intelligently and easily the people's life in a commune takes shape. The more developed the social base, the less need there is for a government; we fear people, we consider them far worse than they are – monarchy has taught us this. Be assured, love is as natural to man as egoism; don't interfere with his egoism, and he will love; don't threaten him all the time, and he will be just, for injustice is as repugnant to man as every lie, every false tone. (V, 363–5)

Herzen denounced the Provisional Government for failing to show any such faith. Certainly the revolution was ill-prepared, and the people would have done better to choose leaders from within their own ranks. But the real blame must rest with Lamartine and his colleagues. In his article 'The Year LVII of the Republic, One and Indivisible', Herzen devoted a brilliant passage to the daring and faith that were necessary. 'How can one go, not knowing where to; how can one willingly lose, not seeing the gain! If Columbus had argued thus he would never have set sail. It is madness to take to the ocean not knowing the way – on an ocean which no-one has crossed, to sail to a country whose existence is in doubt. By this madness he opened a new world' (VI, 51). Every step revealed the Provisional Government's doubt in man's capacity for freedom without an 'impudent government' overlooking him. The idea of freedom had

---

authority to the fundamentally different stance of being willing to bear with a government, whatever its form, provided it was open to pressure for major social reform.

taken root deeply enough in Paris for the government to give a lead had it dared. But, making an idol of universal suffrage, refusing to let the enlightened, the liberated, the true revolutionaries of the capital lead the rest, it handed France over to mere children, wild and dark.

However, as the reactionary summer of 1848 wore on, Herzen's indignation at the failure of the Provisional Government to exploit a superb opportunity began to fade. The frustration of 'After the Storm' gave way to a more reflective appraisal of the situation. And the view Herzen now took evolved from the basically contradictory position he had adopted hitherto. For on the one hand he had damned the government for lack of faith in man, in the people; on the other he had blamed them for failing to exploit the power of the state over the people in order to transform the social fabric and enlighten the peasantry. He now began to stress the destruction that was necessary before France could be free. Though he could still praise the energy and nobility of relatively genuine republicans such as Ledru-Rollin, he now saw their aims as unreal. For they failed to see that the true republic and the 'old world' were utterly incompatible. 'I am convinced that Europe cannot disentangle itself from the contemporary struggle on the basis of its civilisation, its citizenship' (XXIII, 105). The present civic framework, the massive centralised state, the dualistic culture that permeates it – all are antithetical to equality, fraternity and freedom. The old regime, 'feudal and monarchic Europe', parliaments and liberal constitutions, a system that depends upon standing armies – unnecessary, financially ruinous and fatal to civil liberty – must be uprooted entirely. 'I completely deny any possibility of getting out of the contemporary impasse without the destruction of what exists' (XXIII, 111). Drawing once again on the analogy with the fall of Rome, the infiltration of the Nazarenes, and the invasion of the barbarians, he makes a far more intransigent demand for the death of the old world than he had before the revolution. Everything from government to the old domestic values must be destroyed. It is worth pointing out that there was no hint in this of a whirlwind in the form of a Russian invasion. 'There is no need for the barbarians to come out of dense woods and unknown countries,' he told Ogarev, 'they are ready at home' (XXIII, 106). A Provisional Government which merely replaced the personnel in charge could not possibly achieve this total uprooting of the system.

So far as his role was concerned, the conclusion Herzen drew was the need to separate himself from unrealistic republicans and idealists. He likened his position to that of an early Christian, uninterested in 'Imperial squabbles', in the surface political issues of the day, in the ultimately trivial differences between old-fashioned republicans and their conservative rivals.[15] He was very conscious that he might be accused of choosing the easy and spurious role of an idle observer. But he insisted that the role of bystander was not natural or agreeable to him: it was the consequence of historical conditions. It would be hypocritical for him to take sides in an irrelevant struggle. Moreover, he argued that to understand the situation is itself to act. To grasp and accept the truth is not superfluous but a crucial step towards liberation; blind love for 'humanity' is too vapid a motivation to be useful without knowledge. And clear vision reveals that this is not the moment for external action.

This would remain an element in Herzen's conception of his role until 1852. But during 1849 and 1850 his letters and essays gave expression to a growing ideological tension and unease. This cannot be explained in terms of pessimism about the prospects of revolution. On the contrary, throughout *From the Other Shore*, the collection of sketches and essays in which he described his reaction to 1848, he remained generally optimistic that transformation was indeed imminent. France's lack of national honour, the prominence of a man like Cavaignac, the malaise in literature and art – all pointed towards the end of a civilisation. 'We are present at a great drama ... neither more nor less than the decomposition of the Christian–European world' (XXIII, 111). In May 1849 he told Granovsky that he wished to stay alive, not only because he had heard that modern science had discovered it is no longer necessary to die,[16] but 'because the sight of this falling world is peculiarly interesting' (XXIII, 138). In the following year he pointed out to the German radical, Moses Hess, the symptoms of 'decadence, of approaching cataclysm' (XXIII, 287). And in March and April, 1850, in the last articles that compose *From the Other Shore*, he pointed to the desperation of the conservatives and the estrangement of free men from both warring sides as evidence that a form of social life was perishing (VI, 115–42). It might be expected that this confidence that the hated old world was indeed dying would have inspired Herzen with delight and enthusiasm. At last the obstacles to real liberation would be uprooted and the individual could be vindicated in all his grandeur. But this was not the case at all. One

[15] See *'Vixerunt'*, VI, 62–85. Variations in the earliest known version can be found in VI, 442–52.
[16] Herzen was amused by the optimistic speculations of the German physiologist, F. G. Henley.

depressing factor was the undeniable evidence that for the moment reaction was triumphant all over Europe. But this, and the occasional doubt about the approach of cataclysm to which it gave rise, were not the root cause of his gloom. Indeed he is at his most oppressed and pained when he is most convinced that he is witnessing the death of a society. The root cause was his sense of estrangement from the masses.

At the beginning of 1848, impressed by the dignity of the Roman crowds and the 'socialist' workers of Paris, his estimation of the western masses had reached new heights. He had acknowledged the conservative reaction of the French peasantry, but had considered this the result of a very superficial delusion which a vigorous Provisional Government could have swiftly dispelled. However, partly under the influence of Proudhon, in 1849 Herzen's electoral apologetics gave way to the most complete contempt for universal suffrage. 'In general 4/5ths of all France and $4\frac{3}{4}$/5ths of all Europe consist of orangutangs not developed into people. Universal suffrage, the last banality of the formal–political world, gave a voice to the orangutangs, and you cannot make a concert from these' (XXIII, 111). Apart from its brief appearance in attenuated form at the end of 1847, this view of the masses was new. They are no longer the pure citizens of an imminent golden age, temporarily duped by the bourgeoisie. The socialists of Paris are now dwarfed by a violent, instinctive mass bent upon destruction as such, with no creative end in mind. His attitude to the purely destructive phase is necessarily ambivalent. He does not simply condemn the old civilisation. If in the past the minority were able to lead rich, spacious lives and the majority accepted it, the form of life was justified: the conditions that made possible the appearance of Pushkin and Goethe were worthwhile. 'We' enjoyed the blessings of civilisation at 'their' expense. On the other hand, the moment the majority realises the injustice and the democratic principle sweeps through the lower classes, the old form is doomed. Only sheer force can prolong it, and it is no longer justified by tacit consent. Since its demolition can open the way to a socialist era that generalises the breadth of the aristocratic life, Herzen welcomes it. But during the summer he became increasingly conscious that the masses were not ready to differentiate between what was unjust and what was of value in the old civilisation.

At the end of 1849, he criticises those who expressed acute disappointment with 24 February – a disappointment he had himself shared

– since a deeper study of the conditions of the French people would have shown that more than a superficial overthrow of the regime was necessary to build a true republic. Unlike in 'Before the Storm', he is confident that Europe is indeed seething – *'semper in motu'* is the motto of the age (VI, 72).[17] Yet the distinguishing feature of this 'movement' is not the creation of a socialist utopia, but destruction. Democracy is its characteristic, and democratic ideas act as an acid in the old social body, fatal to privilege and hierarchy. In December he is still more or less confident that out of the ashes of the old world will emerge not a perfected socialist state, but an era over which socialism will preside. His consciousness of change, of the limited life of blueprints, and even more of the difficulties of describing a total political formula that would not sacrifice some of the freedom he sought, contributed to the slight note of caution in his optimism. But more important was his growing awareness that the masses were so unprepared.

In *'Consolatio'*, the dialogue he completed on 1 March, 1849, this is most strikingly illustrated. An idealistic young woman argues with a wise, middle-aged 'doctor', a character based on the coldly analytical Doctor Krupov created in *Who is to Blame?*[18] The essence of Krupov's message is lack of faith in the masses. He is not indignant at their failure to achieve freedom because he has studied them and recognises them for the untutored, elemental, semi-conscious beings they are. They lack the education, the painful process of brain growth that the few have undergone. 'I do not believe in their capacities, nor in all those aspirations which are invented for them' (VI, 95). It is the few who cannot bear the degradation of the many; satisfy the masses materially and they will be excellent bourgeois citizens. They totally misunderstood the teaching of the Gospel and of the great Revolution. 'All that was clear and simple was beyond their comprehension' (VI, 98). To his companion's accusation that he is an aristocrat, Krupov retorts: 'Truth belongs to the minority . . . In the present as in the past, I see knowledge, truth, moral strength, the craving for independence, the love of beauty, in a small group of people set against, lost among a crowd that does not sympathise with them' (VI, 101–2). When the young woman points out that such great men as Schiller, Rousseau and Byron preferred to perish rather than

---

[17] The Latin phrase only appears in the later editions of *'Vixerunt'*, but it is true to the spirit of the original.

[18] Herzen had reused the character in his short story 'Doctor Krupov' written in the mid-forties.

accept an abyss between themselves and the masses, he replies that they enjoyed the consolation of faith in the masses. But in his time it is impossible both to believe and to think. Men are born to be free no more than fish are born to fly. Doubt, scepticism, knowledge are not more enjoyable but more painful than faith. But once one has looked behind the scenes it is impossible to conjure up belief again. 'Could you explain to me, please, why belief in God is ridiculous, but belief in humanity is not; why belief in the kingdom of heaven is stupid, but belief in utopia on earth is clever?' (VI, 104–5).

Just how far Herzen had moved from the impatient faith of the happier, revolutionary days of 1848 is brought out by the contrast with the young woman. Her understanding of man and the contemporary situation is in essence the outlook he had expressed in August 1848. She is full of sympathy for Rousseau, for those whom Krupov would criticise for believing in man too much. She is disgusted by events in France – precisely because she feels they could have gone so much better. She sees the logic of Krupov's position, but insists that the moment her heart, her feelings enter, she cannot accept it. She is completely unsatisfied by his resignation to the difference between the few and the many. While he accepts that only a handful of men have knowledge and value individual freedom, she insists that the masses do have 'an inspired intoxication' (VI, 97). Even though they could not understand Cicero, they did follow the Apostles. Throughout she asserts that though they may stifle the inner voice with futile distractions, all men do yearn to be free.

This outlook reflects the faith Herzen had demanded of the Provisional Government. It is the necessary position of anarchism. The view expressed by the 'doctor', on the other hand, was totally irreconcilable with anarchist hope. The dialogue reflects the purity and depth of Herzen's self-analysis. He was giving expression to his inner tension, and not, as has been suggested, disposing of various opinions opposed to his own firm stand.[19] The debate was within his own mind – the first edition of *From the Other Shore* was subtitled *Who is right?* And the tension continued after the dialogues had been composed. But it is the 'doctor's' ideas which carry the confirmation of being 'painful'; it is they that are new. Herzen was tormented by Krupovian cynicism. It was in response to this that he redefined his role in the aftermath of 1848.

Herzen acknowledged not only his separation from the unrealistic

---

[19] Ginzburg, 'C *togo berega* Gertsena'. See Smirnova, *Sotsial'naia filosofiia*, for further discussion of this point.

republicans, but also from both sides in a mighty clash between two worlds. He acknowledged the gulf between himself and the masses. And in this situation, cut off from both worlds, he saw himself in a lonely, isolated position. He equated himself now not with the Christians or their allies against the old world, the barbarians, but with the Roman philosophers condemned to witness the clash between the old and the new worlds. Between the destructiveness of the barbarians and the injustice of the establishment, they could not choose. This was not because of indifference but because they could see further than either side. They had faced up to the truth and accepted the lonely consequences rather than deceive themselves with childish dreams. This was the great merit of the Roman philosophers. They could accept isolation and death with dignity.

But there were two more positive dimensions to Herzen's identification of himself with the Roman philosophers. In the first place, as he came to see the masses as an elemental force for destruction which would not respond to men of his stamp, as he became increasingly doubtful that the period following the 'terrible social war' would respect individual liberty, he faced virtual despair. He was to be condemned to live in a period which would deny him not only political freedom but any hope of creative involvement with the great forces shaping the social process. Confronted by this despair, he sought compensation in private life virtually in defiance of society and the struggles within it. In 1850 he looked back over the 'agony' of the last two years: they had been terrible, they had destroyed belief and hope and led to grief and despair. But he went on, 'Now I want to live; I no longer wish to resign myself to such dependence on the world' (VI, 117). While there was a chance that 'the ship might be saved' the anxiety had been frightful, he said, but now that there can be no political freedom for the world without appalling destruction, we can take stock of our situation. We can make the free choice to live out our own lives fully and richly. For man is more free than is usually supposed. A large part of destiny lies in our own hands. The external world *can* obtain our submission, but only when we are unconscious or too weak to assert ourselves. The greater his consciousness, the greater can be the moral independence of man from his milieu. And in the present situation, having studied the masses objectively and concluded that their immediate aims are not our own, we can and must begin our own life, so independent that it will be salvaged even if the rest of the world perishes. 'We shall find no haven but in ourselves, in the con-

sciousness of our unlimited freedom, of our autocratic independence'
(VI, 119). Like the Roman philosophers, we will take comfort from
personal friendship with a few others who have understood, and from the
sun, the sea and the warm climate (VI, 106).

It is this note of defiance, this declaration of independence, which has
led some commentators to equate Herzen's position with an early statement of existentialism, to liken him to Kierkegaard.[20] And he can be
quoted to support a supremely individualistic interpretation. Yet great
emphasis on this aspect of Herzen leads to serious distortion. This is not
only because *From the Other Shore* reflects a transient reaction to events in
1848 and 1849 which does not correspond to his generally very tangible
sense of immersion in his social context. What needs to be stressed is the
other dimension to the isolated role in which he cast himself, even at this
moment of greatest defiance.

For all his emphasis on the individual, Herzen had always, as we have
seen, been deeply conscious of the social commitment and involvement
necessary to the individual. As well as a private side the full life must have
a social and political dimension. In 1849 and 1850, confronted by a cul de
sac in the socio-political sphere, he seemed to be abandoning this broader
dimension. But in fact he did not do so. When he accepted that he could
make no immediate contribution to either side in the social struggle, he
conceived of his private life itself serving as his mode of intervention in
'general affairs'. It had to bear the weight of his frustrated social idealism.
He saw in an independent private life a political act. This was reflected in
the explanation he gave to his Russian friends in March 1849, for his
decision to stay abroad and if necessary never to return to Russia. The
first, though as we shall see not the sole, reason he gave was that only in
the west was it possible for a free man to live. In the west, despite the
reaction, there was an openness about the struggle, a chance of free
speech which was completely absent in Russia. Only there could the
flame be kept alight. To keep it alight was his mission. When he asserted
that 'The liberty of the individual is the greatest thing of all', he immediately went on: 'Upon it, and only upon it, can real freedom develop in the
commune. Man must respect his own freedom inside himself and honour

[20] See R. M. Davison, 'Herzen and Kierkegaard', *Slavic Review*, XXV (1966),
    191–209, and the comments by E. Lampert and H. J. Blackman on
    Davison's article, 210–17. Malia (*Alexander Herzen*, pp. 381–2, 471 n. 30)
    points out that Herzen was first likened to the existentialists by G. Shpet,
    Filosofskoe mirovozzrenie Gertsena (Petrograd, 1921); Smirnova, *Sotsial'naia
    filosofiia*, pp. 126–40.

it no less than in his neighbour or in the whole people. If you believe this, then you will agree that to remain here now is my right, my duty. It is the sole protest which one of us can make' (VI, 318). It was his right because he too was an individual: it was his duty because of the mutual dependence of individuals.[21]

This protest found fullest expression in Herzen's life and work in the winter and spring of 1849–50. Reviewing the events of 1849, he saw his predictions of a mighty clash, of 'blood and madness' being realised, and asked 'What shall we do with ourselves?' (VI, 113). Although they could share neither senility nor infancy, there was no escape in emigration for the few free men. They were too deeply rooted, in everything other than convictions, in the old world around them. 'We recognise frankly that we would be poor Crusoes' (VI, 114). The few should remain and let their enemies know that there exist independent human beings who will never cease to proclaim the principle of freedom, who will never surrender free speech. Europe is passing through a rare phase of traumatic change in which an old social form is perishing, but the future goes its own way and the free man is unable to see his aspirations fulfilled or devote himself to concrete political action towards realising them. Even the 'liberators' of mankind, who denounce Proudhon because he is an atheist and an anarchist, who 'need an overseeing authority because they do not trust themselves', are more immediately relevant than free men since the masses are uninterested in free speech and individual freedom (VI, 124). Pursuing his analogy with ancient Rome, he observed that although the wisest Roman philosophers may have scattered and seemed to vanish from the scene, in fact they were the victors, the sole free, powerful representatives of the dignity and independence of the human personality. Similarly in present circumstances, by seeking a private freedom and sustaining their independence of outlook and life, the few will vindicate human dignity.

In 'Omnia Mea Mecum Porto' (April 1850), in which Herzen struck his most individualistic notes, the positive socio-political affirmation he saw in his role was clearly visible. For at the very same time as he declared his independence of society, he reaffirmed the socio-political analysis in terms of which this private life was a political act. The individual free life will protest against the central crime of both the reactionaries and the

---

[21] Herzen's insistence on this point bears out the cosmopolitan stance he still adopted in the period immediately after 1848. He would be the Russian spokesman of an international *avant-garde*.

masses – the sacrifice of the individual to society, to the people, to
humanity, to an idea. Despite the political and ideological trauma
through which he had passed, he reaffirmed his faith in the essentially
integrated, social and yet splendidly individual creature man *can* be. 'We
are egotists and therefore we strive for independence, for well-being, for
recognition of our rights; that is why we thirst for love, seek action . . .
and cannot deny the same to others without obvious contradiction' (VI,
129). Far from being the opposite of brotherhood, egoism is its necessary
corollary. But this is precisely what convention denies. Men refuse to risk
giving rein to their own instincts and judgement. 'How the whole centre
of gravity, the point of support of our will, our morality, lies outside us!'
(VI, 128). It is in this context that Herzen's famous and apparently
atomistic declaration that 'the free man *creates* his own morality' must be
seen (VI, 131). He assumed that the moralities thus created would be
mutually compatible. Certainly he had incorporated into his idealism
about the essential nature of man the idea that the harmony of the
individual and society is not achieved in a cold, dead formula, but grows,
becomes with each life and with each society. But fundamentally he
could only make such seemingly atomistic and reckless statements
because this basic assumption remained unchanged. Similarly, the
apparently self-centred, individualistic life he recommended derived its
validity in his eyes primarily from its affirmation of a social principle:

> *Perhaps* this denial will begin a new life. In any case it will be a
> conscientious act. Three centuries ago a whole population left
> their homeland, because they found in it no tolerance, no place
> for their religious beliefs . . . they left in order to continue the
> struggle with Old England across the ocean. The fugitives laid
> the first stone of that enormous state, the only one in our
> fateful epoch in which it is still possible for a free man to live.
> This state, arising from the protest against the absorption of
> the individual by the state is the only one which has, so far as
> is possible at present, realised the great idea of individual
> independence. (VI, 132, 475–6)[22]

---

[22] Herzen deleted the reference to America in editions subsequent to the
original German one, as he took a less sympathetic view of America. His
comments on America are discussed by A. Kucherov, 'Alexander Herzen's
parallel between the U.S. and Russia' in J. S. Curtiss, ed., *Essays in Russian
and Soviet History* (Leiden, 1963). For further evidence of the social
commitment Herzen saw in this role, see his letters to Mazzini (XXIV,
139–41), and to A. Kolatchek (XXIV, 167), 'It is not negative individualism
I preach . . . not cold and disdainful abstention – but a free devotion.'

This, then, was the role which gave meaning to Herzen's life in the west in the period immediately after 1848. He resolved 'to start a new life, at least personally' (V, 209). He had recommended 'internal emigration' when he discovered stagnant France in 1847. The idea had quickly been lost amidst the hopes of 1848. But the desire for a personal affirmation now took a very deep hold on him. And this time it did take on concrete form.

Since 1848, the Herzens had developed a close friendship with the German poet, George Herwegh. Herwegh was personally attractive and, as a delicate romantic spirit as well as an unsuccessful revolutionary, he aroused the protective instincts of both Alexander and Natalie.[23] He became an almost daily visitor while they were in Paris in 1849. He admired Herzen passionately, and Herzen was delighted to find an intelligent western European who shared his political views – even in his account of the bitter denouement to the friendship, Herzen recalled that Herwegh and he had 'the same or very similar understanding of things in general' (*Past*, 869). He identified himself completely with Herwegh in negotiations with Proudhon over establishing the journal *Voix du Peuple* in 1849: 'We want to know the measure of our moral participation.'[24] It was to Herwegh that Herzen addressed his first essay on Russia written in the west. He introduced his analysis by equating their historical positions. Herwegh had left 'this stagnant and decrepit world' and thus 'arrived at the same point as I who have come from an unfinished world still absorbed in childish sleep and unconscious of itself . . . One cannot live in a hospital or a crèche' (VI, 150). The friendship, which extended though with less rapport to Herwegh's wife, Emma, was Herzen's closest outside Russia and played an important part in integrating him in the west.

At the same time as he was elaborating the political ideas which led to it, this 'new personal life' took shape in Herzen's mind in the form of a life shared with George and Emma, away from France, perhaps in the backwater of Nice. To bring out his treachery, Herzen would later stress that Herwegh 'dreamed of going with us somewhere far away and thence calmly watching the fifth act of the dark European tragedy' (*Past*, 869). According to Herzen, it was Herwegh who 'talked of nothing but our leading a pure and earnest life together, far away from the crowd and full

[23] See Carr, *The Romantic Exiles*, pp. 43–107, for the development of the triangular relationship.
[24] 'Six lettres de Herzen à Proudhon', published by M. Mervaud, *Cahiers du Monde Russe et Soviétique*, XII (1971), no. 3, 309.

of harmony' (XXIV, 244). It takes two to make a conversation and this dream was of course in fact not only shared by Herzen – it was the product of his own political and emotional reaction to 1848. The plan evolved in the voluminous correspondence they carried on early in 1850. Herzen was busy in Paris trying to extricate his mother's money from Russia. Herwegh was impatiently awaiting him in Zurich. The two men discussed the reunion of their families in the most idealistic terms. Herwegh's enthusiasm was fuelled by his growing passion for Natalie, whereas Herzen took the project much more seriously as an experiment on a small scale with the free communal life of the future. George's capricious and touchy reproaches irritated him, and he criticised him for being less than kind to Emma. But Herzen's strictures were designed to pave the way to this communal existence. He warned Herwegh that 'no communal life is possible without the complete liberty and autonomy of the individual' (XXIII, 259). And a week later, insisting in still more earnest terms that total mutual frankness is an invaluable preparation, Herzen explained that 'The real meaning of this long correspondence is very simple – before engaging ourselves definitely and irrevocably to a communal life, we [Herzen and Natalie] wanted to divert you from the disruptive element that you introduced amidst the great and true sympathy that unites us' (XXIII, 265).[25] Despite Herwegh's complaints and suspicions of a lack of warmth, Herzen genuinely delayed in Paris no longer than his business affairs demanded – and he assured Herwegh that their financial fates were bound together (XXIII, 309). Meanwhile Natalie, for reasons that Herzen did not yet know, was rapturous about 'the two little maisonettes' on the Mediterranean, and the possibility that Ogarev and his future wife, Natalie Tuchkova, would come to complete 'our little commune, our holy commune' (XXIII, 269). Although the source of Natalie's eagerness was very different from his own, Herzen was not insensitive to her excitement and it increased his own enthusiasm for this concrete manifestation of the 'new private life'.

A large house was eventually found in Nice and Herzen let the upper floor to the Herwegh family at a nominal rent. From Nice Herzen composed what would be the twelfth in his series of *Letters from France and Italy*, dated 10 July 1850. The tone was sad as he reviewed the disappointment of 1848 and his disgust with France, but he took comfort

---

[25] Herzen's letters to the Herweghs in this period are collected together in *Literaturnoe nasledstvo*, 64 (1958), 9–258, with an introduction by Ia. E. El'sberg.

from his retreat to the sidelines.'Before my window lies the Mediterranean, I am on the holy shore of Italy. I enter this haven peacefully, and I will draw an ancient pentagram around the entrance to my home to keep out the spirit of agitation and human madness' (V, 200). For a year he wrote nothing of importance on Europe.

In essence what Herzen had achieved was to shore up his heady idealism from the most devastating consequences implicit in much of what he had said since 1848. He had created a shell within which he could indulge his vision of himself as the prototype of the future society despite the visible reaction around him. Because he made no immediate demands for political confirmation of his idealism, the depressing events in the outside world could not penetrate his 'pentagram'. Despite evidence to the contrary, despite the scepticism and cynicism he had himself expressed, he could still assume the natural goodness of man and the inevitable triumph of socialism. It was within the context of these precariously preserved assumptions that he wrote his first essays on Russia.

4

Russia from Paris and Nice

Between the summer of 1849 and the summer of 1851 – during precisely the period in which he preserved his optimism by resorting to the 'pentagram' of a new private life – Herzen wrote his first explicit analyses of Russian social and political prospects. It was in these works that he laid the bases of his theory of 'Russian Socialism'.[1] They are the founding texts of Russian revolutionary populism of which he is rightly seen as the father. He depicted a brilliant socialist future in Russia. The peasant commune, the character of the people, the intellectual progress – all foretold the realisation of a new world in his homeland. Most commentators have recognised that this blossoming of his hope in Russia was organically connected to the failures of 1848 in the west.[2] The traditional view holds that because the west had now let him down, Herzen transferred all his undiluted utopian fervour to Russia. To quote Lunacharskii, for instance, 'As earlier from our dreary north-east he turned wistfully to the west from where he expected blinding lightning, reanimation of the world, so now gradually the westerner Herzen, living in the west, still more wistfully looks into the mists of the Russia he left.'[3]

---

[1] It was at the end of the fifties that Herzen adopted the title for his vision of rural socialism in Russia.

[2] Malia of course goes very much further and argues that even before 1848 Herzen was impatient to pronounce the west dead in order to give free rein to a nationalistic messianism evident long before he left Russia. (*Alexander Herzen*, pp. 337–46). To depict Herzen exempting Russia from a xenophobic concoction of pessimism designed to condemn the west to stagnation is seriously misleading. More satisfactory are Malia's qualifications of this main thesis, pp. 410–12.

[3] A. V. Lunacharskii, *Sobranie sochinenii* (8 vols., Moscow, 1963–7), I, 145–6. See also, for example, V. P. Volgin, 'Sotsializm Gertsena', in V. P. Volgin *et al.*, ed., *Problemy izucheniia Gertsena* (Moscow, 1963), pp. 50–64.

In part this is valid. Certainly Herzen was no longer so preoccupied by the prospect of imminent success in the west, and hope in Russia did offer some compensation for western disappointments. But the sequence of events suggests that his political 'return to Russia' was less straightforward than may at first appear.

Three main points should be made. In the first place, the dominant motif of Herzen's works on Russia in this period was that of vindication of his native land. He was not in the grip of euphoric faith but was working to establish, to gain acceptance of his view of a powerful revolutionary germ in Russia, against the prevailing view of Russia as a totally benighted backwater. The second point is that when he looked back to Russia between 1849 and 1851, his western experience had already made a significant impact upon the nature of his utopianism. The commune was not merely that 'new world' he had hoped to see born in the west writ Cyrillic. Finally, and most important, his analyses of the west and Russia were still so interwoven that events in the west which took place after these essays were written were able to have a crucial impact on the role he subsequently adopted in Russia. Until 1852 he did not set up a sharp dichotomy between the basic situation in Russia and that in the west. He made the same fundamental assumptions about the historical process at work in each. And in each he saw basically the same role for himself.

During this period immediately after 1848, Herzen's confidence as a Russian was growing. He was acquiring respect in western revolutionary circles, and the very failure of 1848 made Russia's relevance seem less subordinate. The possibility that Russia, instead of languishing indefinitely in backward stagnation, could take a leading role in the advance to socialism, attracted him more and more. But the strident note of these first essays on Russia must be seen within the context of the circumstances in which Herzen wrote and the audience he addressed. The general image Russia projected among the European Left in the mid-nineteenth century was not flattering. She was seen as little more than a nation of slaves ruled by the mainstay of European reaction, the autocrat Nicholas. And although he drew on individual Russians like Bakunin and the Decembrist N. I. Turgenev, Herzen's view flew in the face of conventional wisdom among his friends at home too. In his 'Farewell' of March 1849, written after he had refused to obey a summons home from the Russian government, he still addressed his Moscow circle as if they shared his socialist and revolutionary vision.

His permanent emigration, he told them, would initiate that political emigration which precedes most revolutions, and he would be their uncensored voice (VI, 321–2). But in fact, far from supporting his account, Granovsky, Korsh, Ketscher and the others reacted coldly to the clandestine copies of his work which they saw.[4] Belinsky was dead, Bakunin had disappeared into prison, Ogarev was living quietly on his estate, and the rest of his friends were well to the right of him. His contact with Russia was in fact falling off in this period. Herzen stood alone. And however fierce his aspiration, the apparent stability of the establishment in Russia presented a constant denial of the movement he claimed to see. It was his word against a world of visible evidence. He was seeking, therefore, to confirm his own hopes. The very act of publishing his historical and social account of Russia gave it an authenticity in his own eyes. As he expressed it in his essay of 1851, 'Things one does not dare to say only half-exist' (VII, 84n.). This element of self-persuasion formed the bridge between careful, scholarly analysis and conscious, aggressive propaganda – both of which are visible in the essays.

It was the need for confirmation, rather than any expectation of active help for Russia, which made Herzen so anxious 'to acquaint Europe with Russia' (VI, 322). For an outside audience, an objective observer to recognise the embryonic, almost elusive phenomena would establish them as more certainly real in his own eyes. The western radicals, whom he refused to treat with the veneration he so despised in his compatriot Sazonov, were, none the less, still his intellectual peers if no longer his masters. He therefore devoted his energies not to any form of intervention in Russia but to propagating his account in the west. All his essays of the period were addressed to the west: three were published letters to Europeans – to the German Herwegh and the Italian Mazzini in 1849, and to the Frenchman Michelet in 1851 – and the fourth was the long essay published in German and French in 1850 and 1851, 'On the Development of Revolutionary Ideas in Russia'. With the aid of his considerable wealth, and the help of Proudhon as well as Mazzini and Michelet, Herzen was able to give his works wide publicity among western left-wing readership.

In essence he was throughout answering the question, as he phrased it in his essay of 1850, 'Where is the proof that the Russian people can recover, and what is the proof to the contrary?' (VII, 99). In arguing the

---

[4] In a letter to Michelet, Herzen lamented the poor reception his work had received in Russia (VII, 302).

case he was determined to make his audience share his transcontinental
approach to revolution, shed their western arrogance, and respect the
revolutionary potential in Russia. Accordingly, the articles were sharply
polemical. The doubts that afflicted him about the destructive and
communist rather than socialist instincts of the people, and the vast gulf
between the elite and the masses were restrained – though even within
these essays they were not entirely absent. And the advantages with
which he credited Russia were highlighted. The untapped sources of
intellectual and political vitality in Russia gave her a unique freshness
and 'virginity' as she entered the mainstream of an historical current
running towards socialism. The commune was a fertile basis for socialism
and provided more solid evidence than in the west of the socialist and
revolutionary potential among the masses. But what Herzen was trying
to do was to claim equality and not exclusive salvation for Russia. Even
though the west was still in the vanguard she should no longer dis-
dainfully ignore Russia (VI, 154). Their fates were inextricably bound up
together. The aspect he stressed was Europe's need for Russia to be free,
but equally he recognised that 'Russia's future has never been so tightly
tied to the future of Europe as it is to-day' (VII, 124). This is not to suggest
that Herzen was insincere about Russia's socialist promise: the prospect
excited him increasingly during these years. The point is rather that the
aggressive note he struck in these essays concealed a pioneering claim to
recognition rather than unquestioning messianic fervour. 'Europe has not
solved the antinomy between the individual and the state,' he wrote, 'but at
least she has posed the question. Russia approaches the problem from the
other side, but she has not solved it either. It is in confronting this question
that our equality begins' (VII, 112).

It was because his approach to this central problem confronting society
had changed significantly since he left Russia that Herzen was now able
to eulogise the Russian peasant commune. In the mid-forties, as we have
seen, he had turned away from the commune on the grounds that it
constricted the individual. And in these first essays on Russia this criticism was still quite explicit. As he told Herwegh in 1849,

> The life of the village, like all communism, absorbs the
> personality completely. The individual, accustomed to rely for
> everything on the commune, dies scarcely ever separated from
> it; he grows weak, he finds in himself neither the strength nor
> the motivation for activity; in the slightest danger he hurries to
> hide behind this power which in this way keeps its children in

a condition of perpetual immaturity and demands passive
obedience from them. (VI, 167)

He criticised Haxthausen for failing to recognise that it was precisely this
negative side of the commune that made possible the growth of the
autocracy and the loss of freedom in Russia. But for the lessons he had
drawn from his experience since leaving Russia, he might still have
rejected the commune as retarding to the personality and hence both
aesthetically and politically insupportable.[5] Yet he did not make the
break. Far from it, he integrated the idea of the commune into the very
fabric of his vision of socialism in Russia.

Two alterations in his outlook enabled Herzen to overlook, without
denying, these objections to the commune. In the first place, his expectations had been lowered. The failure of 1848 had destroyed his hopes of
participating in the inauguration of a socialist order which would fulfil
that breadth of personality of which he was himself the model. The ideal
solution no longer seemed so easy to perceive let alone realise. Even
though he still expected revolution, he was now more ready to picture it
in terms of a 'communist' uprising from which socialism would eventually arise.[6] He accepted for himself the position of an intermediary, the
flower of a doomed civilisation, the lonely forerunner of a new order
which must pass through a destructive, anti-individualist phase. He
found an outlet for the demands of his own personality in the new life in
Nice. These demands, which emotionally had lain at the root of his
rejection of the commune, therefore no longer constituted a barrier. It
was the withdrawal of these demands from his immediate political search
which made possible what Lampert has called his 'descent from the
sublime to the ridiculous', from the most crucial problems of life to
the peasant method of dividing strips of land.[7] His social projections
for the near future, in the west and in Russia, were now no longer compelled to embrace the total freedom of the individual, the perfect context
that he had previously sought.[8] The ultimate utopia would still

[5] For further evidence of his reservations, see his equation of the Russian
commune with Fourier's phalanstery, 'a military colony on civil footing' (VII,
123). See also VII, 112.

[6] Like other non-Marxist socialists, Herzen used 'communism' to describe a
primitive form of socialism which would not respect the freedom of the
individual.

[7] Lampert, *Studies in Rebellion*, p. 244.

[8] And indeed after the final catastrophe in his private life – Natalie's death in
1852 – his reservations on this score, though they never disappeared, became
even less urgent. See 'Russian Serfdom', XII, 44–5.

resolve the antinomy between the individual and society, but it was out of reach and would be realised by history in 'a thousand ways' and not by a cold blueprint (V, 186, 216). His immediate speculations were less impatient. The commune was imperfect but he adopted it as a priceless seed for a rural people from whom he was fully conscious he was cut off.

But not only had he become more resigned to this imperfection since he left Russia, his priorities had been positively altered. Direct experience of the poverty in France, amidst a luxury and commercialism with which he had no sympathy, and of western concern for the loss of social values and for the casualties of economic individualism, refocused his attention on the apparent answer that Russia provided to this problem. It was under the immediate impression of the French bourgeoisie, of its 'death in literature, death in the theatre, death in politics', and the helplessness of the poor, that, in 1847, he made his first reference to the commune since leaving Russia (V, 245). He found the walled-off gardens and fields of private property intolerably offensive, a constant reminder to the poor man that 'he is a beggar, that even the view into the distance is not for him'. He remarked that Europe had nothing like the peasant commune to prevent this situation: 'Hail the Russian village – its future is great!' (V, 250). His enthusiasm for the political independence of municipalities in Italy in contrast with French centralisation prompted comparison with the potential in the peasant organisation, and the fiasco of French universal suffrage in the following year encouraged him to stress the system of direct decentralised democracy he saw in it. The idea grew in his mind that Russia had preserved a fertile socialist seed, a protection from western social dissolution and the deception of universal suffrage. On both counts the peasant institution seemed to provide concrete grounds for the vindication he passionately believed was the Russian people's due.

In his letter to Herwegh of August 1849, the first of his works on Russia, he devoted a large section to the commune. With approval he quoted Haxthausen that 'Each rural commune is, in Russia, a small Republic, which governs itself in internal affairs' (VI, 162). He firmly rejected Haxthausen's analogy between the president of the commune and the Tsar. The president's functions are purely administrative, and even then his power can be removed by a united commune. Matters beyond administration and simple policing are decided either by custom, by the council of elders, or by a general assembly. But the central point

that Herzen made about the commune in these first years was that it
provided a guarantee against the pauperisation he had seen in western
society. 'At her first step in the social revolution, Europe encounters this
people which presents her with a solution, rudimentary, half-savage, but
still a solution of a kind, that of the continued sharing out of the land
among its cultivators' (VII, 291). Those who do leave the land – car-
penters, masons and other artisans – form 'mobile communes' while they
are away. In the village, each member has an absolute right to the use of a
share of the land, and when he is too old to work it, the commune takes
care of him. Russia has enough land to sustain its population for a
hundred years by this system of repartition, and by then 'the burning
question of possession and property will have been resolved one way or
the other'. He had fully absorbed the emphasis of early socialism on equal
distribution rather than communal production. The apparently static
nature of Russia's economy made it unlikely that he would have done
otherwise. With equanimity he acknowledged that the short periods of
tenure involved would retard improvements in technique, but he
explicitly argued that this was a fair price to pay to avoid 'the horrible
situation of the starving proletariat' (VI, 168). From his western vantage
point, this problem seemed overriding: 'Is there in the nineteenth century any interest, any question, as serious as the question of communism,
of the sharing out of the land?' (VII, 282).[9]

The commune, then, assumed a greatly increased importance in
Herzen's thought. He was delighted by the way it corresponded to a vital
aspect of socialist society, by the apparently ready-made answers it
offered to the problem of poverty and social atomisation. But the function of the commune in his thought must be understood within the
framework of his general assumptions about the historical process at this
time. Soviet commentators have interpreted these first essays on Russia,
with their eulogy of the commune, as Herzen's attempt to go beyond the
'utopian socialism' which he had seen through. 1848, they argue, had
shaken his faith in the correlation between reason and the direction of
history. But this was what Lenin called 'the break-up of *bourgeois illusions*

[9] This major impulse behind Herzen's adoption of the commune implies a
    corrective to Walicki's emphasis on 'how little he was worried by the prospect
    of the proletarianization of artisans and peasants', and on his purely
    aristocratic criticism of bourgeois society. A. Walicki, *The Controversy over
    Capitalism: Studies in the Social Philosophy of the Russian Populists* (Oxford,
    1969), p. 11.

in socialism':[10] his disillusion was not with history and revolution in general but with bourgeois revolution.[11] This, they assert, was the point of departure for his search for a materialist base in history guaranteeing socialism: the commune provided him with just such a guarantee in Russia.[12] It has even been argued that his faith in the commune in this period was already so great that he suspended his quest for political revolution and was willing to cooperate with the Tsarist government in developing it.[13] These interpretations exaggerate the weight he placed on the commune, the dynamism he credited it with, and they anticipate his disillusionment.

Certainly in the aftermath of 1848 he contemplated the possibility that there was a complete divorce between the rational conception of the ideal society and the actual course of history. In the dialogues of *From the Other Shore*, completed in 1850, he was plagued by the idea that there might be no correlation between the dreams of the elite and the movement of the masses. But, as the dialectical structure of that book suggests, and as his letters and other works of the period confirm, he did not allow this fear to harden into conviction. The tension in his thought is conveyed by an incident in 1849 which he later described in his memoirs. His former university friend, Sazonov, came to urge him to join a popular demonstration led by such figures as Ledru-Rollin, Lamartine and Louis Blanc. Herzen explained that he shared neither the assessment nor the hopes of these men. But when Sazonov chided him for preferring the safety of sceptical journalism to action in the market-place, he replied:

'But what makes you imagine I am not going?

'I concluded that from your words.'

'No: I said it was stupid, but I didn't say that I never do anything stupid.' (*Past*, 672)

The basic optimism we have seen preserved within his image of an exemplary personal life enabled him to resist the political implications of this scepticism. He suppressed his doubt. In 1855, by which time he had accepted the uncertainties of history, he recalled that 'At the end of 1849

[10] V. I. Lenin, *Polnoe sobranie sochinenii* (55 vols., Moscow, 1958–65), XXI, 256.

[11] Ia. E. El'sberg, *Gertsen: zhizn' i tvorchestvo* (Moscow, 1956), p. 421.

[12] See for example, Volodin, *V poiskakh revoliutsionnoi teorii*, pp. 62–9; Koz'min, *Iz istorii revoliutsionnoi mysli*, p. 590; G. V. Teriaev, *A. I. Gertsen – velikii myslitel', predshestvennik russkoi sotsial-demokratii* (Moscow, 1962), pp. 89–98.

[13] Vilenskaia, *Revoliutsionnoe podpol'e*, pp. 51–65.

I was stunned by them . . . I still frantically and obstinately sought a *way out*' (Past, 748). He continued simply to assume that irrational social structures are doomed to face revolution, and that the rational society perceived by the most advanced thinkers will be realised because men, the masses, although they may be temporarily backward, are naturally good. This was as true for Russia as for the west. The way forward for Russia, too, was mass revolution. He considered the destruction of the existing political structure to be necessary in both societies. As he told Mazzini in 1850, 'In Russia I don't believe in any revolution other than a peasant war' (XXIV, 141). This was in fact the premise of his whole vindication of revolutionary Russia.

That he sought a 'way out', that he still relied upon mass revolution between 1849 and 1851, and not upon the organic growth of the commune or a *modus vivendi* with Tsarism, is borne out by his attitude to France and her prospects. Though at times he announced that she had forfeited her revolutionary leadership, in this period his hope in her continually returned. This is a point that has been widely overlooked and needs particular emphasis in placing both his faith in the commune and his alleged 'messianism' in context. In the spring of 1850 he was thrilled by republican gains in the French elections – however marginal such shifts should have seemed in terms of his own cataclysmic analysis (XXIV, 7). He considered adding an optimistic supplement to '*Omnia Mea Mecum Porto*', and significantly proposed calling it 'The Prologue'. After the 'death' of 1848 and 1849, he wrote, the time had come 'to preach the day after the funerals, to look to the heritage and the inheritors' (XXIII, 326). This was in response to the evidence of a swing to the left in France: he had in mind not Russia but the socialist heirs of the west. On the same day as he wrote of the 'inheritors', Herzen remarked that

> The great question of the future has changed completely.
> France is democratising herself before our eyes, and the
> elections of 10 March [1850] constitute a complete revolution.
> It is very likely that the government, leaning on the Orleanists
> and the *bourse*, will make yet another attempt at reaction, and
> it is even quite possible that it will succeed. But in the long run
> it is doomed. The complete change in the political religion of
> the petty bourgeoisie and the mood of the soldiers bodes no
> good for the monarchic principle. Germany is preparing for war
> . . . and in Berne the radicals are triumphing. (XXIV, 7)

He declared that he was 'reconciled' to the French people (XXIII, 301).

As late as the summer of 1851 he told his Russian admirer, A. Chiumkov, that it is in Paris and Lyon that 'the true hope of history and humanity lie'. The great strength of the French people is their 'consciousness of social injustice, anger and an amazing unity'. They 'are certainly not ready for socialism, for freedom – but they are ready for revolution . . . The French people are an army, not of democracy, as the Montagnards imagine, but an army of communism' (XXIV, 199).[14] Europe's immediate future depends on the outcome of the French elections scheduled for May 1852 – like many radicals Herzen had hopes of a republican victory in this poll which in fact was never held. But even if reaction succeeds now, it can only last 'fifteen to seventeen years'. Herzen's expressions of greatest gloom over Europe's future were usually reserved for his essays propagating Russia's claims to attention. In general he concluded not at all that Europe was doomed to stagnation, but that he was fated to live through her age of transition.

During this period, then, Herzen expected revolutionary transformation where the commune did not exist at all. The commune was not the necessary motor-force behind progress to socialism. He did not see economic or institutional developments as the dynamic power which would bring it about. Indeed he continued to view economics as basically static. 'Economic questions are extremely important,' he wrote in June 1849, while preparing the first of these essays on Russia,

> but they only constitute one side of the whole [socialist]
> conception which, along with the abolition of the abuse of
> property, aspires to abolish on the same basis everything
> monarchic, religious – in the courts, in government, in the
> whole social structure and, above all, in the family, in private
> life, around the hearth, in behaviour and morality. (V, 179)

The commune was a hopeful omen and a useful point of departure. But it was passive, it had quiescently endured endless oppression and left to itself might continue to do so. 'It can neither defend itself from tyranny nor free its members; to survive it must go through a revolution' (VII, 38). It was the product, perhaps the proof in western eyes, of a more basic force for socialist development in Russia. As Herzen wrote in 1849,

> It seems to me that there is in Russian life something higher

---

[14] This remark typifies Herzen's inconsistent use of 'the French': he uses it variously to mean the whole nation, the establishment, and the mass of the people. For further evidence of his continued hope in France, see XXIV, 161–2.

than its commune and something stronger than its power; this
something is difficult to put into words and still more difficult
to point at with one's finger. I speak of that internal force, not
entirely conscious of itself, which sustained the people so
wonderfully under the yoke of the Mongol hordes, and of the
German bureaucracy, under the oriental knout of a Tartar and
under the western truncheon of a corporal; I speak of that
internal force, with the help of which the open and beautiful
countenance and the lively intelligence of the Russian peasant
has been preserved, in spite of the degrading discipline of
serfdom, and which, at the imperial command to civilise itself,
replied, after a century, with the colossal phenomenon of
Pushkin; I speak of that force, finally, and of that confidence in
self which ferments in our breast. This force independent of all
external circumstances, and in spite of them, has conserved the
Russian people and protected its impregnable faith in itself.
(VI, 162–3)

It was belief in this 'internal force' which inspired Herzen's optimism
about the approach of revolution and the advance in the direction of
socialism in Russia. This force was the social equivalent of that individual
respect for self to which he attributed revolutionary potential. Conscious
of their own worth, the people will reject the social and political oppression of the old world and will ultimately overthrow that world. In essence
this was Herzen's version of the belief in natural virtue, the natural
aspiration towards freedom on which much early socialism depended for
its optimism. And it was in terms of the presence or absence of this
internal, psychological intransigence that he assessed the prospects for
revolution in both the west and Russia between 1849 and 1851.

He equated the Russian peasantry directly with the Parisian proletariat: 'The man of the coming Russia is the *muzhik*, just as in regen-
erated France it will be the workman' (VII, 291). He attributed to both a
remarkable colour and richness of personality. He made use of sources in
Russia comparable to those, such as the theatre, that he had used in Paris.
He detected in the plaintive tone of Russian chants a vitality which could
not find sufficient scope within the existing social order. 'In spite of his
position, the Russian peasant has so much strength, so much agility, so
much intelligence and beauty' (VI, 172). Categorically he told Michelet:
'There is one fact which no-one who has closely observed the Russian
peasantry can dispute. The peasants rarely cheat each other. An almost

boundless good faith prevails among them, they know neither contracts nor written agreements' (VII, 286). The continual and harmonious repartition of land bore this out. As a class they had the qualities for uncoerced cooperation, true freedom.

Equally strongly Herzen emphasised the Russians' defiance of the *status quo*, which he saw corresponding to this breadth of character. In the chants of brigands – and popular admiration for the brigand – he found not a cry of melancholy but resistance arising from a sense of freedom within. The Russian people had internal integrity, an unbroken disrespect for all that was not simple and human – and this was profoundly revolutionary. He wrote his most passionate defence in reply to Michelet's imputations of Russian acquiescence in his *La légende Kosciuszko*. Herzen freely acknowleged that the Russian peasantry deceive the nobleman and the official. But this, he said, is not dishonesty: it is an intelligent recognition that they are the enemies of the peasantry. He conceded that the Russian peasants, like all ill-educated people, are superstitious, but insisted that their disrespect for religion and priests, despite external compliance, demonstrates that they have not internalised these beliefs. His defence of their apparent veneration for the Tsar was the same. There is no longer any emotional attachment to a real entity, as there is among many westerners for their sovereign. The Europeanised bureaucracy has assisted in creating an estrangement between throne and people evident in 1812 when Russians fought not for their Tsar or Orthodoxy, but for their native soil (VII, 284–8).

Because they respect themselves, they do not respect the state, the law, a religion and conventional morality which deny their dignity. They are immune from the dualism which has penetrated Europeans and makes them voluntarily sacrifice themselves to false idols, to such barren absolutes as 'order'. The Russian peasants have not acquiesced in their position: they have preserved their dignity in a recalcitrance reflected in the periodic murders of noblemen, and the growing discontent in the country. The people bows to external force, but its spirit of resistance is unbroken. It obeys 'because it fears, but it does not believe' (VII, 110).

In the case of Russia, Herzen elaborated this central core of his vindication – the peasantry's innate and incorruptible rejection of the existing order – in two directions. He argued that Russia had achieved nothing; she was an abhorrent military dictatorship supported by a servile nobility suppressing a serf population. But precisely because she had achieved nothing, she had a greater chance of total revolution and full socialist freedom. For unlike the west, she had nothing to lose: the forces of conservatism therefore lacked the depth and resources of their equivalent in the west.[15] Where later generations would see the advantages for economic development of Russia's backwardness, Herzen saw in it potential for upheaval and destruction. He also reaffirmed the idea that Russia was young and full of untried promise, that she had only entered the 'historical stage' in 1812 and therefore had the energy and freedom from the past necessary for total revolution. Youth might be no guarantee of a future, young men do die, but it is not the usual thing. In the same way he drew encouragement from the analogy between the nineteenth century and the fall of the Roman Empire. Just as Christianity and barbarism destroyed the old classical world, so socialism and the new 'barbarian' masses would destroy the old regime now. Initially he had been attracted to the parallel by its dialectical character – the clash between the old world and the rebellion it provoked issuing in a new era of socialism. The importance of the dialectic in his thought receded at the end of the forties although his ideal remained a form of synthesis between a richness of individual development epitomised by the aristocracy of the past and the communism he attributed to the contemporary revolutionary surge. But the essential point of the analogy became the fresh, untainted, totally estranged character of the 'barbarians'.

Both these arguments could be applied to a whole country, building on the notion that each nation constitutes an organism with a limited capacity for change and innovation. Russia could be seen as the heir to an exhausted west. Undertones of this idea were already visible in these essays: 'Men are uneasy, agitated; they ask themselves whether Europe, that decrepit Proteus, that worn-out organism, can still find enough strength to bring about its regeneration' (VII, 273–4). But in fact it was only under the impact of the personal and political debacle he experienced in 1851–2 that he virtually wrote the west off altogether. As yet he only applied the argument to all classes in France and Europe

---

[15] Herzen continued to reject Slavophile criticism of all western achievements. But he argued that it was just because of the progress the western ruling classes had made towards liberty that they were reluctant to risk jeopardising it for true freedom. Conventional morality and law were not guaranteed by force alone but were at least partially accepted voluntarily. The consequent lack of aspiration was reflected in the impoverished, stunted personalities of educated Europeans. He was bitter in denouncing 'this western dullness, which you can penetrate with neither logic nor feeling, this narrowness of a falling nature, this agonising cretinism' (XXIII, 138).

when he was most concerned to vindicate Russia, when he was at his most polemical. Generally he could and did separate the revolutionary masses from the establishment in the west and credit them with advantages similar to those of Russia. He saw in the west 'a world rotting and collapsing about a cradle', along with the 'chaos' and 'demented agony' he saw 'the pangs of giving birth' (VII, 275).

Further proof of the potential for change in Russia Herzen saw in the emergence of a critical intellectual minority. He drew encouragement from this development for two seemingly paradoxical reasons. On the one hand, when he had first come to the west he had asserted that the Russian begins where the European ended, and had stressed that Peter the Great had 'consolidated our right of inheritance'. It was a question of Europe's 'garret being our *rez-de-chausée*' (V, 21). On the other, the failure of 1848 led him to conclude that socialism could not be built upon, but in fact required the complete overthrow of, the old civilisation. Intransigence, defiance and complete independence of the old world were at a premium – and he found evidence for these among the elite as he had among the peasantry. The basic framework was the same. He argued that they too manifested an internal confidence, a respect for self which depended on no external criterion and which prevented them from venerating external idols, even the achievements of the west. It was this sense of independence, which he genuinely experienced himself, that enabled him so blandly to associate Russians of such widely varying political opinions. The point is epitomised in his comment on Gogol, who had become explicitly conservative before 1848. The anguished, bitter exposure of Russian life in *Dead Souls* reflects for Herzen a frankness in admitting one's own faults which can only proceed from an inner self-assurance. 'In order for such a cry to escape from one's breast, it is necessary that there remain something healthy and a great power of rehabilitation. He who frankly recognises his weakness and insufficiencies feels that these are not the essence of his nature, that he is not completely absorbed by them, that there is in him still something which escapes and resists downfall' (VII, 99). The scope and richness of Pushkin, the irony and intransigence of Lermontov, the beauty of the entire literary movement: all reflect a vitality and strength corresponding to the unbroken spirit he divined in the people. It is the refusal of Russians to compromise that inspires Herzen's hope. 'The great act of accusation that Russian literature addresses against Russian life, this total and passionate negation of our faults, this confession of horror at our past, this bitter irony which makes us blush at the present, this is our hope, this is our salvation, the progressive element of the Russian nature' (VII, 117). The point to stress here is that he explained this 'tragic emancipation of conscience' in terms of total independence, not just from Russia's past, but from the history and civilisation of the west. It was to Michelet in 1851 that he wrote his most memorable passage on the subject:

The emancipated Russian is the most independent man in Europe. What could stop him? Respect for his past? ... But does not the modern history of Russia begin with an absolute denial of nationalism and tradition? ...

On the one hand the past of you western European peoples serves us as a lesson and that is all; we do not regard ourselves as the executors of your historical testament.

Your doubts we accept, but your faith does not rouse us. For us you are too religious. We share your hatreds, but we do not understand your devotion to what your forefathers have bequeathed to you; we are too downtrodden, too wretched, to be satisfied with a half-freedom. You are held back by caution, restrained by scruples; we have neither caution nor scruples; all we lack at the moment is strength ...

It is from this, Monsieur, that we get the irony, the fury which exasperates us, which preys upon us, which drives us forward, which sometimes brings us to Siberia, torture, banishment, premature death. We sacrifice ourselves with no hope, from distaste, from tedium ... There is indeed something irrational in our life, but there is nothing vulgar, nothing stagnant, nothing bourgeois.

Do not accuse us of immorality because we do not respect what you respect. Since when has it been possible to reproach foundlings for not venerating their parents? We are free because we are beginning from our own efforts. We have no tradition but our organism, our national character; they are inherent in our being, they are our blood, our instinct, but by no means a binding authority. We are independent because we possess nothing; we have hardly anything to love. All our memories are filled with bitterness and resentment. Civilisation and learning were held out to us at the end of a knout ...

We are dragging about too many chains that violence has fastened on us to increase the weight of them with others of

our choice. In this respect we stand precisely on a level with
our peasants. We submit to brute force; we are slaves because
we have no means of freeing ourselves; from the enemy camp,
none the less, we accept nothing.

Russia will never be Protestant. Russia will never be
juste-milieu. (VII, 298–300)

Herzen was not striking a false note. The intensity and eccentricity of
the critical elite of the 1840s are well attested. When he told Granovsky
that his closest friend, the German Herwegh, 'is the only Russian, i.e.
man, among the foreigners', he was expressing an experienced contrast
between the excited, perhaps naïve, but deeply committed atmosphere
among his circle of friends in Moscow, and what seemed to him the
relatively distant, dispassionate character even of radicals in the west.
The impression made upon him was real. And yet here too the rigid
separation between Russia and the west was more polemical than
thorough-going. Having asserted that Russia was no mere dim shadow of
the west, and having made his protest against the entire fabric of
bourgeois civilisation, Herzen demonstrated with equal urgency and
sincerity that the Russian elite were inseparably connected with and
deeply involved in contemporary western thought.

Herzen did not claim politico-philosophical originality for his
countrymen – he acknowledged the west as the source of the most
advanced ideas of the age. He reproved the Slavophiles for disdaining the
west 'which alone can enlighten the abyss of Russian life' (VII, 113). And
since it was an implicit assumption of his 'utopian socialism' of these
years that the development of revolutionary ideas was a gauge for the
approach of revolution itself, he was anxious to show that the Russian
elite were abreast of this *avant-garde* thought. This was an essential
element in Russia's claim to equality. He therefore stressed the
similarities and links between the revolutionary elites of Russia and the
west. 'The hopes and aspirations of revolutionary Russia,' he wrote,
'coincide with the hopes and aspirations of revolutionary Europe, and
anticipate their alliance in the future' (VII, 125). He saw proof that the
Russian elite was indeed 'contemporary' in the embryonic political emigration – Ivan Golovin, 'who has been equally appreciated in France, in
Germany and in England'; Sazonov, 'one of the most zealous defenders
of democracy' and expelled from France in 1849; and above all Bakunin
who, 'succumbing at the same time as the German revolution, and going
to [exile in] Siberia for Germany . . . will serve as a guarantee and proof of

that sympathy which exists between the people of the west and the revolutionary minority in Russia' (VII, 403).[16]

Herzen himself personified a unity between the affluent and urbane revolutionary in both historical situations. A man of the forties, his perception of and aspiration towards the new world was, as we have seen, cosmopolitan. The two societies with which he was concerned, the Russian and the western (primarily French), were intertwined in his thought by the very nature of his historical setting. His physical emigration had further guaranteed that he would view them within the same framework. Living in the west, he was deeply involved in the drama of 1848, and his personal relationships and intellectual milieu were now as much European as Russian. His utopianism was too deeply rooted in French speculation and French socialist prospects for the reversal of 1848 alone to cause him to set the Russian situation completely apart. His analysis of historical development in terms of ideas and 'internal strength' enabled him to see Russia and the west at a comparable historical crossroads, and to deny the necessity of Russia's social fabric passing through western phases. In this period between 1849 and 1851 he made the analogy between the 'hospital' of the west and the 'crèche' of Russia absolutely explicit. And while this analogy held, he arrived at the same conclusion about his role in both societies. The identification between the man of the west and the man of Russia is the striking feature of both *From the Other Shore* and *Letters from France and Italy*, completed respectively in 1850 and 1851.[17] And his essays on Russia were interspersed between his work on fragments of these books. The *modus vivendi* of the new personal life corresponded as much to his sense of isolation and helplessness in the Russian context as the western.

After 1848, as we have seen, Herzen came to see the masses in the west as hostile not only to the political and economic edifice that he too abhorred, but also to the achievements in terms of artistic and individual development which he himself cherished. The masses were still a

[16] Bakunin was arrested after the Dresden uprising of 1849, and later handed over to the Russian authorities.

[17] This is not to deny that Herzen's willingness to accept his isolation in the western context was enhanced by his sense in some moods of 'belonging physiologically to another world', i.e. Russia. See for example his letter to Moses Hess in March 1850 (XXIII, 287–8). But the great bulk of his letters and work bear witness to his identification with the predicament and preoccupation of western revolutionaries. In the same month of March he even told Herwegh of his plans to write a series of articles on German philosophy for the French (XXIII, 292).

revolutionary force and therefore progressive. But he became increasingly conscious of how different their aspirations were from those of educated individuals in the west who wanted revolution. The social abyss separating them from their more affluent sympathisers had appeared in unprecedentedly sharp relief in their class war with the bourgeoisie in 1848. It was an important element in Herzen's reaction to the debacle that he confronted this problem head on. He was concerned to convince western revolutionary circles of the existence of this gulf between them and the masses. He saw the pretence that their ideals were shared by the people as not only false but reactionary. This was the point he made to Proudhon when discussing the policy he favoured for their newspaper, *Voix du Peuple*: the old world, he said, 'is within the revolutionary camp' (XXIII, 176). He had seen through the Republic of 1848; the June Days convinced him that the differences were too great to be bridged. The true revolution would be brought about by the union of workers and peasants; it would totally destroy the old civilisation and would be communist in character – which alarms the 'old believers'. He heaped scorn upon them, the 'Don Quixotes' of revolution, men of books who knew the people only on paper, and were too immersed in that civilisation to see that it was in essence anathema to the people.

He presented a very similar analysis of Russia. In both countries he saw an approaching struggle between outright reaction and popular communism. He equated the Russian regime with those of the west as 'variations on one and the same theme' (VI, 185). And despite his greater emotional involvement with the Russian peasantry, his enthusiasm for both was qualified by fear that their communist instincts would restrict the individual. He saw the workers in the west and the *muzhiks* in Russia as the worthy but unpolished heirs to the future. 'The masses, like the Slavs, are not ready for a harmonious entry into possession of the fruits of civilisation, but the masses are not ready, on the other hand, to be patient ... and hence the character of the explosion will be terrible' (XXIII, 113). In fact – not surprisingly given the actual social structure – he saw the problem of the gulf between the elite and the people as in a sense *more* acute in Russia. This is not to deny that he was very conscious of the need for the elite to communicate with the people, and that he called upon them to awaken the slumbering consciousness of the masses, 'to make them aware of their dismal situation' and inspire them to rebel. 'Who should do this,' he asked, 'if not those who represent the intelligence of the country, these organs of the people by which it seeks to understand its own position?' (VII, 113). He dismissed the objection that the elite is too small, and cited the innovations and great revolutionary example of the Decembrists as evidence of the power of a few individuals. Before Russia could enter the phase of revolution, she has only her education to get, he remarked, and she is getting that at this moment. He told Michelet that those Russians who have passed through European civilisation must act 'as a means, a leaven, interpreters between the Russian people and revolutionary Europe' (VII, 291). Yet in practice he saw this rapport with the masses as the vocation of his successors and not of himself and his contemporaries. For he was painfully conscious that at present the elite were totally estranged from the masses. Praising Pushkin's *Eugene Onegin* for depicting the isolation of the 'superfluous man', he reflected gloomily that 'We are all more or less Onegins' (VII, 74). The predicament of the critical minority is 'very tragic; it is separated from the people because for some generations its fathers have been attached to the civilising government, and separated from the government because it is civilised. The people see them as Germans, the Government – as Frenchmen' (VI, 178). The prime weakness of the Decembrists had been precisely this total divorce from the people.

During this period between 1849 and 1851, in spite of his vehemence against the 'old believers', Herzen recognised that he was himself tainted by the old world. Despite his insistence to Mazzini that 'What I demand, what I preach is complete rupture with incomplete revolutionaries' (XXIV, 140), he recognised that 'We ourselves belong by life, by habit, by language, to that literary–academic and political sphere which we repudiate' (V, 208). He humbly admitted that the revolutionary intellectual, however sincere and intransigent in aspiration, had roots in the doomed order which made it impossible for him to become part of the new society. At his more buoyant he saw this in terms of being born before his time, of superiority rather than inferiority. He implied that he felt in himself an aspiration blended of the richness of individual life, of the literature and art, the culture that he associated with it – the best part of the old world – and the justice and solidarity of the revolutionary masses. He accepted that the immediate future was more likely to be communist than socialist. At the very end of 1851 he told Proudhon that 'France, falling back into childhood, and Russia not yet emerging from it – both under a degrading yoke – have arrived at the same level. Russia has gained nothing and France has lost everything. Despotism will create tremendous possibilities for communism' (XXIV, 216–17). And in these

circumstances he suggested that as free individuals they should move
away from both to England. But whether he stressed the dignity or the
taint of his position, his interpretation of the limited nature of the
historical role he could play was the same.

Until 1852, Herzen experienced the same paralysis in the Russian as in
the western context. It was in the last two of his *Letters from France and
Italy* that he gave the fullest and final expression of this understanding of
his role. And these letters represent a self-definition in terms of a fusion
of his role in Russia and in the west.

He reaffirmed his belief that revolution was the sole way forward and
that the people were indeed moving towards it. He saw 'barbarians
coming from everywhere: from Paris and from Petersburg, from below
and from above, from castles and from huts' (V, 211). But the painful
truth is that the people has no need for and does not respond to men of his
stamp:

> The people suffers much, life weighs upon it, it hates much,
> and passionately foresees that soon there will be a change, but
> it does not await ready-made workers, but the *revelation* of
> what secretly broods in its spirit, it awaits not books but
> apostles, people with whom faith, will, conviction and strength
> coincide – people who have never broken away from it – people
> who have not left it but are really in it and with it, with open,
> unshakeable faith and with none of this distracted devotion. (V,
> 208–9)

Even those who had made the ideological break from the old world are
separated by a vast chasm from the people. 'Where the people learn, it is
hard to say – only not from books, the people read little ... What we
work out by long theoretical labour, they suddenly embrace whole and
apparently without effort' (V, 203–4). The people have no use for elabor-
ate principles, critiques and doubts. They 'scarcely know the spectres
against which we struggle' (V, 208). His concept of the people possessing
an internal integrity which gave them a direct, spontaneous relationship
with 'the truth', made any idea of gradual conversion from outside, by
men of his generation and milieu, superfluous.

The elite had made the theoretical break, the insight into total destruction of the old civilisation which socialism implied. This was their
contribution. He did not denigrate it. Indeed, he saw it as an essential
step towards freedom. Despite their isolation, they had perceived 'the
idea of the future revolution' and it could not now be suppressed. But on

this act of rebellion 'we spent our greatest strength, on it we spoke our best words, and now we can only be strong in the struggle with men of books and the pharisees of the conservative and revolutionary world . . . To leave speech and turn to the people is a great act: but we are incapable of it' (V, 208). Helplessly separated from the people, and unable to take part in the world they would introduce, since 'our spoiled lungs cannot breathe any air other than this corruption', Herzen proclaimed his *'Morituri te salutamus, Caesar!'* (V, 209).[18]

Herzen's first vision of 'Russian Socialism' took shape within the context of this resignation. His vindication of Russia, his hope of her transformation and rural socialism left him in precisely the same impotent position as in France. He felt himself peripheral. He could do no more than argue on the speculative and literary plane. It was this that made it possible for him calmly to contemplate emigrating to America, no less. The likelihood was never very great, but the conclusion was logical.

However, he did not emigrate, he did not devote himself to purely theoretical argument. On the contrary, he found a wholly new role for himself: direct agitation for peaceful emancipation of the Russian serfs. This represented a dramatic departure in his understanding of himself and of the historical process, and a significant shift in the degree to which he concentrated on Russia. It was only possible when the outlook which hitherto had informed his attitude to his role in both Russia and the west was altered. His reorientation was precipitated by the ordeal he suffered in 1851 and 1852.

[18] There had been moments, and would be again, when Herzen thought Russia was about to go to war, and that events might therefore move fast in his homeland. See, for example, his letter to Mazzini of 20 November 1849, when war with Turkey seemed possible and he became very overstimulated, predicting that 'The taking of Constantinople will be the beginning of a new Russia, a *democratic and social* Slav federation' (VI, 224–30). But in this period he generally accepted that the hour of creative action in Russia was probably still far off (VII, 301).

5

The tragedy

Between the New Year of 1851 and the summer of 1852, Herzen underwent a series of devastating blows. His private life was virtually destroyed during the very period that expectations of early Republican advances in France were finally dashed. Early in 1851, Natalie confessed to her love affair with George Herwegh, the man with whom the Herzens were sharing a house. In November Herzen's mother and his younger son, the deaf-mute Kolya, were drowned at sea. Natalie fell dangerously ill. And at the beginning of December Louis Napoleon perpetrated his *coup d'état*, destroying Herzen's recurrent hope that he would, after all, witness dramatic progress in France. The effect of this first instalment of disaster was to undermine his morale, but it served to confirm his judgement that he was doomed to be a bystander in the confrontation between communist masses and dictatorial governments. It was the second series of blows, suffered in 1852, which triggered off a basic shift in his outlook and activity. In January 1852 Herwegh had the effrontery to challenge him to a duel, tormenting him with reflections on the ecstasy he had shared with Natalie. To make matters worse, Herwegh spread the news of his challenge and the details of his insults. Herzen was deeply shaken and at the same time was subjected to the curiosity of mutual friends and acquaintances. In the heat of the struggle which ensued for public sympathy among western democrats, Natalie died.

Although these events have often been outlined, commentators have paid scant attention to their impact upon his political and ideological development.[1] The cavalier treatment of the drama through which

[1] See for example; El'sberg, *Gertsen*, pp. 318–23; Smirnova, *Sotsial'naia filosofiia*; Volodin, *V poiskakh revoliutsionnoi teorii*; after a detailed commentary on Herzen's development, Koyré apologises for treating him as a thinker rather than as a man (*Études sur l'histoire*, p. 221). The fullest and best account of the drama is in Carr, *The Romantic Exiles*.

Herzen passed *after* 1848 is epitomised in the major western study by Malia. 'Herzen's family drama led him to question none of his principles,' says Malia; 'rather it moved him to reaffirm them all ... Total negation of the existing world and at the same time unlimited affirmation of the ego's autonomy, in spite of all that oppressed it, was the only way out of the crisis, both political and personal, to which his new life in Europe had brought him.'[2] That the personal tragedy led him to reaffirm any such principle, and that it had no other major effect, are both demonstrably false. Malia's conclusion rests in part on his basic interpretation of Herzen. He credits Herzen with a deep-seated nationalism which made him welcome France's failure in 1848, and totally dissociate himself from the troubles of a dying west immediately thereafter. Malia is thus not open to the major impact that the events of 1852 had on what was until then in fact a profoundly cosmopolitan involvement. But Malia's conclusion also rests on a strange rearrangement of the sequence of events. He dates Herzen's knowledge of Natalie's infidelity from the beginning of 1850 – a few months before Herzen arranged that he, Natalie and Herwegh should live cosily together in the same house.[3] And he places Natalie's death in 1851 whereas in fact she died in 1852.[4] Far from leading Herzen to reaffirm 'the autonomy of the ego', the trauma undermined precisely that conclusion and the sense of withdrawing behind a private 'pentagram' which he had based on it. Herzen himself was deeply conscious of the interaction between his personal experience and his general outlook.[5] And although the particular interpretation he gave of the interaction cannot be accepted uncritically, this terrible period did shape the rest of his career and reverberated throughout much of his work and thought. It transformed his concept of his role.

The commune that the Herzens and the Herweghs had established in Nice in 1850 did not last long. That summer Herzen completed his essay 'On the Development of Revolutionary Ideas in Russia'. But as autumn approached, his calm began to be overshadowed by suspicion. Natalie was pregnant and on 20 November gave birth to a daughter, but her passion for Herwegh was by now in full flow. Herwegh himself became increasingly nervous, and as the tension grew Herzen became irritable

---

[2] Malia, *Alexander Herzen*, p. 387.
[3] Natalie successfully allayed Herzen's early suspicions.
[4] Malia, *Alexander Herzen*, p. 386, 387, 393.
[5] This is one of the most striking characteristics of his memoirs. See especially *Past*, 857–8; see also the various prefaces to different parts of the work, and his final dedication to Ogarev, *Past*, 1858–66 and xliii–xlvi.

and bitter. In his memoirs he describes a scene which captures the emotionally charged atmosphere of those days. Natalie had shown him a picture of their house with herself in the background that she had commissioned.

> I thought that the sketch was meant for me, but Natalie said that she meant to give it to Herwegh as a New Year's present ... I was vexed.
>
> 'Do you like it?' asked Natalie.
>
> 'I like it so much,' I said, 'that if Herwegh will allow it I shall order a copy to be made for myself.'
>
> ·From my pallor and my voice Natalie understood that these words were both a challenge and evidence of a violent storm within me. She looked at me, and there were tears in her eyes. 'Take it for yourself,' she said.
>
> 'Nothing would induce me to. What a trick.' (*Past*, 877)

The truth came out shortly afterwards. Herzen learned not merely that Natalie had been unfaithful to him, but that she had carried on a sustained love affair with his best friend in the west. And he had shown himself totally blind. Herzen was outraged.

However, both Natalie and Herwegh acted in the way most certain to soften the blow. By imploring him to stay with her and agreeing that Herwegh should leave the house next day, she shielded him from the most wounding, corrosive threat – humiliation. Before he could be submerged in self-pity and embarrassment, her helplessness, her 'look of infinite suffering, of mute agony' (*Past*, 880), forced his attention away from himself. At the very moment he learned of her betrayal, he begged her to forgive his rage. Her behaviour made it possible for him to see only Herwegh's treachery and not Natalie's implicit dissatisfaction with himself. And at the same time Herwegh treated him with awe. He hid upstairs when the storm broke. He begged Herzen to kill him. He sent grovelling messages through Emma and Natalie, threatening to take his own life because he had offended Herzen. He slunk away from the house when Herzen ordered it, without protest, without confrontation, without any pretension to equal standing with his rival. Inadvertently, he did everything to protect Herzen's ego, to leave him feeling powerful, magnanimous and ultimately victorious over Natalie's heart.

This is not to deny either that Herzen was deeply hurt or that he became profoundly melancholy during the next six months. He did. 'How many times we came in to dinner,' he recalled in his memoirs, 'alone in the evening and, neither of us touching anything, and not uttering a word, got up from the table wiping away tears . . . Idle days, sleepless nights . . . misery – misery. I drank whatever came to hand' (*Past*, 886). He reproached Natalie for valuing their past, their intimacy so little. In June he lamented 'I have not found the peace I wanted, the quiet haven.' 'For a long time,' he went on, 'I thought it was possible, at least personally, to begin a new life, to retreat into oneself off from the gabbling market-place. It is not possible – if there is just one man around you with whom you do not break off all ties, the old world with all its vice and debauchery, its cunning and treachery, will return through him' (V, 201). It was in this mood that he felt most tainted by the old civilisation that was to be destroyed; it was in June that he proclaimed his '*Morituri te salutamus, Caesar!*'

The worst moment in this first act of his tragedy came in July when he discovered that Sazonov had heard Herwegh's view of the whole tale. For a moment he saw himself ridiculed as a reactionary husband compelling his wife's obedience against the dictates of her heart. But when he furiously demanded an explanation from Natalie, she hurried to reassure him. And this time the rapprochement was lasting and probably more sincere on Natalie's side. Herzen recalled this period as a second honeymoon. 'I am thankful to destiny for those days and for the four months which followed them. They made a triumphant ending to my personal life. I thank her, the eternal pagan, for crowning the doomed victims with a sumptuous wreath of autumn flowers and strewing their path, if only for a time, with her poppy and her fragrance!' (*Past*, 893). The euphoric description may well have owed something to Herzen's need for 'poetry' in his life when he wrote it. But the wounds had begun to heal. For some months he enjoyed complete peace from his rival. Natalie had ended her correspondence with Herwegh, and had apparently satisfied Herzen completely of her renewed devotion. She was again pregnant.

The first blow of discovering Natalie's infidelity, then, was to some extent deflected. It did increase Herzen's sense of being at once 'the corpse and the murderer, the sickness and the dissector' of the old world. And the most extravagant aura with which he had surrounded his 'new life' was lost. But his outlook and interpretation of his role were not fundamentally altered. In the summer and autumn of 1851 he still firmly asserted that France represented the revolutionary *avant-garde*. In November, looking forward to the elections to be held in May, he enthusiastically thanked Michelet for dispelling his apathy and assured him 'I have faith again in 1852' (XXIV, 203).

His recovery was quickly undermined. On 16 November, his mother and his younger son, Kolya, were drowned at sea. The Herzens were stunned. Natalie never fully recovered. Herzen felt himself visibly aged. 'The physical world,' he told Michelet, 'is semi-organised chaos, consolidated disorder, wandering, blind, stupid and senseless' (XXIV, 210). And a fortnight later, as if to confirm his assumptions about the inseparable links between private fortune and public history, Napoleon's *coup d'état* demolished hope of Republican victory. 'We had scarcely begun to recover and get used to the personal blow of 16 November, when there was suddenly no family,' wrote Herzen, 'and a whole country goes to the bottom, and with it, perhaps, the century in which we live' (XXIV, 213–14). With any hope of imminent progress in France lost, and with the 'commune' in Nice destroyed, Herzen's dejection was profound. He now made his most lurid prophecies of 'thunder and lightning, the flames of burning palaces, the ruins of factories and offices'. 'Communism,' he said, 'will fly past violently, passionately, bloodily, unjustly, quickly' (V, 216). Yet even now he saw not the death of Europe's ultimate prospects, but the violent overthrow of the old regime, ruthless confrontation between reaction and communism. And correspondingly he still sought some comfort in private life, and at the end of 1851, urged Proudhon: 'Let us separate ourselves from the painful sight of this demented world and try to free ourselves, let us save ourselves even if we cannot save the world' (XXIV, 21). The scene was set for him to leave a continent likely to endure a violent struggle for the rest of the century. It was in this condition, demoralised by the tragedy at sea and the coup of 2 December, that Herzen was confronted by Herwegh's fateful re-emergence on the scene and the final episode in his tragedy. It was this episode which was to mark the crucial turning point in his concept of his own role.

After the original fracas, Herzen had refused to read his rival's letters and returned them unopened. But one morning, soon after the New Year of 1852, a letter arrived from Herwegh with the envelope marked '*In re* an honourable challenge'. Herzen decided he must open this letter. It gave full vent to Herwegh's indignation and frustration at the ignominy of his position. For a year he had brooded over his undignified departure from Nice, over Herzen's cold contempt, unread letters returned, and the sheer injustice of Herzen apparently escaping unscathed. He was bent

upon revenge. To regain lost ground and establish his status as lover, he
challenged Herzen to a duel.

Herzen never re-read the letter, so great was the impression it made
upon him, and later he ceremonially destroyed it. But a draft survives
and is worth quoting at length:

> Knowing your brutal methods I am communicating with you
> once more through *this* channel. I wish to exhaust all peaceful
> means – and if these fail, *I shall shrink from no scandal*. I shall
> be obliged to bring a third party into the dispute. Be assured
> that my voice will drown the voice of this child of incest and
> prostitution which you wish to display to the world as a
> triumphant proof that you are what people say you are! There
> is your greatness of soul – the solution which you seek at the
> price of the degradation of her whose possession you dispute
> with me! Yet you know from her *own mouth* that she never
> belonged to anyone but me, that she remained virgin in your
> embraces despite all her children – and she remains so still.
> You know how we were together at Geneva, at Nice, day after
> day. You have been told of this union of soul and senses, those
> vows which only the most unspeakable love could transfigure
> and sanctify, you find her lips still hot with kisses of my whole
> body; you know that in the transports of her love she conceived
> a child by me at Geneva; and I shall never believe that you did
> not even then suspect, like everybody else – you are not so
> much deceived as you pretend. You know – but you do not
> understand – that she was unhappily compelled to accept
> another child by you, that she begged my forgiveness for it,
> that I forgave her, that my friendship for you was then almost
> as great as my love, that I could not see you suffer, that we
> took Emma into our confidence, but begged her on bended
> knees to sacrifice herself in silence. She saw our love; she saw
> our affection for you; and she was willing that she alone should
> be unhappy. But you only know how to *insult* women when, by
> every kind of falsehood, hypocrisy and manoeuvre, you have
> succeeded in driving away the men. You know that the object
> of life of Natalie and myself was to repair the unfortunate
> accident at Geneva, that she dreamed and thought only of
> getting a child by me, that our whole future lay in that hope,
> that when she spoke to you she thought she had succeeded;

perhaps you do not know that I only remained in the neighbourhood because she had sworn that she meant to escape.

Enough! You will not continue this prostitution of a being whom I did not steal from you, but whom I took because she told me that you had never possessed her; at any rate I shall not survive it if you do. To your gratuitous insults to Emma you have added the infamy of pretending that I seduced your wife. There are enough wrongs to justify me in demanding satisfaction . . .

Let us tear each other's throats like wild beasts – since we are to be no longer men – and show for once (if you have it) something else besides your purse.[6]

Each insult was piercing. The primary purpose of the letter was to torment, to humiliate and to incite Herzen. It succeeded brilliantly. 'This letter was the first insult I had ever received in my life,' Herzen recalled three years later in his memoirs. 'I leapt up like a wounded beast with a moan of fury.' Beside himself, he resolved to 'go and kill him like a dog' (*Past*, 903). Although a year had passed since he first discovered Natalie's infidelity, it was only now that Herzen felt the full weight of the blow dealt him. Not only were the old wounds reopened: they were cut infinitely deeper. Not only did Herwegh repeat the tale that Herzen had heard from Sazonov – that Natalie intended to leave him once he had calmed down – but he added the most poignant, intolerable insult possible, the all too convincing account of Natalie's infatuation and ecstasy. He claimed that Natalie herself had said she 'remained virgin' in her husband's embraces. The baby Natalie was carrying, whose birth Herzen had hoped would bury the past and open a new chapter, was besmirched by Herwegh's taunts. The depth of Natalie's betrayal and commitment to her lover had not and never would again be so powerfully forced before Herzen's eyes. The insipid light it cast over their relationship was unbearable to Herzen. For, as we have seen, his romantic view of their love, their rich, idyllic family life had cast a glow over his whole view of life. Since their courtship and marriage, her devotion and admiration had become the cornerstone of his enormous self-confidence. 'I was so completely at peace, so sure of our deep, perfect love,' he recalled in a passage of his memoirs, 'that I never spoke about it; it was the great *assumption* upon which all our life rested; a serene

[6] Quoted in Carr, *The Romantic Exiles*, pp. 96–7.

consciousness, a boundless conviction of it excluding doubt or even distrust of myself, constituted the basic element of my personal happiness.
Peace, repose, the aesthetic side of life, all that . . . rested on her, on her,
on her!' (*Past*, 473). Shortly before the debacle in Nice he had told a
friend that 'only one woman had played a part in my life, and that part
had been an enormous one' (XXIV, 243). She was his 'bliss', his
'heaven'. He had come to take her love for granted, but that only made
the shock greater. It was his most anguished reproach to Natalie that her
actions showed such contempt for the past, that they left nothing 'sacred'. The deepest wound of all was the contempt she had shown for him.

'Horrified at the thought that the doubt would always remain' that
Herwegh's account might be true, Herzen frantically questioned Natalie
(*Past*, 908). She denied it, but it is probable that she knew Herwegh was
telling the truth and that her denials were deprived of much of their
weight. Just a week before she died she secretly wrote to Herwegh,
reproaching him not for implicating her but for degrading their affair by
trying to shirk his share of the responsibility for the initiative. Nevertheless, her reassurance was desperately necessary to Herzen, both for his
own peace of mind, and as a riposte to Herwegh. He refused to correspond with 'the creature' himself, but he passionately wanted the
picture Herwegh had drawn of Natalie's feelings to be repudiated at first
hand. This was done in a letter Natalie wrote Herwegh five weeks after
the challenge, on 18 February. Carr has noted that it 'reflects in every line
the inspiration of Herzen's masterful pen',[7] and the style and tone are
undoubtedly quite unlike those of the letters she wrote him both before
and after this one.[8] The letter therefore reflects above all Herzen's
preoccupation – the need to crush at source the campaign to humiliate
him. To the 'hideous nakedness' of Herwegh's 'perfidious' character, the
letter contrasted 'Alexander's dignity and devotion . . . My unhappy
infatuation has served only as a new pedestal on which to raise my love for
him . . . Have I not always told you that I could not for one day survive
parting with him? that if he left me, even if he died – I would remain alone
to the end of my life?' (*Past*, 908). But for the time being Herzen was
deprived of the satisfaction even of this retaliation. Herwegh sent the
letter back apparently unopened, and it was not until nearly five months
later, when Herzen's wounds had had time to fester, that the letter was

[7] *Ibid.* p. 99.
[8] Much of Natalie's correspondence with Herwegh can be read in the review by
L. P. Lanskii, *Literaturnoe nasledstvo*, 64 (1958), 259–318.

forcibly read to Herwegh and it was discovered that he had indeed read it but had resealed the envelope.

Natalie's death itself set the seal on the tragedy. The slate could never now be wiped clean. Just when Herzen needed her most to demonstrate to himself and to the world where her true loyalties lay, just when he would need most her warmth and support to ward off the disillusion and bitterness which threatened to encompass him, he saw her weaken and die. The last scenes of her death made an indelible imprint upon his mind – 'those frightful, inhuman nineteen hours', the death of the newly born baby, Natalie's painful hope that she would live, his own sheer help-lessness (*Past*, 917).[9] Her death left him desolate. 'My moral weariness and insignificance has no limit,' he wrote to a friend (XXIV, 275).[10] He felt himself declining into apathy and reaching the point of suicide. Yet he was prevented from retreating into himself to recover his composure. For she had died in the heat of his struggle with Herwegh for the support of public opinion.

Herwegh's campaign to shake what he saw as Herzen's complacency was not limited to an intensely private, personal insult. Not only did he himself jeer at Herzen as a cuckold, but he made sure that the tale was widely known, so that on top of the virulent abuse from this rival who had made his trust look so blind and foolish, Herzen suffered the fear of scorn from common acquaintances. Hearing the story from Herwegh's side, they would see Herzen in the doubly damning light of attempting to conceal his humiliation. 'I had been astounded at Geneva when I heard from Sazonov of the scoundrel's gossip,' he wrote later, 'but how could I have thought that round us, close at hand, the other side of the door, everyone knew, everyone was talking of what I regarded as a secret buried among a few people' (*Past*, 902). The challenge to a duel was designed to add weight both to the private insult and the public scorn to which Herweigh was subjecting Herzen. The move later lost some of its force when Herwegh proved less than adamant, but initially it was masterly. By making his challenge common knowledge, Herwegh seemed to have forced Herzen either to refuse and run the risk of adding cowardice to his damaged reputation, or to accept and concede to the 'scoundrel' the status of lower and equal rival for Natalie.

[9] Herzen devoted a whole chapter to 'The Last Scene', *Past*, 912–20.
[10] See Herzen's letters to M. K. Reichel throughout May and June 1852, XXIV, 275–92.

Herwegh's vendetta therefore compounded the assault on his pride Herzen had already endured from Natalie's betrayal. Whatever the truth about the depth of his wife's desertion, about the real motive for his refusal to fight a duel, Herzen suffered from gnawing doubt about the real or imagined criticism of others. His previous life, his success and popularity, his predominance in his Russian circle, had given him no preparation for this experience. He was peculiarly vulnerable because of the enormous dimensions of his ego. He therefore felt an intense need for confirmation of his view of the saga, for support from friends and the radical circles in which he moved. His self-esteem, his whole concept of himself, was at stake.

Having made sure the contents of Natalie's letter to Herwegh were publicly known, he devoted himself to the struggle for the support of a growing public opinion. This centred on the question of the challenge to a duel. Herzen's attitude was complex. He had a real desire for vengeance, a deep hatred of his rival. But he was also fully aware that to accept the challenge would be to restore Herwegh's dignity and position. This he refused to do all his life. The whole picture he created of Natalie's innocent part in the affair rested upon Herwegh being no more than a cunning and deceitful seducer. Moreover, Herzen despised duelling – and he made the point long before the issue became so pressing – as an aristocratic relic of male chauvinism. He made great play of his insistence that Natalie should have the opportunity to vindicate herself, and not be fought over as a dumb chattel. And his most impassioned argument rested on a much broader principle. He saw the defence of 'honour' as obedience to a humiliating external authority, the tyranny of public opinion. 'We may boldly demand that the decision should be left to ourselves when we are to bow the head to an idol which we do not believe in, and when to appear in our full stature as free men and, after battling with the god and the authorities, to dare to throw down the gauntlet to the medieval tribunal' (*Past*, 904). Duelling itself might be disappearing, but fear of public censure for cowardice was not. 'I was conscious that I was taking my stand against a monstrous and merciless force' (XXIV, 258). He reaffirmed the guiding precept of his political and social outlook. 'The principle that regulates a man's actions should lie within himself, in his own reason; if it lies outside him, he is a slave, however valiant he may be' (*Past*, 905). The ideological defence of his refusal to fight a duel was eloquent and wholly consistent with his principles. Yet for all the independence that he wished to assert from one tenet of public opinion, he very naturally minded passionately what was said and thought about his feud with Herwegh. He must explain his motives and not simply allow himself to appear a coward and a hypocrite who, when it came to the test, insisted upon his bourgeois rights as a husband. Although he declined the opportunity to try to kill Herwegh, he intended to do the next best thing – to annihilate him as a personality within their shared milieu.

By the time of Herwegh's letter, Herzen had lived for five years in the west and intended to remain there for the rest of his life. The drama had taken place in the west and concerned western people. Though his view of western revolutionary circles had become less romanticised, he had taken his place among them. He had become personally integrated among these French, German and Italian idealists and had steadily lost contact with his friends in Moscow. Apart from detailed explanations of the whole affair to such close friends as Ernst Haug and V. A. Engel'son, it was to his western comrades at large that he turned for support. He appealed to Proudhon, to Mazzini, to Willich, to Wagner, to Michelet. 'I belong to this new society to which you and your friends belong,' he told Proudhon, 'I belong to the revolution to which Mazzini and his disciples belong' (XXIV, 325).[11] He denounced Herwegh as slanderous and depraved, he explained his refusal to fight a duel, and he appealed to the solidarity and power of the forerunners of 'the new society' to decree Herwegh's 'moral death' (XXIV, 297). His campaign culminated in his attempt to establish a 'court of honour' to decide the issue. The plan was suggested to him by the Italian Orsini, but the energy and hope Herzen concentrated on securing a formal judgement from the circles of idealists illustrate his sense of an almost concrete community among them.[12] He composed a remarkable address which he circulated to the democratic camp in July 1852:

> I take you for my judges.
> I have refused a duel.
> A duel with M. Herwegh.
> Why?

[11] Similar letters to Wagner and Michelet are preserved, XXIV, 295–7, 307–10.
[12] For an interesting portrayal of the sense of international solidarity among revolutionary circles, see M. Gershenzon, 'Gertsen i zapad. Glava iz biografii A. I. Gertsena', *Obrazy proshlago* (Moscow, 1912) pp. 175–282. Although he overrates Herzen's feeling of integration in London after 1852, Gershenzon pieces together some useful evidence on the atmosphere among the radicals after 1848.

I will speak frankly. Treachery, hypocrisy, cowardice and
exploitation are crimes. Crimes must be punished or expiated.
A duel is neither an expiation nor a chastisement.
A duel is compensation.
To condemn and stigmatise crimes which, by their very
baseness, escape the processes of our official enemies, I turn to
the only tribunal I recognise, a jury of correligionists, expecting
from it justice against the infamous wretch whom I denounce
before it – a sentence all the more solemn and terrible for
having as executioner the conscience of all men of good will.
Our brothers of European democracy, responding
spontaneously to my appeal, unanimous in their condemnation,
have declared themselves ready publicly to damn a man who
has forfeited his honour . . .
Let the verdict be pronounced and justice be done for the first
time without solicitors or policemen, in the name of the
solidarity of peoples and the autonomy of individuals. (VII,
386–7)

All his correspondents offered warm sympathy, and his closest friends
devoted time and energy to pursuing Herwegh. A group of Italian
followers of Mazzini did announce their verdict in Herzen's favour, and
Mazzini added his name. But as the weeks went by after Natalie's death
in May, Herzen's hope of achieving a consensus so tangible that it would
vindicate his whole version of the affair and restore his self-esteem,
gradually faded. Piecemeal expressions of support did not carry enough
weight to give him back his peace of mind. As he explained to Michelet,
his desire to take his personal affair before 'our own court' had only half
succeeded. 'My friends nobly supported me with their sympathy, but
they are still too weak to defend their own brothers' (XXV, 120). In
October he decided that he could achieve nothing more in this direction.
He was despondent. 'It frightens me,' he told Marie Reichel, an old
friend and fellow emigrant who took care of his children during this
period, 'that I have become so base and cowardly, that I am afraid of
quiet, like badly brought-up children are afraid of being left in a dark
room. I feel all the faint-heartedness of my behaviour – but everything
is so terribly broken inside, that I don't want to see or feel' (XXIV,
323).

A decisive turning point had been reached in his career. He had lost his
way; he had lost his *raison d'être*. 'I have lost everything,' he wrote at this

time, 'I have lost my mother and one of my sons in a shipwreck, I have lost my wife. Struck down even in my own home, after terrible, bitter experiences, I wander with neither occupation nor aim, from one country to another' (XXIV, 342). The private life in which he had placed so much of his moral capital since 1848 had been destroyed. And at the same time the social milieu in which he had moved in the west had failed to provide consolation. Late in 1852 he wrote one of his now rare letters to his Moscow friends giving his version of the tragedy, the public row and his own role in it. 'I am only to blame,' he said, 'in that I believed too completely in the new society. I wanted to show the world how a man propagating our principles should act' (XXV, 110). In acknowledging that his aim could not be achieved through an appeal to the international fraternity of prophets of the new society, he felt he had rid himself of his 'last illusion' (XXV, 120). The result was to weaken sharply that sense of identification with French, Italian and German democrats which had characterised both *From the Other Shore* and his *Letters from France and Italy*.

The break was marked by his departure for London in August. England was the major European country which had always aroused least emotion in him – and in his revolutionary contemporaries Bakunin and Belinsky. He felt a warm sympathy for the Italians, France was the first home of revolution and socialist thought, and despite his distaste for much that was German, he was tied to her through his German mother, through personal friendships and through intellectual debt. But England, for all the respect she inspired, was strangely peripheral to his view of the world. He set her in a world apart from both Russia and France – she was tolerant, conservative not reactionary, but above all dull. He did not become involved in her political affairs and even if he had, life there was likely to consolidate his sense of separation from the affairs of the continental west. The fact that he stayed there for twelve years reflected an entirely new detachment from western Europe. She did offer relative political freedom, but his immediate concern was with her peace and calm and sheer distance from the scenes of painful memories. 'At last the consternation and alarm encompassing me, that I myself evoked, are abating,' he wrote;

> the people round me grow fewer and, since we are not
> travelling the same road, I am left more and more alone. I shall
> not leave London. I have nowhere to go and no reason for
> going . . . I was driven and cast up here by the waves that so

pitilessly whirled and smashed me, and all that was dear to me
. . . And here I shall stay for a little, to catch my breath and
try to be myself again. (*Past*, 1858)

It was in this condition, with an acute sense of loneliness, personal and
political, that he developed what he called 'a frenetic desire to write a
memoir' (XXIV, 359). At first his intention was simply to write a
memorial to Natalie, a devastating rebuttal to Herwegh's slanderous
account of the drama. He would vindicate Natalie and himself. When his
friends encouraged him to write not a memoir but his 'Memoirs', he
refused – to do so, he said, would be to distract attention from the main
issue. But as time passed he found himself giving way. When he sat down
to write he decided that he would begin with a 'brief' account of his early
life. In fact, as it turned out, this was all he completed in the next three
years, and ultimately constituted almost half the book. 'I have no illusions,' he wrote at the time. 'To write memoirs instead of a memoir is
almost to abdicate, to perjure, almost to betray – and to cover with
literary success a moral fall. I despise myself for that – why then do I do
it?' (XXIV, 361). The answer to Herzen's question lay in his need for his
own sake, and not for the sake of Natalie, or justice, or revenge, to go
back into and bring alive his early life.

One reason why he turned to his early memories first was that they
were Russian. He was experiencing the need so often felt by expatriates –
especially unhappy expatriates – for the motherland, and inherent in his
return to those years was an imaginative and emotional return to Russia.
He did not actually wish to live again in Tsarist Russia, nor would the
authorities have given him a warm welcome. But he did feel an intense
urge to affirm his nationality, his roots. He had felt the urge the previous
summer when he was recovering from the first blow of discovering
Natalie's infidelity. 'I have never felt more clearly how Russian I am
before these last years,' he told a Russian correspondent (XXIV, 197).[13]
But after the final tragedy and the failure of the western democrats to
console him, the urge became a deep yearning. It was to satisfy this
yearning that he began *My Past and Thoughts*. He would later recall that
the idea with which he had come to London was 'to seek the tribunal of

---

[13] That same summer of 1851 he had also written a 'Dedication' to Ogarev of
the collection of his works he was planning to arrange. Its tone of nostalgia
for the past and near apathy towards the future foreshadows the mood in
which he began *My Past and Thoughts* the following year (VII, 269–70). See
the commentary on this 'Dedication' in *Literaturnoe nasledstvo*, 61 (1953),
23–4.

my own people'. The problem he discovered, when the court of honour failed to materialise, was that

> in order that there may be a tribunal of one's own people one must first of all have a people of one's own. Where were mine?
> . . .
>
> I had had my own people once in Russia. But I was so completely cut off in a foreign land; I had at all costs to get into communication with my own people; I wanted to tell them of the weight that lay on my heart . . . Books would get through of themselves; writing letters was impossible . . . and little by little I set to work upon *My Past and Thoughts*. (*Past*, 1023–6)

Granted Herzen published his memoirs in French, German, Danish and English as well as his native tongue. But it was first and foremost as a Russian that he spoke.

This was reflected in his interpretation of his tragedy. For as the book took shape, he came increasingly to re-cast his whole experience in terms of his alien nationality. Previously, as we have seen, he had seen himself as a socialist pioneer, a member of a cosmopolitan *avant-garde* of the new world, set apart from that old world which still dominated the west and Russia alike. And at first he saw his private tragedy in corresponding terms. 'Just as the aberration of the stars reflects in miniature an eclipse, so the sad history that has taken place around my hearth,' he wrote in November 1852, 'reflects precisely the 24 February of all nations: good intentions, an energetic spirit – a brief breath and a halt, like death in the mud' (XXIV, 361).[14] But as he turned back to the past, he reinterpreted his experience as the result of a clash between fresh Russian blood and the degenerate west. He had been betrayed by his closest western friend, the European who had pretended to share his 'new personal life' of a prototype socialist. His unpolished, perhaps naïve, but strong and genuine Russian nature and family life had been traduced and destroyed by western corruption. His reaction was epitomised in the introduction he wrote in 1857 to the section of his memoirs devoted to his personal tragedy.[15] He recalled an historical novel he had read called *Arminius*, set in the first centuries of Christianity and the fall of Rome. It had described the meeting and collision of two worlds, not on the 'official' level, but in

---

[14] The reference is, of course, to the French revolution of February 1848.
[15] Herzen probably wrote most of the chapters on his private tragedy in 1855 (X, 446–9).

terms of 'the fortunes of the persons who were directly dependent on them'. He went on:

> It never entered my head that I should be caught in a similar collision, and that my own hearth would be desolated, crushed at the meeting of two wheels of world history.
>
> Whatever may be said there, similar sides exist in our relationships to Europeans. Our civilisation is skin-deep, our depravity is crude, our coarse hair bristles up under the powder, and the sunburn shows through the ceruse; but we are far behind the hereditary, intangible subtleties of West European corruption . . .
>
> And that is how it is that we readily yield to a man who touches upon our holy things, who understands our secret thoughts, who boldly utters what we are wont to pass over in silence or to speak of in whispers to the ear of a friend. We do not take into account that half the sayings which set our hearts beating and our bosoms heaving have become for Europe truisms or mere phrases; we forget how many other corrupted passions, the artificial senile passions, are entangled in the soul of a modern man belonging to that effete civilisation. (*Past*, 857–8)

Even after 1852, of course, Herzen continued to have western friends – the Italians Orsini and Saffi and the German Karl Vogt, among others. He continued to respect such men as Proudhon, Michelet, Garibaldi and Mazzini, and sought their help in 1852 when establishing his Russian journal, *The Polar Star* (*Poliarnaia zvezda*). But his tragedy, and Herwegh's treachery, cast a shadow over his relationship not simply with the bourgeois establishment, which he had condemned long before, but with the west as a whole. That distinction he had drawn between the true revolutionaries of the west, with whom he had identified, and the false, 'incomplete' revolutionaries, lost its importance. His scathing criticisms were directed at the whole western world, and behind the portrait of the seemingly liberated European character which he drew on several occasions in the later fifties, the ghost of Herwegh is clearly visible.

> He is himself a placard, a living decoration, a lie personified. He elicits sympathy and gives nothing in return – and even if he wanted to he has nothing to give . . . Apart from danger to himself . . . only one thing can curb him – the pit, public

opinion. Leave him alone and he would not wash his
hands . . . By opinion he is radical, he hates the aristocracy
and especially bankers; but he desperately wants money . . .
This being, gilded outside and depraved inside, with whom
every feeble passionate impulse is developed, and not one
passion, brings death and misery into all circles of simple and
frank people . . . He is the chief culprit for the disaster
befalling Europe recently. He attracts the masses by his phrases
. . . in order to betray them at the first danger. (XII, 335–6)[16]

From the western continent that produced such figures, Herzen dis-
tanced himself. This is not to say that he dismissed Europe's chances of
regeneration. Even at his most pessimistic, when he was willing to
endorse Mill's fear of permanent 'conglomerated mediocrity' in the west,
he exonerated 'the people' of the west from the charge of corruption and
considered the overthrow of the establishment quite possible.[17] But in
the aftermath of 1852 he ceased to identify himself with and feel closely
involved in the fate of the west. The sharpest contrast he drew was
between the European and the Russian of his own stamp. He came to
define himself as a Russian rather than as a socialist.

The need to re-establish his separate Russian identity was an important motivation behind his return to the past. But this was only one
dimension of a more general need to find again that self-esteem which had
been so devastatingly undermined. And it was in evoking and reliving his
early years that he regained his sense of meaning in his life, that he found
himself again. Throughout his life, literary articulation had afforded him
a necessary outlet for his greatest enthusiasms and his most bitter disappointments. 'For this free speech,' he had told his Russian friends in
1849, 'I give up everything' (VI, 317). As Herzen himself said – and the
point is important in understanding his development generally – it was
on the printed page, in the process of articulating, of describing that he
felt the full impact of events in his life. Because of this, personal reminiscences retained a quite unusual resonance for Herzen. The very process
of recall, spelled out in the most compelling prose, could rehabilitate
him. It is essential to grasp this function of *My Past and Thoughts* to

[16] This passage is taken from 'Both are Better', published in Russian in 1856.
The characterisation is ostensibly of Horace, the hero of George Sand's novel,
but the vices Herzen describes are those he saw in Herwegh.

[17] Herzen's review of Mill's *On Liberty*, written in 1857, can be found in *Past*,
1075–85. See his reference to the English working man at the end of the
review.

appreciate both the nature of his recovery and the early parts of the book itself. 'I determined to write,' said Herzen in 1854,

> but one memory called up a hundred others: all the old, half-forgotten things came to life again – dreams of my boyhood, hopes of adolescence, my far-away youth, prison and exile – early misfortunes that had left no rancour in my heart but had passed away like the storms of spring, and by their blows my young life had been refreshed and fortified.
>
> I had not the strength to repulse these shadows: let them, I thought, encounter the patches of light . . .
>
> So I began to write from the beginning, and while I was writing the first two parts several months passed rather more calmly . . .
>
> The tenacious vitality of man is more visible than anywhere else in his almost incredible capacity for abstraction and for turning a deaf ear; futile to-day, frightening yesterday and indifferent to-morrow; man diverts himself by looking over the distant past, playing in his own graveyard. (*Past*, 1861–2)

Herzen conjured up a picture of his youth that vibrated with all the hope and self-confidence and 'poetry' that Natalie's betrayal and Herwegh's campaign to humiliate him had submerged. He returned 'to the bright, warm, lovely memories of early youth' (*Past*, 54). He recalled the emotion and fresh enthusiasm that had fired his idealism, his *joie de vivre*, and his utopian socialism. He really immersed himself in his past. He recounted in close detail instances of his father's caustic wit. He found himself apologising for the length at which he described the lighter side of life at university and before his exile to the provinces – 'one prolonged feast of friendship, exchange of ideas, inspiration, carousing' (*Past*, 139). Very delicately he touched on the birth and flowering of his relationship with Natalie, on that new chapter of his life 'full of purity, serenity, youth, earnestness, secluded and bathed in love' (*Past*, 294). He vividly recalled the opposition to their marriage from the older generation, their sublimely romantic correspondence, and the danger and thrill of his visit to Moscow, while still exiled, to elope with her. In virtually every episode Herzen himself emerged in the most flattering light. Even actions that he might regret were suitably reinterpreted. An example of this was his description of the incident in 1842 when he seduced a maid serving in his house in Moscow. Because he thought Natalie had overheard and might be suspicious, he decided to confess to her, confident that his frankness would disarm her. He was horrified to find that she was profoundly shaken and lapsed into a morbid depression. Looking back he regretted that she could not distinguish between infidelity that means something and infidelity that means nothing. 'To reproach a woman for her exclusive view of things,' he remarked generously, 'is hardly just. Has anyone ever tried seriously, honestly, to shatter their prejudices?' (*Past*, 475). And he exonerated himself from blame for any serious offence. It has been argued that this special pleading reflected not his own pride but his deliberate intention of creating a revolutionary prototype to inspire young Russians – a revolutionary hero who must emerge unscathed. Herzen portrays himself as happy and preserves himself from humiliation because of a deliberate political purpose in constructing the hero of *My Past and Thoughts*.[18] But this interpretation seems to underrate the crisis Herzen had reached when he began the book. His flattering self-portrayal served a deep psychological function in restoring his self-esteem. And in this respect his return to the past was highly successful. His prose was charged with the inspiration he derived from these memories – which doubtless lost nothing in the telling. He regained his impassioned sense of

> How rich the human heart is in the capacity for happiness, for joy, if only people know how to give themselves up to it without being distracted by trifles. The present is usually disturbed by external worries, empty cares, irritable obstinacy, all the rubbish which is brought upon us in the midday of life by the vanity of vanities, and the stupid ordering of our everyday life. We waste our best minutes; we let them slip through our fingers as though we had heaven knows how many of them. We are generally thinking of to-morrow, of next year, when we ought to be clutching with both hands the brimming cup which life itself, unbidden, with her customary lavishness, holds out to us, and to drink and drink of it until the cup passes into other hands. Nature does not care to spend a long time offering us her treat. (*Past*, 366)

By savouring the richness and value of his past life, Herzen came to terms with his ordeal, he recovered his composure. But nothing could restore his former 'confidence in life', in the future. The contrast

[18] L. Ia. Ginzburg, '*Byloe i dumy*' *Gertsena* (Leningrad, 1957) pp. 294–303. Despite underrating Herzen's need for self-assertion in the early stages of his work, Ginzburg's study throws a great deal of light on Herzen's memoirs.

between his expectations and the tragedy that had awaited him remained acutely painful. And though melodramatic, the inscription of his first dedication of the work was heart-felt: 'Under these lines,' he wrote in 1852, 'rests the dust of a forty-year-old life, which came to an end before its death. Brothers, receive the memory of it with peace!' (*Past*, 1858).[19] In the middle of a happy memory, he would make the melancholy remark that 'I have lived my life and now am trudging downhill, broken and morally "mutilated"' (*Past*, 318). The text is repeatedly brought back to the present, to the atmosphere of loneliness and resignation. 'Should one touch with wrinkled hands one's wedding garment?' (*Past*, 277). After Natalie's death, Herzen's private life never regained that flavour which had enabled him to attribute to it such broad social significance. If he was to find a role it would be elsewhere.

An essential feature of Herzen's return to the past was that he reconstructed that past in the most political terms possible. He gave full rein to his sense of the interlocking of the private and the public. The autobiography opens with Napoleon's invasion of Russia, his father's unique role in carrying a message from the French Emperor to the Russian Tsar, and his own presence (as a baby) in Moscow. He recounts his education in political idealism, his precocious interest in the French Revolution and his emotional involvement in the heroic protest of the Decembrists. His experience in his father's home of the relationship between master and serf 'awakened in me from my earliest years,' he said, 'an invincible hatred for every form of slavery and every form of tyranny' (*Past*, 35). He recalls his adolescent friendship with Ogarev with the greatest possible emphasis on their shared political commitment. He describes the enormous historical significance they attributed to their friendship and their sense of each other as '"chosen vessels", predestined' (*Past*, 68). He describes their excitement on discovering the works of the Saint-Simonists. There opened before them 'a whole world of new relations between human beings; a world of health, a world of spirit, a world of beauty, the world of natural morality and therefore of moral purity' (*Past*, 150). He recalls how at Moscow University, 'We were persuaded that out of this lecture-room would come the company which would follow in the footsteps of Pestel and Ryleev, and that we should be in it. They were a splendid set of young men in our year' (*Past*, 105). He dwells on his own clash with the state, his imprisonment and two periods of

---

[19] Contrary to the footnote inserted by the revision editor, H. Higgens, the reference is not to Natalie's life, but to that of Herzen himself.

exile. He conveys the revulsion he had felt in Russia for the vulgarity and pettiness of provincial and bureaucratic life, and for the ruthlessness of the establishment based on serfdom.

The picture that emerged, as has often been pointed out, portrayed the young Herzen as far more consistently and committedly political than was in fact the case.[20] The mood he described in the 1840s, the bitterness of his second banishment, the intense political and philosophical debate in Moscow, the clash with the Slavophiles and the rifts among the Westerners, is broadly authentic. But the first three parts of the book, those written in 1852 and 1853 on the period up to 1840, certainly anticipate the date at which his frustration fastened so clearly and definitely upon the political struggle. The point to emphasise, however, is that, as with his recollection of his private life, this exaggeration made an important impact on his own morale. When he began the book, he had lost the energy and willpower to involve himself in the political struggle. 'Finding in myself neither strength nor freshness for new labours,' he wrote in 1853, 'I am writing down *our* memories' (*Past*, 72).[21] It was by dwelling upon the political content and mission of his early life, that he reinvigorated his commitment and regained his sense of belonging to a dynamic movement. His most personal recollections became permeated with his outrage at the arbitrary autocracy, the inhuman institution of serfdom, and the irresponsible privileges of the nobility. The glamorous version which he gave of his early private life could not, as we have seen, overcome his sense that his personal life was over. But this flattering account of his political past played a very significant part in giving him the confidence for the particular pioneering political role he would adopt in the future.

Herzen's return to the past after Natalie's death and the failure of the 'court of honour', then, restored his sense of the private sparkle there had been, and the historic significance there still was in his life. And he found both in a Russian context. His heart had of course always beaten faster for

---

[20] See in particular M. Partridge, 'The Young Herzen: a Contribution to the Russian Period of the Biography of Alexander Herzen', *Renaissance and Modern Studies*, I (1957), 154–79; E. J. Brown, *Stankevich and his Moscow Circle. 1830—1840* (Stanford, 1966), pp. 32–40; various corrections in detail are made in the notes to Herzen's memoirs, VIII–XI; sympathetic accounts of the greater social truth Herzen expressed by riding rough-shod over details and chronology may be found in Ginzburg, *'Byloe i dumy' Gertsena*, and Putintsev, *Gertsen – pisatel'*, pp. 234–56.

[21] Herzen placed great emphasis on his friendship with Ogarev as fundamental to his life, and he dedicated the work to Ogarev.

things Russian. He had always insisted that his children must be brought up as Russians. He had seen his role among the international revolutionary elite as that of Russian spokesman. And yet it was this process of self-definition at a moment of total loss that turned his full attention towards Russia.[22] Success in his 'new personal life', even in spite of triumphant reaction, could have led him to sustain a cosmopolitan view of his role and a cosmopolitan journalistic career. But it was not a success and he was forced back to the source of his self-esteem. That source lay in Russia.

As he wrote the first part of his memoirs, in late 1852 and 1853, he began to be caught up in his effort to establish a Russian press in London. In November he wrote an article on Russian serfdom for the English paper *The Leader*, but in February 1853 he made quite explicit his determination henceforth to focus his energy on propaganda within Russia. On 21 February he published his announcement of the opening of the Free Russian Press. He said that his inclination to speak with foreigners had passed; he had told them about Russia; he had done what he could. 'I return to my native language' (XII, 62). Recalling that he had had the idea of starting some form of Russian press as long ago as 1849, he explained that he had been delayed by persecution (in France) and by private tragedy. But above all, he admitted, he had been fascinated by western affairs: he had spent time, energy and emotion upon them. Now he no longer felt himself involved there. 'To be your organ,' he told the Russians, 'your free, uncensored voice – this is my aim' (XII, 64). And the ordeal of 1852 played a crucial part in shaping the nature of this 'organ'.

---

[22] It was with reference to this moment of despair in 1852, and not to the period immediately after 1848, that Herzen would write later (1858) that 'Faith in the future of Russia saved me on the brink of moral ruin' (V, 10).

6

Alone in England

The 1850s were for the radical left in Europe a period of disillusionment. The surge of 1848 had been repulsed. The establishment was fortified by the economic boom which started at the beginning of the decade. The democratic alliance between middle class progressives, the urban workers and the peasantry had broken up. The peasantry had come to the aid of reaction. Sectional interests and conservative power seemed to stand immovably in the way of constructing the rational society. Herzen shared this disillusion, and his resonant articulation of his own experience of it, as well as his particular focus on Russia, made him a highly significant point of intersection of the historical forces generating the European mood. His blend of seemingly realistic patience and uncompromising utopian principle evoked a response in Russia in the period leading up to the Great Reforms. The political expression he gave to the conclusion he drew from his disillusionment afforded him an enormous influence in Russia for a decade. The literary expression he gave to the whole experience afforded him an international influence far beyond.[1]

It was during his first years in England, before his Free Russian Press blossomed at the end of the Crimean War in 1856, that Herzen came to terms with his disillusion and that the crucial transition in his career took place. His private ordeal, coinciding as it did with Napoleon III's crushing of radical hopes in the west, did more than predispose him emotionally towards exclusive concentration on Russia. It forged the nature

---

[1] Central to *My Past and Thoughts* was the portrayal of this disillusionment. The failure of 1848 is the pivot of the work, while, as Herzen himself said, it was to give an account of his personal tragedy that he wrote all the rest.

of his intervention on the Russian scene. It transformed the politico-philosophical air he breathed. It is essential to grasp how much faith Herzen had to lose, in order to appreciate the change wrought in the whole aura surrounding his perception of the world and of himself. A real imaginative effort is required to grasp just how deeply his outlook had been permeated by the assumption that he stood among the *avant-garde* of a predestined socialist regeneration. The instincts of the masses might be communist, their concern might be equality not liberty, there might even be a painful hiatus before revolution began. But there was a fundamental correlation between the ideals of the elite and the movement of the masses, the course of history. He stood in the mainstream of an historical current flowing inevitably towards socialism. This was the very premise of his role of theoretician and commentator, upholding, in private life and intellectual argument, the principles of the true republic, hailing the future socialist world, discerning the mood of the masses, exposing the illusions of those 'Don Quixotes' who still believed that the people would *immediately* institute socialism. Merely to understand, he had said, 'is already to act, to accomplish' (VI, 83). This was his contribution to the revolution. The practical, physical process of transformation could be left to look after itself.

Herzen's essays on Russia between 1849 and 1851 had reflected these optimistic assumptions. Taking for granted inevitable triumph at some unspecified date, he had devoted himself to informing the west, vindicating Russia, affirming her revolutionary promise. This seemed to give weight to the forces for socialist change inside Russia. Purely 'theoretical', intellectual activity was sufficiently absorbing to discourage him from questioning the assumption that the actual process of revolution would materialise without more practical assistance from Herzen himself and men of his stamp and generation.

After 1852, however, although he did periodically publish similar portrayals of Russia in the west, his attitude changed.[2] And it was not simply that the message had ceased to be new. The purpose of these foreign addresses no longer seemed so tangible. 'We have told them what we can about Russia and the Slav world; what could be done has been done,' he said in 1853 (XII, 62). Now he felt the need for more concrete, direct intervention in Russia itself to bring about change. This reflected in

[2] The most notable of these, the series of letters written to the English republican, W. Linton, at the beginning of 1854 and entitled 'Russia and the Old World', will be discussed below (pp. 124–5).

part his disenchantment, following the failure of the 'court of honour', with the community of international democrats. They had been shown to be as feeble in personal affairs as in public.[3] But it also reflected a deeper change in his understanding of the historical process and of his role in it.

Herzen's repudiation of his previous role in both the Russian and the western contexts arose primarily from his ordeal of 1851–2. For the ordeal struck at the emotional source of his assumptions about the inevitable triumph of socialism: that ebullient ego with which he had developed from his earliest days in Russia. It was this which had inspired his grandiose personal and socialist aspiration, and his sense of the approach of a new world, elevated enough to satisfy the demands of his personality. He had carried over much of the exalted personal romanticism of the thirties into his breathtaking social idealism of the forties. His historical optimism was bound up in his irrepressible belief in himself, in his own capacity for the most exquisite life. He felt himself to be the pioneer in thought and private life of a new society. And so long as this image of himself remained intact, purely cerebral scepticism could not shake his underlying optimism or the political activity based on it. His life with Natalie, his lofty sense of superiority over the doomed world around him, counteracted the effect of gloomy political developments. If the success of reaction checked his euphoric vision of the immediate future, he remained the harbinger of a utopia that would presently be realised. The period of withdrawal to Nice with the Herweghs reflected the vitality of his sense of this new life. Then too 'everything breathed of hope, everything strove and strained ahead' (*Past*, 1859).

This confidence in life, and with it his complacency about the direction of history, was destroyed by his personal tragedy. That Natalie's infidelity and the public humiliation brought upon him by Herwegh dealt a devastating blow to his ego has already been demonstrated. The point to stress here is the consequence of this blow for his political outlook. For along with his self-esteem and his romantic view of himself, his assumptions about the world around him were also destroyed. He had seen through the philosophic bases of belief in the socialist millennium before 1848; he had admitted the sombre implications of the political events of 1848. But so deeply rooted in his personality was his optimism that it required personal catastrophe, touching him at the deepest level, for these perceptions to make an impact upon his basic approach to

[3] Herzen suggested the analogy while he still had hope of gaining a decisive verdict against Herwegh (XXIV, 306).

historical development. The decisive chapter in his disillusionment was in 1852. 'The last year,' he wrote early in 1853, 'has cost me dearly, and not only financially, but in terms of half my vitality' (XXV, 52). The dream was broken. The rare atmosphere which had been engendered in Russia, and which until now had informed his works and his whole perception of the future, of human nature, of revolution, was dispelled. There was a change in the tone of his writing: in place of high-flown portrayals of himself as a Roman philosopher caught between two ages, and of cataclysmic communist upheaval, appeared what was basically a new realism. The outbreak of the Crimean War at the end of 1853 rekindled occasional portentous visions, but these were the last notes of heady, melodramatic prophecy. Herzen himself felt the striking contrast between his earlier works and his new mood. It was at the end of 1852, recalling his departure from Russia, that he told his Russian friends, 'I was then in my prime: my previous life had given me such pledges and such trials that I fearlessly went from you with my rash pre-sumptuousness and overweening confidence in life.' Looking back over his first attempt at autobiography in the late thirties, he remarked that since those days there had been time enough 'not only to develop my powers, to fulfil my boldest dreams, my most unrealizable hopes with amazing splendour and completeness, but also to destroy them, to over-turn everything like a house of cards, everything both private and public' (*Past*, 1859–60). Announcing the establishment of his Free Russian Press in February 1853, he warned his friends that they would no longer find his words 'so youthful and so warm with that bright and happy flame and that clear faith in the near future, which forced its way through the censor's grill. A whole life is buried between then and now' (XII, 65).

   The interaction between his personal life and his political thought now had its most far-reaching consequence. At last Herzen exorcised the assumption he had made hitherto – however often he had apparently questioned it – that the irrational society is doomed and the rational must triumph. It was in the context of the tragedy culminating in Natalie's death that he himself placed his final abandonment of his illusions. 'Now I am accustomed to these thoughts,' he wrote in 1855,

> they no longer frighten me. But at the end of 1849 I was
> stunned by them; and in spite of the fact that every event,
> every meeting, every contact, every person vied with each other
> to tear away the last green leaves, I still frantically sought a
> *way out.*

That is why I now prize so highly the courageous thought of
Byron. He saw that there is *no way out*, and proudly said so.

I was unhappy and perplexed when these thoughts began to
haunt me; I tried by every means to run away from them . . .
like a lost traveller, like a beggar, I knocked at every door,
stopped people I met and asked the way, but every meeting
and every event led to the same result – to *meekness* before the
truth, to self-sacrificing acceptance of it.

Three years ago I sat by Natalie's sick-bed and saw death
drawing her pitilessly, step by step, to the grave; that life was
my whole fortune. Darkness spread around me; I was a savage
in my dull despair, but did not try to comfort myself with
hopes, did not betray my grief for one moment by the
stultifying thought of a meeting beyond the grave.

So, it is less likely that I should be false over the general
problems [of society]. (X, 123)

And to Herzen the most important product of his experience, and of
the experience of his generation, was the realisation that 'logical truth is
not the same as the truth of history . . . the idea is impotent, that truth has
no binding power over the world of actuality'. He departed from a
fundamental tenet transmitted from the Enlightenment and German
idealism. The Jacobins and indeed all revolutionaries until now had
suffered from their failure to see that reason 'does not have any means,
physical or fancied' by which to impose itself upon society.

We are only now beginning to feel that all the cards are not so
well prearranged as we had thought, because we are ourselves a
failure, a losing card . . . As though someone (not ourselves)
had promised that everything in the world would be just and
elegant and should go like clockwork. We have marvelled
enough at the abstract wisdom of nature and of historical
development; it is time to perceive that in nature as in history,
there is a great deal that is fortuitous, stupid, unsuccessful and
confused. (*Past*, 743–5)

Before turning to the implications for his role in Russia of what Herzen
called his 'painful discoveries', it is instructive to look at their effect on
his attitude to the west. Little attention has been paid to the finer points
of this view because after 1852 his gaze was predominantly fixed upon
Russia. And it is true that he was no longer predisposed towards a role in
the west and therefore did not labour to analyse what part the intellectual

revolutionary could play there. But his reflections on the west in this period provide the backdrop against which the evolution of his stance in Russia may best be understood. For it is in contrasting the impasse he depicted there with the role he carved for himself in Russia that the operative difference may be highlighted.

As early as 1849, Herzen had concluded that there could be no progressive steps towards socialism in France and the west of the Continent without mass revolution. The possibility of republican electoral success, as we have seen, had made him suspend this judgement more than once. But after Napoleon's *coup d'état* he was adamant. 'Europe must be transformed, must decompose to enter into new forms ... We have reached the limit of patching up; it is impossible to move within the ancient structures without making them snap. *Our* revolutionary idea is completely incompatible with the present state of affairs' (XII, 134–5). Herzen had no use for the existing institutions. There were no concrete concessions, no piecemeal reforms for which he considered a sincere socialist could usefully work. There was nothing he wanted from the establishment other than its own demise. Any progress, therefore, depended on the revolutionary mass – which in the west in this period he identified as the workers. 'The worker can save the old world from a great disgrace and from great misfortunes [i.e. from stagnation]. Saved by him, the old world will not survive a day. Then we shall see *militant* socialism – and the question will be resolved positively. But the worker could also be crushed as in the June Days' (XII, 135–6).

Whether or not there would be successful revolution, Herzen no longer claimed to know. On the whole, and especially during the Crimean War, he was hopeful. His sense of the injustice of the present was as strong as his sense of the stability of the *status quo*. He believed that there was a clash of interests between the people, peasants and workers, and the bourgeois establishment, which could not simply be smoothed away. What evolved from any upheaval might well not be rational, but he was still inclined to foretell 'terrible events gathering over the west' (XII, 64). Despite sacrificing all honour and the vestiges of freedom, the bourgeoisie had failed to crush 'the onset of the passionate aspiration to create a new social order' (XII, 85). The Crimean War itself seemed a possible point of departure for these terrible events. Sharing the contemporary exaggerated view of Russia's military might, he predicted doom for western regimes – however great Nicholas's power 'he cannot prevent Russian intervention being the *coup de grâce* to all the continental monarchs, to the whole reaction, and being the beginning of the armed, terrible, and decisive social struggle' (VII, 18). Russia provided a guarantee: if Europe did not destroy her own *status quo*, Russia would do it for her. As the war progressed and Russia's stability became more questionable than Europe's, his attention was distracted from the west and he dropped this idea. But he still welcomed such events as the international meeting organised by the Chartists at the beginning of 1855 as an encouraging sign.[4] Throughout all the oscillations in his mood he would insist, as he did to Ernest Coeurderoy in 1854, 'I have never denied that in the depths of the populations of the European states, there is a *savage* element, disinherited by the civilisation of the minority, which has the strength, the seed to produce a new social form' (XXV, 183). At times his assertions became so positive that he appeared to be overlooking his 'painful discoveries'. 'All Europe has now reached the inevitability of despotism in order to uphold somehow the existing order,' he wrote in the mid-fifties, in a passage for his memoirs, 'against the pressure of social ideas striving to instal a new social structure, towards which western Europe, though frightened and recalcitrant, is being carried with incredible force' (*Past*, 529). Herzen's own verdict on these notes of optimism was given a few years later. 'It was not that I retained various inconsistent convictions, but *they remained of themselves*, though I was theoretically emancipated. I outlived the romanticism of revolution, but the mystic belief in progress and in humanity lasted longer than other theological dogmas' (*Past*, 794). And against these hopeful notes can be set innumerable warnings that western Europe might simply stagnate. 'This problem will be solved by events,' he wrote in 1857: 'it cannot be solved theoretically. If the people is overcome, the new China and new Persia are inevitable. But if the people overcomes, what is unavoidable is a *social revolution*' (*Past*, 1084).

What needs to be stressed here is that it was not in terms of a xenophobic pessimism about the west's chances of producing revolution that he depicted the impasse for the intellectual revolutionary there. He felt Russia's need for Europe, for her thought and at times for her revolutionary initiative. He feared the consequences for Russia's prospects of change if the west remained as it was. He himself personified the

---

[4] His speech to the meeting, arranged in London in 1855 to commemorate the great revolutionary movement of 1848, is in XII, 241–52; see in particular the closing paragraphs.

dependence of progressive opinion in Russia on conditions abroad. And in fact, despite a stability that disabused less sceptical natures, he continued intermittently to predict upheaval well into the 1850s. The problem was that either way he saw no role for the intellectual elite. He had lost his sense of identity, through intellectual participation, with the revolutionary masses. The form of political intervention he had undertaken hitherto was made redundant.

The point was illustrated at the end of 1854. He was asked to make a contribution to an almanac being prepared by refugees in Jersey. His response was an article entitled 'Dualism is Monarchy'. It was simply a recapitulation of the critique of modern society elaborated in *From the Other Shore* and *Letters from France and Italy*. 'As monarchy relies for its strength on lack of faith and contempt for man,' he wrote, 'the republic has as its sole dogma and faith confidence in human nature . . . Make men believe that they are imbecile, that they are unable to carry on their own affairs, this is the secret of all governmentalism. In fact, the direction of public affairs, when it has emerged from its passive role, will be very simple' (XII, 219). Man is naturally sociable, he naturally seeks and gives love – not in spite of but because of his egoism. The critique and aspiration in the article were still truly Herzen's. But his whole attitude to this kind of work had changed. In a letter of introduction to the editor, he remarked: 'I send you some new variations on very old themes for your almanac of the scholastic revolutionary.' He would have sent 'something more practical, more topical' but while the Crimean War inflames public opinion against the rational discussion of real problems, 'I think I will be allowed to talk of philosophy, of abstractions, of socialist dogma, of revolutionary doctrinairism.'[5] The sarcasm was biting. Yet what else could he say? The Crimean War might explain why he did not talk more about Russia; but it constituted no restraint whatsoever on his producing 'something more practical, more topical' on western revolution. In fact in this period he wrote no articles at all devoted primarily to western affairs. This was not for want of time or a publisher. His silence reflected above all the paralysis of an approach to political change built upon historical optimism and finding expression in a personal declaration of faith in human nature – the paralysis in the 1850s of an idealism shaped in the rarefied atmosphere of early nineteenth-century Russia. When he wrote to Marie Reichel in 1853 that 'From this spring I have completely ended all intervention in western affairs', he was registering, besides his per-

[5] *Literaturnoe nasledstvo*, 61 (1953), 222–3.

sonal 'return to Russia', his sense of the helplessness of the intellectual revolutionary confronted by a rigid regime (XXV, 45).

Herzen continued the same letter: 'In the future I may end all [intervention] in eastern affairs.' And the impact of his disillusionment on the way he had hitherto approached the question of Russia's future was as profound as its effect on his western outlook. It is this which the standard Soviet interpretation obscures. Soviet scholars see his 'painful discoveries' preceding and giving rise to the Russian Socialist vision spelled out between 1849 and 1851. They therefore overlook the impact that these discoveries in fact had upon his Russian Socialism.[6] His faith in Russia, too, had been based on the ultimate correlation between history and reason, between the revolutionary spirit of the masses and the socialist ideal, and not on the dynamic power of the commune. That faith was now undermined.

He began to spell out the implications of his disillusionment not immediately after the debacle of 1852 but in 1855, in the pages of 'Il Pianto', written as a chapter for his memoirs. His remarks were the fruit not of heated reaction but of considered reflection. He accepted the fissure between the realities of power, the flow of history, on the one hand, and the rational, the ideal, on the other. And he accepted the melancholy truth not as a diagnosis restricted to the failing west but as a philosophic truth about mankind. 'We were angered, moved to fury by the absurdity, by the injustice of this fact,' he wrote. But

> the anguish will pass with time; its tragic and passionate nature will calm down: it scarcely exists in the New World of the United States ... [The contentment that will be achieved there] will be duller, poorer, more arid than that which hovered in the ideals of romantic Europe: but with it there will be neither Tsars nor centralisation, and perhaps there will be no hunger either.

Anyone who is able should leave for America. Those who cannot will stay to live out their lives 'as patterns of the beautiful dream dreamt by humanity. They have lived too much by fantasies to fit into the age of

---

[6] Smirnova, for example, analyses the development of Herzen's Russian Socialism without noting any turning point in 1852 (Sotsial'naia filosofiia, pp. 144–71). El'sberg's biography does at least observe the change in Herzen's life that took place in 1852, but does not relate the creation of the Free Russian Press in London to the simultaneous change in Herzen's approach to the historical process (Gertsen, pp. 362–84).

American common sense. There is no great misfortune in this: we are not
many and we shall soon be extinct' (*Past*, 744–5).[7]

Herzen was not using his disillusion with utopian socialist faith to
bring out a contrastingly guaranteed faith in Russia. He was not
polemicising, he was not dramatising his conclusions with an ulterior
motive, he was no longer jeering at the 'Don Quixotes' of revolution. He
was expressing above all his personal sense of the bankruptcy of an
idealism which had relied upon the inexorable process of history for its
fulfillment. There was no guarantee either in logic or in the historical
process. And this was as true for Russia, for the land of 'Tsars', as for the
west.

It is not surprising, therefore, to find that after 1852 he was very much
less assertive about Russian Socialism. He saw that it was no more than a
theory and a hope; that an elite relying upon its inevitable triumph was as
impotent and superfluous as the intellectual socialists in the west. The
commune's future development was an open question.

> Should we [re]*organise* our *obshchina* on the basis of the abstract
> independence of the individual and his autocratic right to
> property, eradicating its patriarchal communism and family
> mutual guarantee, or, on the contrary, should we *develop* it on its
> popular and social bases, trying to conserve both the content of
> personal independence, without which there is no freedom, and
> the social bonds of mutual guarantee, without which freedom
> becomes the monopoly of the property-owners? (XII, 310)

In the face of criticism, he continued to stress the advantages the commune offered Russia. But his characteristic approach underwent a shift.
In discussing it he became protective. He sharply rejected liberal–westerner suggestions that its destruction would facilitate development. Foreshadowing later populist polemics, he argued that it would be
misleading to suggest that the removal of its protection would create
peasant revolutionaries: 'To be hungry and proletarian is certainly not
enough to become a revolutionary' (XII, 109). He insisted that the

---

[7] Ginzburg has rightly pointed out that the mood of '*Il Pianto*' recalls the
atmosphere and the 'hero' of *From the Other Shore*. It was the denouement to
the disputes contained in those dialogues. It is also true that Herzen no
longer identified himself as merely one of these disabused 'romantics'. Since
he wrote *From the Other Shore*, he had redefined himself in terms of a new
and purely Russian role. But that role was based on precisely the open-ended,
sceptical view of history expressed in '*Il Pianto*'. Ginzburg, '*Byloe i dumy*'
Gertsena, p. 287.

imperfections of the commune were not sufficient grounds for abolishing it. It would be sheer folly 'to destroy the communal base, towards which contemporary man strives, because it has not yet developed the free personality in Russia' (XII, 112). As the difficulties of creating socialism were borne in upon him, concrete institutions which existed not in speculative theory or popular aspiration but in reality could not fail to carry weight with him.[8] He still drew great encouragement from the proof it seemed to offer of a spirit of hostility to private property among the peasantry. But he now saw it merely as a tangible element in the Russian political scene – which it was. It had no guarantee in the future; its past was irrelevant.[9] He still believed that without the most intense provocation from outside, it might continue to accommodate itself for ages to a harsh regime (XII, 248).[10] Far from finding in the commune a material guarantee of a utopian future, Herzen was wholly undogmatic about Russian Socialism.[11] In 1854, exhorting his son to continue his commitment to Russia, he bequeathed his own discoveries. They were, he said, not solutions but hard-won truths. 'We do not build, we destroy, we do not proclaim new faith but we expose old lies' (VI, 7).

Herzen's disillusion, therefore, deprived him of his role as revolutionary theorist in Russia as in the west. It was not enough to criticise the *status quo* and analyse what the future *should* hold, it was not enough to demonstrate as a logical theorem the necessity and compatibility of both egoism and social sense. Nor was it enough to argue the existence of, and therefore rely upon, a correlation between the socialist ideal and peasant practice. 'Internal work, contemplation, study gave you much,' he wrote in 1853 in one of the first pieces published by his Free Russian Press, 'but now they can give you nothing more. Thought so outstrips events. Thought without deeds is as dead as faith. The more it departs from life,

---

[8] This was reflected, too, in the respect he was beginning to show for English institutions – it was with reference to his new refuge that he remarked, 'It would be mad to begin the revolution with the destruction of free institutions because in practice they are only available to a minority' (XII, 112).

[9] Herzen had little time for the debate over the origins of the commune (XII, 431).

[10] For his passive view of the commune in this period, see also *Past*, 526–8.

[11] In his essay on Herzen in the west, Plekhanov recognised that Herzen was far from seeing in the commune a guarantee of socialism. G. Plekhanov, *Sochineniia* (24 vols., Moscow, 1923–7), XXIII, 431–2. But in his essay on Herzen's philosophy, he adopted what was to become the standard Marxist view that Herzen believed he had found an objective guarantee in the commune (*Ibid*. XXIII, 403).

the more it becomes cold, dry, dispassionate ... Fruitless indignation, learned arguments, noble aspirations, yearnings for freedom and all this revolutionary epicureanism and lyricism no longer suit us, we have outgrown them' (XII, 92). He scorned the theoretical preoccupations of his former Moscow friends, of the contributors to *The Contemporary* (*Sovremennik*). He criticised the article his friend Engel'son wrote for the first edition of his journal *The Polar Star* – what was needed was 'practical advice, and not philosophical treatises *à la* Proudhon and Schopenhauer' (*Past*, 996). As he wrote to Proudhon himself in 1856, 'There is a certain stagnation of thought; it recognises itself to be so completely useless, so completely superfluous, so completely overthrown, crushed underfoot by the only genuine reality – by *force majeure* – it has nothing to say or to suggest' (XXVI, 14).

Now, although Herzen had resigned himself to the impasse he perceived confronting the revolutionary intellectual in the west, he was not willing to do so in Russia. But it was if anything because he became *less* preoccupied with his utopian vision, because after 1852 his view was *less* concentrated upon the prospect of Russian Socialism, that he did find a new role. Both the means and the immediate end of his activity were transformed. He approached Russia from a new perspective. His attention became focused upon the immediate, overwhelming blemishes of Russian life. Hitherto, the prospect of revolution and the realisation of the socialist dream had distracted him from the worst aspects of the *status quo* in Russia. The manner in which the problems of serfdom and censorship had been taken for granted in his works before 1852 is remarkable.[12] They were not specific obstacles, but part of the backwardness of Russia from which she might leap so much further than the west had done. It was not that in his concern to vindicate Russia he had concealed them deliberately, rather they had seemed relevant only as evidence of the suffering of the people and the emptiness of the regime. He had looked over and beyond those questions: the revolution would do so much more than emancipate the serfs and remove censorship. It was the blows he suffered after he had formulated his vision of Russian Socialism which made possible his reorientation. His confidence in the future, his faith in intellectual activity and his preoccupation with the socialist dream – all had been undermined. Instead he became convinced

---

[12] Smirnova points out Herzen's virtual silence on serfdom before 1852, but offers no explanation for his abrupt shift of emphasis at the end of that year, *Sotsial'naia filosofiia*, p. 156.

that nothing at all could be done without concrete reforms in Russia. The future of the commune could not even be discussed until free speech had been won, and its practical development was impossible while serfdom existed (XII, 310–11). The first piece he wrote after the dramas of 1852 – in November of that year – reflected a wholly new concentration on the primary problem of serfdom: he protested to an English readership that since they were so concerned about slavery in America, they should spare a thought for Russia's equivalent. 'The whole *Russian question*,' he began to realise, 'for the present at least, may be said to be included in that of serfdom. Russia cannot make a step in advance until she has abolished slavery' (XII, 8).

Herzen's sweeping political idealism, his fiery rhetoric and his passionate devotion to the revolutionary cause in the five years since he had come to the west suggested that he would now concentrate on active steps to bring about revolution: having lost faith that revolution was inevitable, he would devote his energies to ensuring that if not through the impersonal exigencies of history, then through conscious effort and forethought revolution would be instigated. That he did not do so may partly be explained in terms of the stability of the regime and the difficulty of revolutionary agitation from his isolated position in far-off London.[13] But these realities did not automatically impinge upon the author of *Letters from France and Italy*, 'The Development of Revolutionary Ideas in Russia' and 'The Russian People and Socialism': that they did so at all itself reflected his new realism after 1852. And in fact he still considered a *Pugachevshchina* (peasant war) quite possible, and for a brief period in 1854, as we shall see, he demonstrated that he saw no incongruity in direct revolutionary agitation from abroad.[14] The explanations offered in terms of the development of his own thought dwell on his dislike for violence after the experience of 1848, and his illusions about the possibility of thoroughgoing reform from above.[15] While both

[13] This explanation is favoured by Soviet scholars. See for example Teriaev, *A. I. Gertsen – velikii myslitel'*, pp. 89–98. Teriaev insists that Herzen was acting in as revolutionary a manner as was possible in the early fifties.

[14] It is because Herzen did consider mass upheaval quite possible that Lenin's oft-quoted explanation that he 'could not see the revolutionary people' is unsatisfactory. Lenin, *Polnoe sobranie sochinenii*, XXI, 261.

[15] See for example Ia. I. Linkov, *Revoliutsionnaia bor'ba A. I. Gertsena i N. P. Ogareva i tainoe obshchestvo 'Zemlia i volia' 1860–kh godov* (Moscow, 1964), pp. 52–3. Linkov also cites Herzen's doubts about the possibility of successful revolution after the failure of 1848; Smirnova, *Sotsial'naia filosofiia*, p. 163; Koz'min, *Iz istorii revoliutsionnoi mysli*, pp. 591–2.

of these are relevant, neither seems to go to the heart of the matter. After all, he was quite willing to justify violence, and he always presented his hopes of reform from above as no more than qualified: they were the consequences rather than the cause of his reluctance to work for immediate revolution.[16] For Herzen, the only authentic form of revolution was mass revolution. The underlying factor on which his attitude towards revolution depended, therefore, was the way in which he perceived the peasantry and the way in which he related to them. An important shift in this respect has been obscured because it has not been recognised that the crucial chapter in his disillusion was in 1852, *after* his most forthright revolutionary statements of 1848–51.[17]

In the years before 1852, as we have seen, he had recognised the gulf separating the revolutionary elite from the masses. But at the same time he had enjoyed a sense of identity with the revolutionary masses: he was making a valid contribution through intellectual labour to the preparation of the revolution which they would carry out. The separation had been spirited beyond the mists of the approaching upheaval. After the debacle of 1852, however, this complacency was upset. His gloomy sense that socialism might never triumph, and that his intellectual effort and private affirmation of the future society might have been mere dreaming, forced him to confront the reality of the difference between the elite and the masses. And in these first years in England he made the occasional extremely 'Krupovian' remark. The elite were isolated 'by their culture – they represented the highest thought of the age, but not its general consciousness, not the thought of all.' And in explaining this isolation and how the 'general consciousness' could have become so out of step with the development of the people, he reached his most depressing conclusion. 'For conviction to be *right*,' he wrote in 1855, 'is not enough ... something more was necessary – *mental equality*.' The effective majority since 1789, the petty bourgeoisie, had not attained this equality. But this was not because of any warping effect of the unjust privileges

---

[16] It is true, however, that it was only when his hopes of reform from above became forlorn, at the end of the fifties, that he felt the need to expound in very much more detail his attitude towards revolution.

[17] This oversight may derive from the tendency for Soviet authors to seek to demonstrate Herzen's more or less steady progression towards – without ever achieving – historical materialism, and total commitment to mass revolution. Though they recognise his 'waverings' in the fifties, they deny that these related to the deepest problems in his thoughts: the evidence to the contrary is passed over by a sudden switch from close analysis of his thought to emphasis on the *objectively* revolutionary effect of his activity.

they enjoyed over the lower classes. On the contrary, it was because they were themselves underprivileged. Their customs and traditions had grown up narrow and contorted, wholly alien to the revolutionary idea, because they had been retarded and repressed under the aristocracy. Only a few men, enjoying 'their monopoly of an exclusive culture . . . the mental superiority of the well-fed castes, the leisured castes that had time to work not only with their muscles' had grasped and preserved the revolutionary idea. The implication was of course that not only the detested bourgeoisie, but also the much-loved people, 'whose muscles, under a constant strain, cannot spare one drop of blood for the brain', lack brain equality (*Past*, 743–6).

Herzen was confronting a tension implicit in much nineteenth-century idealism: the simultaneous assumption that man in the person of the most developed thinkers was achieving full consciousness, and that the masses, who had palpably taken no part in this intellectual progress, were somehow abreast of it. Philosophical evolution confronted the noble savage. It was a tension, not a contradiction: ethically, and in the capacity for free and harmonious social life, the philosopher could well have struggled to the height of the unspoiled savage. But Herzen's disillusion led him to contemplate the less exhilarating possibility that the masses were inherently, biologically incapable of grasping the revolutionary idea. 'Not through propaganda but through chemistry, mechanics, technology, railways, may [the masses] adjust the brain which has been cramped morally and physically for ages', he told his compatriot, Pecherin, in 1853 (XXV, 55).[18] His impatience with immediate injustice and oppression was always too intense for him to concentrate his own energies on long-term evolutionary solutions. And it was not until after 1856 that he would discuss the problem in detail. But already, despite remnants of full-blown revolutionary rhetoric, a new note of caution and realism entered his political thought. This was reflected in his attitude towards revolution.

As in the west, popular revolution had hitherto been the means by which Herzen had assumed Russia would be transformed. The revolution would be a social catharsis in which the injustice and irrationalities of society would be swept away and replaced by a new world: a leap of

[18] Herzen reproduced this letter in *My Past and Thoughts*. His comments related as much to Russia as to the west: he was addressing a Russian and the letter coincided with complementary remarks on the Russian peasantry in 'Baptised Property', XII, 94–117.

consciousness, a dramatic recreation of social, property, power and personal relations as men rose to their full height as free beings. And even when, after 1848, he was inclined to see the immediate revolutionary prospect as communist rather than socialist, he welcomed it as the first step from which socialism would arise. It was this assumption which enabled him to hail an initial communist whirlwind, in the west or Russia, as part of the grand historical march towards socialism. Although he might not himself live to see the utopian goal realised, the *Pugachev-shchina* would be the chosen vehicle, the masses complementing the idea worked out by the intellectual elite. After 1852, Herzen no longer saw revolution in this exalted light. The dream, as we have seen, had been broken. He was no longer confident that such an upheaval would be creative. In the event of a *Pugachevshchina*, he told the gentry, 'You will perish, and with you that education which you have attained by a difficult path, with insulting humiliations and great injustices' (XII, 83–4). Mass upheaval was a practical possibility, one conceivable political contingency – and not the ordained midwife of socialism. Herzen had lost that sense, which as Lichtheim pointed out, remains an integral element of the revolutionary philosophy of Marxism, of the role that the actual process of revolution must play in the birth of socialism.[19] Not that Herzen abhorred the prospect. He warned the gentry that if they made no move, and the peasants did take matters into their own hands, 'Our hearts will bleed for the innocent victims, we mourn for them in advance, but, bowing our heads we will say: let the terrible fate which they were unable or unwilling to avoid befall' (XII, 84). If there was no other way to emancipation, he would consider bloody revolution fully justified. But whether or not it came about, he did not see his role either as instigating or as participating in it. His attitude was precisely parallel to his attitude towards revolution in the west. He still believed early revolution was quite possible. And in his occasional addresses to western audiences, intent upon demonstrating the difference between the Russian regime and the Russian people, he emphasised the likelihood. In the first article he wrote after his private tragedy he prophesied that since the gentry's 'cruelty is tempered only by the knife or the axe of the peasant', and since neither nobles nor government are doing anything to improve matters, 'the difficulty of the situation will probably be thus cut through' (XII, 13). On the other hand, he recognised that the peasantry had failed hitherto to overthrow the regime and might continue to do so. But either way he felt

[19] G. Lichtheim, *Marxism*, p. 54.

himself to be an onlooker. The gulf between himself and the masses was too great. A revolution of untutored destruction could offer no role to Herzen.

It was on completing this article that he first mentioned, in a letter to Marie Reichel just before Christmas 1852, 'a wonderful project now turning in my mind – to begin agitation for the emancipation of the peasantry' (XXIV, 375). Six weeks later he was convinced that 'The main thing now is propaganda about the emancipation of the *muzhiks*' (XXV, 16). He committed himself to direct political action in the form of agitation to press the establishment into making concessions, in order to achieve the concrete political objective we have seen he now focused upon. For Herzen this marked a major departure. He could only have adopted this practical role after the disillusion of 1852, after his loss of faith in the inevitable triumph of reason and in the creative drama of revolution. The idea of publishing 'books' in Russia had occurred to him before 1852, but the purpose then had been the exchange of politico-philosophical ideas with the intellectual elite, the stimulation of 'internal work'.[20] As late as September 1851 he had told Michelet, 'The day of action for us may be still far away; the day of consciousness, of thinking and speaking, has already risen. We have lived long enough in sleep and silence; the time has come to tell our dreams, and the fruits of our meditation' (*Past*, 1675). After 1852, this was inadequate: 'consciousness' and 'dreams' were no longer enough. The time had come for direct intervention in political affairs.

The establishment of the Free Russian Press in London in February 1853, embodied Herzen's 'wonderful project'. He launched his campaign to galvanise all progressive Russian opinion in exerting pressure upon the establishment for emancipation. His appeal was broad: he offered to publish anything 'written in a spirit of freedom' (XII, 63), and he specifically invited the Slavophiles to contribute, despite their conservative faults. 'Together,' he told his readers, 'we will seek means and solutions' (XII, 64). He hoped his old friends in Moscow would begin to send him material for the agitation immediately, but until it was forthcoming he would publish his own propaganda. He was in the process of writing *My Past and Thoughts* and this provided him with a context for

[20] He planned an edition of his works in 1849, 'for *Russians* in *Russian*' (VI, 149). But the plan was not realised, and even if it had been, the only works he could have included would have reflected precisely that preoccupation with 'contemplation' and 'study' which after 1852 he ceased to view as valid political activity.

highly charged invective against serfdom. The first article he wrote for his press – 'St George's Day' – was an appeal for emancipation directed to the gentry at large. He addressed them as a class, a social force with concrete political power – not as the 'intelligence' of the nation. He proudly posted a copy to 'the highest bureaucrats' in St Petersburg (XXV, 82).[21] His appeal was in part presented as fraternal advice. 'We are slaves – because we are masters. We are servants – because we are *pomeshchiks*, and *pomeshchiks* without faith in our rights ... It is impossible to be a free man and to have manor serfs, bought like merchandise, sold like cattle.' He exhorted them to stand up for their own dignity. His second line of argument was to warn them that unless they moved towards emancipation, either the Tsar would do so, or the peasants would take matters into their own hands and in both cases they would be destroyed. But this could still be averted. 'If we thought this chalice was unavoidable, we would not address you, our words would be superfluous or irrelevant and malicious mockery.' He implored them not to imitate the fruitless reaction of the bourgeoisie of 1848 who had solved nothing by their sacrifice of all honour and freedom. They must choose whether to swim with the tide or resist and be drowned. But they must hurry – 'There is not an hour to lose' (XII, 81–5).

The conventional account of Herzen's absorption in Russian affairs holds that when the western revolutions failed to fulfil his utopian hopes, he looked to Russia to do so. In fact, however, the Herzen who looked back to his home country after 1852 was a man changed in the deepest recesses of his political character. Russia could not restore what his experience in the west had destroyed. He was forced to come to terms with the problems which his personal euphoria and expectations of revolution had enabled him to escape. Rather than turning back to

---

[21] The significance of this first article, the first use to which he put his press, has been underestimated. El'sberg appears to interpret it as an appeal to the gentry not as a group with the tangible political power to effect emancipation but as the milieu of the intelligentsia (*Gertsen*, pp. 371–3). Linkov stresses only the threat Herzen made of the summons to arms that he could address to the peasantry, and discounts the article as evidence that Herzen opted for peaceful pressure rather than revolution *before* the Crimean War. Ia. I. Linkov, 'Nachalo revoliutsionnoi agitatsii A. I. Gertsena obrashchennoi k narodnym massam', *Istoricheskie zapiski*, 66 (1960), 301–11. It should be noted that in 1852 Herzen had already expressed his astonishment at the failure of Alexander I and Nicholas to realise their apparent desire to emancipate the serfs. In 1853 his appeal was to the gentry, but the seeds of an appeal to a more responsive monarch were already present (XII, 13–14).

Russia to create a new myth, his approach to his homeland when, after 1852, he devoted his full attention to it, was more realistic than ever before. If he was blind to the economic forces working to transform Russia, he perceived that serfdom and censorship had become unstable and that effective pressure could be brought to bear on the political establishment. In fact, far from providing an escape into unscathed utopianism, Russia provided the only context which could afford the battered idealist a satisfactory role. It was Russia's social backwardness, and not a messianic vision, which provided him with his role in the 1850s. At times he admitted this. Though he passionately denied that Russia had to follow the western pattern of development, he was conscious that the immediate necessity was for reforms which parts of the west had achieved long before. In 1857 he lamented that the new Tsar had done nothing positive, and that Russians had to recognise that they were 'the most backward of all the peoples of Europe' (XII, 352; XIII, 24). His frustration was so intense because he saw that such enormous strides could easily be taken by the government. He reproached the Tsar for his failure to take advantage of the fact that 'the present government could do miracles, without the slightest danger to itself. Not one monarch in Europe is in a position comparable to that of Alexander II' (XIII, 29). Once the Great Reforms had disappointed him, the predicament he faced in Russia would gradually fall into line again with that he had already portrayed in the west. He would see revolution as the sole way forward: the problem would once again be that of his relation to and role in that revolution.

To insist that Herzen's deepest disillusion followed the conception of Russian Socialism and profoundly affected it, is not to question his emotional commitment to Russia. As was pointed out in Chapter 5, in the aftermath of his personal crisis of 1852, it was Russia which provided the context in which he could rebuild his self-esteem. Warmth, happiness and hope were associated with the atmosphere of his youth – and that atmosphere was Russian. A widowed and lonely – if gregarious – existence in England did little to distract him. Personal need focused his attention on Russia. The resonance that things Russian had for him provided an essential impulse behind his journalistic activity. Without it he could never have discovered the necessary energy and enthusiasm. Similarly, the possibility that Russia could one day create rural socialism without the agonising process of industrialisation and urbanisation provided him with a hope, an inspiring aspiration. But nostalgia and hope could not of themselves give him a role: they must not be allowed to obscure the impact on his approach to Russia of his politico-philosophical disillusionment.

Events did not at first conspire to encourage Herzen's 'wonderful project'. There was a gloomy silence from Russia and positive discouragement from his friends in Moscow. In 1853 Shchepkin, one of their number, visited him in London and conveyed their disapproval. The outbreak of the Crimean War distracted attention from domestic problems in Russia and rallied the gentry, the power group upon which he had chosen to exert pressure, behind the government. Herzen suspended the embryonic campaign. Apart from exasperation at the lack of response, he was himself distracted. Since 1849 Russia had seemed to all sections of public opinion the dominant power on the Continent. A clash between her and the great western powers could well be seen to promise a mighty cataclysm. Herzen's prediction of this cataclysm, made in the heady days of 1849, suddenly seemed about to be realised. Old hopes were rekindled as events seemed poised to move swiftly. At first he thought Russian intervention would spark off revolution in the west. As Russia's weakness became apparent, he saw more hope of instability at home. It was in the grip of these dramatic expectations that he wrote his last major series of articles addressed to the west – 'Russia and the Old World'. Their tone recalled that of his works before the tragedy of 1852. He readopted the lofty, olympian note of prophecy. Tsar Nicholas must and will strive to take Constantinople, not only to distract the Russians, or strengthen the support he derives from the Orthodox church, but also because he acts '*instinctively*, for, ultimately, he too is the agent of *destiny*: without himself understanding it, he continues to realise the hidden designs of history; he works to hasten the calamity which must engulf him or his successors' (XII, 165). He conjured up the possibility of the war constituting a social catharsis, a European revolution.

> Perhaps in the midst of this blood, this carnage, this fire, this
> devastation, the peoples will wake up and, rubbing their eyes,
> will see that all these terrible, disgusting, frightful dreams were
> only dreams ... Bonaparte, Nicholas, a cloak covered in bees,[22]
> covered in Polish blood, the emperor of the gallows, the king
> of the firing squad – none of these exist, and the peoples,
> seeing that the sun has long been risen, will be amazed by their
> long sleep ... Maybe ... but ... In any case, this war will be

[22] Bees appeared on the Napoleonic emblem.

the *Introduzione maestosa e marziale* of the Slav world into
universal history and *una marcia funebre* for the old world.'
(XII, 166)

The possibility of the educated elite somehow 'dissolving' in the mass of
the communal peasantry suddenly seemed sufficiently imminent to have
real meaning for him (XII, 153).[23] And in this mood, at the beginning of
1854, he took what he could see as a practical step towards such a fusion:
he published four articles by his friend Engel'son which aimed to create
immediate revolutionary agitation among the peasantry, and he himself
went as far as an appeal to the Russian army in Poland to disobey any
orders they might receive to suppress risings there.[24] In the excitement of
the moment, his gloomy conclusions about the mental inadequacy of the
people, and the gulf between himself and them, were forgotten.

But as the war dragged on without sparking off exciting political
developments, this euphoria faded for the last time. He became acutely
depressed. In the west he was accused of supporting the Tsar; in Russia
the possibility of early upheaval from below disappeared. He was
reduced to silence. By the end of 1854 his reaction to the war had become
simply that of a humane man revolted by senseless destruction. 'The war
is becoming more and more ferocious; war is the old world, it is all that
we hate, brutal force, exalted *amour-propre*, nationalism manifested in
hatred' (XXV, 209). Instead of being the point of departure for social
transformation, the war was purely negative. It was now that he wrote his
most poignant pieces on disillusionment.

The painful interlude passed, and as his morale recovered, he returned
to the pragmatic position he had reached before the outbreak of the
Crimean War. With the tide turning against Russia, he began to see great
potential for renewed agitation for reform from above. The decisive
event was the death of Nicholas on 2 March 1855. Herzen was overjoyed,
'We are drunk, we have gone mad, we are young again!' (XXV, 242). He

[23] The synthesis of the education and individual development of the elite with
the social structure of the peasantry was the ultimate ideal for Herzen
throughout the fifties. But except during this brief moment of excitement,
the abyss seemed too great after 1852 for the vision to have immediate
practical implications.

[24] These articles are discussed in detail by Linkov, 'Nachalo revoliutsionnoi
agitatsii A. I. Gertsena'. Linkov does not even mention the Crimean War –
the crucial development which evoked this revolutionary response from
Herzen. In July 1853 he had seemed to reject out of hand the idea of such an
appeal to the soldiers (XXV, 82). See Sh. M. Levin, 'Gertsen i krymskaia
voina', *Istoricheskie zapiski*, 29 (1949) 184.

seized upon the hope that Alexander II would prove more malleable than his father. Throughout he had taken great care not to identify himself or his press with Russia's enemies, the enemies of the establishment which he would again make the object of his pressure.[25] This time his propaganda would be explicitly aimed at the Tsar as well as the gentry. He wrote to Alexander appealing to him as more enlightened than Nicholas, as a lover of the people – and threatening him with revolution only if he tried to resist change. 'I am an incorrigible socialist, you are an autocratic emperor; but between your flag and mine there can be one thing in common – love for the people . . . I am ready to wait, to restrain myself, to speak of other things, if only I have real hope that you will do something for Russia.' He asked for free speech and emancipation with land. 'I am ashamed by how little we are ready to be satisfied by . . . Sir,' he concluded, 'if these lines reach you, read them in good faith . . . it is not often that you hear the frank voice of a free Russian' (XII, 273–4). By the end of March he had decided to publish a regular review – *The Polar Star*. His aim was the same as when he had originally founded the Free Russian Press. 'We have *no system, no doctrine*. We extend our invitation equally to *Westerners* and *Slavophiles*, to the moderate and the immoderate, to the careful and the careless . . . so far as means are concerned, we open all doors wide, we summon all arguments' (XII, 296). He would make every effort to stir progressive opinion into action, to unite the widest possible front for emancipation. His objective was pressure on the one effective power-centre in Russia with which he felt able to communicate: the gentry–Tsarist diarchy.

The agitation was recommended. But this time he found himself contributing to a gathering current running in favour of emancipation. Partly in response to the agitation, the government in 1861 would carry through what has rightly been called 'the greatest single piece of state-directed social engineering in modern European history before the twentieth century'.[26] For a brilliant period, Herzen's search for a role was rewarded with a responsive historical situation.

[25] Levin, 'Gertsen i krymskaia voina', 189.
[26] T. Emmons, *The Russian Landed Gentry and the Peasant Emancipation of 1861* (Cambridge, 1968), p. 414.

7

Apogee

Between the end of the Crimean War in 1856 and the promulgation of the Edict of Emancipation in 1861, Herzen played his most effective political role. The ordeal which had led him to adopt this role had also tempered his character for the task. His disillusion had narrowed the fields among which his energy had previously been spread. He believed his private life to be over. He told his friend Malwida von Meysenbug, who had become the governess of his children, that she would be unable to cure him and make him once again expect 'poetry' in his life (XXV, 199). By the end of 1855 he had written his account of Natalie's tragic affair with Herwegh, and considered that dimension of his life to be closed. The point was quickly put to the test. In April 1856 Ogarev and his wife Natalie, came to London and set up house with Herzen. Their arrival marked the beginning of Herzen's most unrewarding and wearisome human relationship. Natalie fell in love with him, and Ogarev did not try to restrain her. She bore Herzen three children, yet after the first few months neither she nor Herzen was happy. She was an unstable character, failed to win the affection of his older children, and did much to poison the atmosphere of their home. But she was in part the victim of Herzen's disillusion. She was only twenty-eight and was deeply mortified by his detachment and the slight importance she found he now attributed to his personal life.[1] Certainly he never romanticised their relationship: describing these years in his memoirs he hardly touched on this side of his life, and never even mentioned Natalie. The integrated view of his personal and political lives, destroyed in 1852, could not be restored by

[1] For an excellent account of their relationship, see Carr, *The Romantic Exiles*, 164–78, 218–41.

this unsatisfactory relationship with the wife of his best friend. What Natalie lost, his political activities gained. He threw himself whole-heartedly into his work.

Not only did Herzen's 'general interests' benefit at the expense of his private life, but those interests themselves became more specialised. Previously his private life had been a positive affirmation of a basically elitist, urban, western way of living and thus a diversion from the peasant affairs of Russia: he no longer felt it to be so. He put down no roots in England, he lived in twelve different houses in as many years, and though he made some political contacts, they were relatively insignificant.[2] He devoted himself to his homeland. In this he acted as an interesting – and self-conscious – barometer of the time. The cosmopolitan aspiration with which he had come to the west, and in the light of which he had become so deeply involved in 1848, was replaced by a deliberate national com-mitment. His home became a centre for Russian visitors. He consciously cultivated Russian habits and the Russian language among his family.[3] He acknowledged a certain justification for a country like Italy placing the national question above that of the Republic (*Past*, 1027–35). He poured scorn upon the journal *L'Homme*, published by political exiles in Jersey, for its anti-national tone: '*Vive l'unité, l'uniformité* – and all those who will not die of boredom!' (XII, 462). This concentration on narrower aims was an element in his reaction against reliance on insubstantial speculation and generalisations. It was a product of the decomposition of that highly integrated view of the world, the different nations, the political, the social and the private spheres with which he had come to the west. He ceased to be primarily either a Russian among an international revolutionary community, or the interpreter of Russian affairs to the west. He became first and foremost a protagonist on the Russian domes-tic scene.

The renewed friendship and partnership with Ogarev, fresh from Russia itself, provided an enormous aid and stimulant to this com-mitment. It was at Ogarev's suggestion that, a year after his arrival, they published the first number of *The Bell* (*Kolokol*), a monthly and sub-sequently a fortnightly supplement to *The Polar Star*. *The Bell* was chiefly responsible for the remarkable stature Herzen achieved in Russia.

---

[2] Those he did make are discussed by M. Partridge, 'Aleksandr Gertsen i ego angliiskie sviazi', *Problemy izucheniia Gertsena*, pp. 348–69.
[3] See Malwida von Meysenbug, *Mémoires d'une idéaliste*, translated extract in *Gertsen v vospominaniiakh sovremennikov* (Moscow, 1956), pp. 366–74.

Its elegant, lively, informed and open columns embodied the role he sought for himself. The basis of his position was unchanged: he sought to create the maximum pressure for three major reforms – the abolition of serfdom, freedom of speech, and the end of corporal punishment – within the existing political structure. To achieve this he would galvanise the widest possible front of progressive opinion. Herzen's triumph during these years has often been described.[4] It is necessary to go over some of the ground here only in order to set in context those developments in his thought which throw light on his inability to sustain his influential position after 1861.

As Alexander succeeded Nicholas and peace followed war, Herzen's appeal to educated Russian opinion bore fruit. Both the government and public opinion accepted the need for reform and emancipation of some description. In this atmosphere Herzen's approach struck the right note. He combined uncompromising damnation of serfdom, censorship, corporal punishment and numerous varieties of cruelty and injustice, with an open mind on the means of achieving reform and an inspiring faith that reform would be achieved. He pursued several avenues. He published personal addresses to the Tsar, appealing to his sense of history, of honour, of justice, of humanity – and of pride. He challenged him to prove his love for Russia, and promised him an illustrious place in history if he did so. These appeals were of course designed to arouse his readers to the possibilities open to the autocrat. But it was an essential characteristic of the heyday of his campaign that he sought to communicate at a direct, personal level with the Tsar himself.[5] He genuinely hoped to inspire Alexander – the enthusiasm of his article 'You have conquered, O Galilean!', when he welcomed the clear decision in favour of emancipation, illustrated the point. Asking I. S. Aksakov early in 1858 if he had seen his panegyrics on the Tsar, Herzen remarked, 'I truly love him, though he does not really suspect this' (XXVI, 161). In November 1858, he wrote a long letter to the Tsarina, urging her to send the Tsarevich to university, like the English heir, instead of giving him a military education (XIII, 354-5). He impressed upon her the great opportunity and

---

[4] See, for example, F. Venturi, *Roots of Revolution*, translated by F. Haskell (London, 1960), Chapter 4; Z. P. Bazileva, *'Kolokol' Gertsena* (Moscow, 1949), Chapter 2.

[5] At the height of its influence, *The Bell* was said to penetrate the Winter Palace itself, though I have found no clear indication of whether or not the Tsar read the appeals Herzen addressed to him.

responsibility she had to serve Russia in this way. He was appealing to
the Romanov family over and above the heads of the chief ministers
and the bureaucracy. In fact from as early as June 1858, when he
told Annenkov that he would remove his 'protection' from the Tsar, his
confidence in his progressive intentions was qualified (XXVI, 186). Yet
the personal form of address gave to his demands throughout the period
an unusual directness and an air of practicality. It enabled him to
publish the most total condemnation of government action without
calling for upheaval. And this was the policy he pursued until after
Emancipation.

He saw publicity itself as the most effective way to rouse public
opinion and influence the regime. A major theme of *The Bell* was the
exposure of the inhuman abuses practised in Russia. He collected and
published specified allegations against all branches of the establishment.
He hoped to make the Tsar himself aware of abuses that might otherwise
be hidden from him. He accused reactionary ministers of attempting to
suppress *The Bell* to keep the Tsar in ignorance. He pilloried the most
reactionary members of the main Committee on the peasant question –
the men he dubbed 'the Black Cabinet'. He saw them as the chief
restraint on Alexander's progressive inclinations and made a special
point of publishing evidence to demonstrate their unjust and obscuran-
tist approach. He poured bitter scorn on the censorship which he
believed they inspired. He justified his concentration on their crimes on
the grounds that if highly-placed villains escaped unchecked, this would
encourage lesser ones. He published evidence to demonstrate the ruthless, irresponsible use of power by the gentry. He was particularly
horrified by the case of a twelve-year-old serf girl allegedly raped by the
landlord and then brutally punished by the landlord's wife (XIV, 74–5).
Hearing that certain serf-owners were forcing their peasants to move
their homesteads to poor soil so that in the event of emancipation they
would have to buy the good land back from the landlord, Herzen
demanded the names of such gentry. 'We will turn the special attention
of the sovereign on to these villains' (XIII, 292). He repeatedly
denounced the use of corporal punishment, both on serfs and on sailors
in the navy. He reserved some of his most biting criticisms for the clerical
hierarchy. He accused them of forcing peasants to convert to Orthodoxy.
He asked sarcastically whether it was true that the Church was about to
use its riches to redeem peasants' land. He denounced the injustice and
tyranny of certain university professors, and in particular attacked the

repressive measures taken against supposedly unruly students.[6] A persistent demand was for reform of the courts, for public hearings, and for government submission to the law. He vigorously protested against the exile without trial of A. M. Unkovsky who had emerged as a leader of the more progressive serf-owners during the consultations over emancipation. Throughout he was preventing progressive opinion becoming complacent about the course the government was taking. He pointed to the censorship and repression in Poland, and the reactionary allies the Tsar chose abroad as evidence that the government could not be trusted. Public opinion must maintain and intensify its pressure.

Herzen's campaign quickly gathered momentum and the circulation of *The Bell* rose sharply.[7] As editor of *The Polar Star* and *The Bell* he became an important figure on the Russian political scene. The analysis of the underlying trends in his thought, however, in this the 'apogee' of his career, is not made easier by the particular nature of the role he decided to play. For he deliberately adopted, in terms of precise ideology, a very low profile. From the very first he had proclaimed that 'We have no system, no doctrine', and had stipulated only that contributors should at least subscribe to what he considered his very restricted programme of reform. His primary aim was not to proclaim 'the truth', to preach the ultimate justice, but rather to provide a forum and a stimulant for the whole range of progressive opinion. In his first major article in *The Bell*, he left open the question of the nature of the new forms and organs which Russia must find: 'We do not know them yet, nor does the government, we are moving towards their discovery; in this consists the tremendous interest of our future' (XIII, 22). His reply to the accusation that he only criticised and created doubt without providing answers, was that 'Those solutions about which you speak, I cannot give, I do not have them. I am looking for them myself: I am not a teacher, I am a fellow-seeker' (XIV, 72). He was seeking to help formulate a broad consensus among the progressive echelons: in 1860 he was still insisting that 'It is necessary that one *opinion* gain decisive preponderance . . . What can you achieve with the axe, when half say the question of communal ownership is decided entirely in the Russian sense, and half believe that it must be decided in the English one?' (XIV, 242). This policy did not reflect a preference for successful journalism above a principled stand. It flowed

---

[6] See, for example, 'The Kharkov Story' and 'An Ugly End to the Kharkov Student Story', XIII, 306–7, 329.

[7] See Bazileva, '*Kolokol' Gertsena*, pp. 134–7.

rather from his judgement of the most useful contribution he could make to Russia at that time. This judgement was, of course, the product of the ideological state in which his western disillusion had left him. And although, as we have seen, he implemented these practical implications before spelling out his new politico-philosophical position, criticism would soon provoke him to give a more theoretical justification for his activity.

Herzen was in any case not wholly absorbed in editorship, in chairing the debate. He explicitly renounced responsibility for the opinions of others for which he provided the publicity. In the case of the most moderate liberal contributions, he published them under separate cover in the series of volumes of *Voices from Russia*. He was too reflective and independent a thinker to be ideologically passive. His own ideas, his general precepts, his view of the world and the political process continued to evolve, and found expression in his letters, his longer polemical and review articles, and the parts of his memoirs written at this time. The danger was present from the start of a clash between his role as editor and his own personal viewpoint of the controversies at issue.

It was with the liberal wing of progressive opinion that Herzen first came into conflict. The dispute arose over the question of the general direction in which Russia's social structure should develop. Herzen, of course, had never ceased to hope that Russia could evolve directly towards socialism, that there was no need for her to imitate western bourgeois development. But he was willing to 'keep silent' about it, to suspend this debate in favour of the immediate issues at hand. In fact controversy over the question could not be suspended in the period before Emancipation. Liberals such as B. N. Chicherin and K. D. Kavelin were urging the western path forward and the creation of a middle class, and Herzen felt compelled to make more explicit his own commitment to the peasant commune, to spell out the case for Russian Socialism. This he did most fully in the long article written late in 1859, 'Russian Germans and German Russians'. Castigating as bourgeois and reactionary the ideas of Westerner intellectuals and bureaucrats, he warned that along the path they recommended, it would take 150 years for Russia to catch up contemporary Prussia! While readily conceding that Russian society was for the moment inferior to western society, he asserted that by developing the full personality within the commune, it was in Russia's power to achieve 'a social structure far superior to that of the west' (XIV, 155). The clash was intensified by liberal objections to Herzen's willingness to countenance a peasant rising if all else failed to bring about emancipation. The open controversy was a result of, and contributed to, the polarisation of opinion in Russia, and it demonstrated how ambitious was Herzen's aspiration that one opinion 'gain decisive preponderance'.

But as yet the polarisation was limited. When Chicherin denounced Herzen it was not only the younger generation but also the moderates such as Kavelin who rallied to Herzen's defence. Nor did the controversy destroy Herzen's sense that he was open-minded in contrast to Chicherin's dogmatic commitment to bourgeois development. Chicherin's programme was the product of elitist imitation of the west, it was arrogant and doctrinaire and would require imposition by a strong central government against what he saw as the authentic development of Russian society. 'You, my learned friend,' Herzen wrote in the draft of a letter to Chicherin, 'know definitely in what direction to go, how to lead; I do not know. And so I feel that it is for us to observe and study, and for you to teach others. It is true that we can say what *ought not* to be done . . . but you can say what *ought* to be done' (*Past*, 627). His own outline of the path Russia should follow, on the other hand, was not a dogma given from on high but a translation of the wisdom proffered by 'the popular life'. It was in fact his defence against the accusation of inconsistency in these years that while others '*lead* the people, *inspire* it, for its own good . . . our strength lies in instinct, by which we guess how its heart beats, when it bleeds, what it wants to say and cannot' (XIV, 257). In the period before Emancipation, the full implications of this respect for 'the people' were not apparent: Herzen continued to be preoccupied by and deliberately to lay stress upon immediate reforms rather than the long-term future of Russia. It was partly because of this that the final rift with Turgenev and Kavelin was delayed until after the unsatisfactory nature of the Emancipation was brought home to Herzen.

If anything, the clash with Chicherin enhanced Herzen's prestige in the eyes of the radicals. But a far more agonising tension between his political role and the direction of his thought in general, this time affecting his relations with these radical circles, lay ahead. His prestige among left-wing opinion rested on his unambiguous demand for the most far-reaching reforms – reforms which constituted a transformation of Russian society – and his consistent affirmation of the justice of a peasant upheaval. As the very limited scope of the government's actual plans became increasingly clear, the logic of his stand led from conditional patience with the regime to outright confrontation and commitment to immediate revolution. But while his demands had encouraged extreme radicals to expect a firm revolutionary lead from him, his thought on the masses, on the role of the elite, and on revolution had not developed in a complementary fashion towards any such commitment. Indeed, in these years leading up to 1861 his attitude towards early revolution was becoming if anything more cold. His commitment to objectively revolutionary demands reflected not a growing willingness to work for immediate revolution, but rather his insistence, at times apparently supported by external factors, at times more patently based on wishful thinking, that these reforms could be achieved without revolution.

Herzen felt that he was working in an intermediary age, in conditions of thaw. In the first issue of *The Bell*, he expressed the hope that the younger generation would see realised in fact what he had perceived only in theory. In the long letter he addressed to the Tsarina at the end of 1858, he showed his concern with the character of the heir to a Tsar who was himself still only forty years old. He hoped that the generation after his own would be rewarded with a truly progressive monarch. To them, he wrote, 'will belong, *perhaps*, the action and the drama. We do not envy them. Our affair is near its end ... Soon we will pass on, exhausted but not overcome by the thirty-year fight' (XIII, 353). Similarly, at the beginning of 1860 he ridiculed Sasha's impatience at the slowness of developments. 'Are you really so innocent that you imagine that the transfer from the despotism of Nicholas to the expropriation of part of the gentry's land and the formation of free-communal *obshchinas* can happen without set-backs, reactions, errors in which, perhaps, not one Alexander II but ten will break their necks?' (XXVII, 9). Shortly afterwards, reproaching the Tsar for his failures, Herzen recalled that it had been his hope to see the 'steel chains' of serfdom removed so that development could become possible. 'The rest it seemed to us would come in its own way – perhaps, or even more probably, after us' (XIV, 216). Emancipation would only be a step in the direction of his ultimate ideal, but it was the greatest step he expected to witness himself. His policy was based on the assumption that this would be the crowning achievement of his generation and of his own efforts.

Accordingly, in the late 1850s, Herzen was proud that he had outlived 'the romanticism of revolution' and wondered 'Does not the revolutionary era, for which we, in the light of the dying glow of the nineties, were striving, and for which Liberal France, Young Italy, Mazzini and Ledru-Rollin were striving, already belong to the past? Are not these

men becoming the sorrowful representatives of the past, around whom
another life and different questions are boiling up?' (*Past*, 794, 1044). He
no longer shared the revolutionary and 'apocalyptic formulae of socialist
doctrinairism' of the exiles whose fate he so scathingly depicted in his
memoirs at this time (*Past*, 1039). 'The age of revolutionary demagogy,'
he wrote in a letter in July 1858, 'has passed. With every day I see more
clearly that the epoch of political revolution is reaching its end – like the
epoch of the Reformation – without having solved the question: can one
say that the religious question is solved? No – yet it no longer interests
anyone' (XXVI, 192–3).

Herzen was therefore sceptical about the relevance of the most idyllic
political structures and about the capacity of revolution to attain those
structures in his era. The theoreticians of these worthy ideals, the
prophets of reason, make a useful contribution in the long run, but not in
the foreseeable future. 'Owen was right, and England will catch up with
him, but of course not in the nineteenth century.' 'Our role', he said, the
role of 'the prosaic workers', concerns the immediate future, the discovery of the next step. 'We are seeking and we wish to act in our own
time, in contemporary Russia – this forces us not to complicate questions
but to try to overcome those which have already arisen' (XIV, 10). The
Russian boat, he said, is afloat. It may yet run aground. That depends
upon the pilots. But at least it has begun with the right question – not that
of political structure but of social content, and above all the question of
the emancipation of the peasant with the land. This was for Russia the
central issue. In the sharpest contrast with his attitude before 1848, he no
longer saw it as 'mere economics'. 'As if the economic question is not the
chief, the vital, the sole salvation' (XIV, 33). He believed that he had
drawn the crucial lesson from Europe's failure: the need to separate the
social question from the political question and to concentrate solely upon
the former. He appeared to elevate to the level of principle the need to
suspend the whole problem of government, of constitutions, and of
revolution: 'That is, again, the social question before the political' (XIV,
14).[8]

---

[8] It is a major weakness of Smirnova's recent interpretation of Herzen that she
rides rough-shod over this aspect of his thought. Reflecting, perhaps, the
common Soviet lack of interest in Herzen's 'liberal illusions' in this period,
she comes to the conclusion that at the end of the 1850s he believed that 'The
social revolution in Russia assumes, in the first place, the destruction of the
existing political forms – the autocracy and the centralised bureaucratic
system of government' (*Sotsial'naia filosofiia*, p. 170).

For a time at least circumstances conspired to confirm Herzen's sense that he had found the key to progress in this formula, that satisfactory emancipation could be extracted from the existing regime. The burst of energy and hope with which the new reign opened misled many radicals. The commitment by the government to emancipation, whatever the details, was remarkable enough. Expectation of substantial reforms was widespread. The Tsar himself lent them active support and some reforms were put in hand. And the very fact that his own campaign evoked such a warm response encouraged Herzen's hopes. No-one was in a better position than he to judge the change of mood in Russia. The silence of 1853 was transformed into a flow of contributions to and a widespread demand for *The Bell* and *The Polar Star*. For a charmed period he stood unchallenged at the head of progressive opinion. And it was his unique combination of exposure and criticism of the evils of Russian society, with an open mind on the political means of achieving the necessary reforms, which gave his call such wide appeal. He provided the most eloquent, inspiring expression of that transitory hope shared for varying lengths of time by men of such different outlooks as Chicherin and Chernyshevskii, that dramatic reforms would be achieved from above. With his left flank covered by an irreproachable record of prison, exile, personal presence in Paris in 1848 and his most uncompromising publications, his blend of principle and patience appealed directly to the liberal wing of Russian society. While shedding the doctrinairism which might have alienated more cautious readers, he remained faithful to the ultimate socialist aspirations of the radical wing. It was widely recognised that, as his liberal admirer, Kavelin put it in 1858, Herzen had become a 'formidable power' on the Russian scene.[9] He could not help but take pride in and be inclined to exaggerate the strength of the movement to which he had contributed so much. And he was determined not to allow the political question to confuse the issue and weaken and divide the pressure of progressive opinion on the regime.

At the same time, Herzen found corroboration for his view that the question of the central regime and revolution could be suspended in his experience of the west in these years. For he saw evidence not just of the poverty of revolution but of the positive progress that could be and historically had been made without revolution. He was struck by the phenomenal strides made by Piedmont in just ten years – and all that had

[9] *Literaturnoe nasledstvo*, 62 (1955), 285. See also Bazileva, *'Kolokol' Gertsena*, pp. 134–58 on the extent of Herzen's influence.

been necessary was 'an unsuccessful war and a series of concessions by the regime to public opinion' (XIII, 22). Living as he did in England, and actively enjoying the freedom she provided, he was acutely conscious of the peaceful progress she had made. What France had achieved in 1789, England had achieved without resource to upheaval. Despite her unrevolutionary record, she was the most 'vibrant' country in Europe. It was she who provided a haven for foreign exiles and firmly resisted the pressure of a reactionary Continent against this policy. The rejection under public pressure of the Conspiracy Bill, which was directed against foreign refugees, made a deep impression upon him. At the end of 1860, just before the enactment of Emancipation, he expressed his admiration for Britain and her police force in a letter to *The Daily News* (XIV, 354). He respected the 'clumsy, ponderous Anglo-Saxon worker, with his sweaty hands, with which he built a hut for himself "into which rain and hail may enter, but the royal power cannot"' (XIII, 232). He considered the age of secret societies to be over in England, arguing that institutions of real worth had been established to be built upon rather than overturned. Where he rejected outright the value of German and French examples for Russia, he turned down the lessons of English legislation because 'it is like a folk song, which is beautiful in its own language, but nonsense in translation' (XIV, 242).

The impact that Victorian England made upon Herzen must not be misconstrued. He never wanted Russia to imitate England. His admiration for England did not mean that he had shed his socialist aspirations: she was to his mind conservative, bourgeois and unjust. He was fully conscious that the main benefits of her achievements were enjoyed by the privileged few, and that in London 'every night a hundred thousand men don't know where they will lay their heads, and the police often find women and children dead of hunger beside hotels where one cannot dine for less than two pounds' (*Past*, 1026). His diagnosis was that England had much worth preserving, but that at present she seemed unwilling to risk losing it for the chance of a much more just society. And yet so far as political means were concerned, his respect for the freedom that she had created for the individual did at least provide ammunition in defence of the policy he was adopting in Russia. She demonstrated that revolution was not the *sine qua non* of progress.

Conditions in Russia at the beginning of Alexander's reign, then, together with Herzen's view of progress in Piedmont and England, encouraged his hopes of reform without revolution. But these factors cannot satisfactorily explain why his attitude remained unchanged even when the government's true nature became increasingly plain from about 1859. The fact that he clung to his misjudgement against growing evidence of the regime's reactionary intentions – which he fully recognised – and that he showed similar tendencies in the later sixties, when circumstances conspired even less to deceive him, must primarily be explained by the ideological basis of his outlook. There was an undercurrent in his thought which made him reluctant, even when he himself acknowledged the evidence, to accept that the political question could no longer be suspended in Russia. The essential features of this undercurrent were visible in his works before 1856. But in order to understand his perception of his role in the period of Emancipation, it is necessary to appreciate that this trend in his thought had taken deeper and deeper root at the very time that 'the revolutionary situation' was developing.[10]

Fundamentally, there was a change in his approach to the human condition. He no longer placed faith in the natural goodness and sociability of human nature – that faith which had inspired his most impassioned critique of western bourgeois and Russian absolutist society. This was well illustrated in the lines he wrote for his memoirs in this period describing a dispute over the education of his son Sasha. Herzen recalled that Ketscher, a close friend in the forties, had very firm views on education and wished to impose them on Sasha. 'He wanted to wrest the child from *artificial* life and consciously restore him to a state of savagery, to that primitive independence in which equality is carried so far as to wipe out once more the distinction between men and monkeys.' Herzen recognised that 'We ourselves were not so very far removed from this view,' but now he roundly condemned it – and with it the 'revolutionary method' in general.

> The savage assumption of the 'normal' man, to which the followers of Jean-Jacques aspired, detached the child from its historical environment, and made him a foreigner in it, as though education were not the grafting of the life of the race onto the individual ... Unfortunately, in education as in everything else, the violent, revolutionary method, while unthinkingly breaking down the old, has given nothing to replace it. (*Past*, 609)

Herzen's description of Serafima, the destitute girl Ketscher married in

---

[10] Following Lenin, Soviet historiography has designated conditions in Russia in the years from 1859 to 1861 as amounting to a 'revolutionary situation'.

the 1840s, reflected the same outlook. Illiterate and impoverished, the girl was suddenly placed amidst a highly cultured circle. But 'on her lay all the blessing and all the curse that lies upon the proletariat, especially upon ours ... We and she belonged to different ages of mankind, to different geological formations, to different volumes in the history of the world' (*Past*, 613). He could no longer expect, as he had once done, the undeveloped masses whom she represented, suddenly to close the gap and forge the rational society to which he aspired. The scepticism he had developed between 1852 and 1856 had increased and whereas before 1852 he had been willing to accept an interregnum which would be destructive, communist, but ultimately progressive, he was now more reluctant to accept it while any other way offered hope. Analysing the way in which Serafima's character became spoiled, self-pitying and complacent, he concluded:

> The mistake we made was again the generic mistake of all
> Utopias and idealisms. When one side of a question is correctly
> grasped, no attention is commonly paid to what that side has
> grown fast to, and whether it can be separated from it, no
> attention is given to the deep-lying tissue of veins connecting
> the raw flesh with the whole organism. We still think like
> Christians that we have but to say to the lame man: 'Take up
> thy bed and walk', and he will walk.
>
> At one stroke we flung the solitary and half-savage Serafima,
> who had not been seeing people, from her loneliness into our
> circle. We liked her originality, we wanted to preserve it, and
> we destroyed the last chance of her developing by removing all
> desire for improvement, assuring her that *she was all right as
> she was*. But she herself did not care to remain simply as she
> had been before. What was the result? We – revolutionaries,
> socialists, champions of the emancipation of women – turned a
> naïve, devoted, simple-hearted creature into a Moscow *petite
> bourgeoise*!
>
> Did not the Convention, the Jacobins, and the Commune
> itself turn France in this way into a *petite bourgeoise*, turn Paris
> into an *épicier*? (*Past*, 619)

That trend towards an evolutionary view of human nature, which we have seen in evidence immediately after 1852, actually became more pronounced in Herzen's thought at the very time the political situation in Russia was moving towards a climax that would demand commitment to immediate revolution. It is interesting to note that in April 1860 he recommended Darwin's *magnum opus*, which had come out the previous year, to Sasha (XXVII, 41). And it was at the end of 1860, immediately before the promulgation of the Edict of Emancipation, that he gave the fullest expression to this trend in his thought. Robert Owen had died two years earlier, and Herzen was provoked by the coldness of a British review of the life and work of the great utopian socialist to give his own more sympathetic account. Sufficient notice has not been taken of this article. The subject gave ample scope for Herzen's own preoccupations. He considered it his best work in the period of emancipation (XXVII, 226). His pride was understandable – the essay contained some of his most memorable passages.

States, he observed, are not houses of people who have lost their senses, but of people who have not yet come to them. 'Reason is the final endeavour, the summit to which development seldom attains' (*Past*, 1218). Even the tsar and the priest were in their time marks of progress. And the greatest buttress of reaction, along with the self-interest of the minority, he considered to be 'the backwardness of the masses . . . who are incapable of understanding' (*Past*, 1224). He was making completely explicit the unwelcome but logical conclusion of that perception at which he had arrived years before and reaffirmed now. 'The development of the brain needs and takes its time: there is no haste in nature . . . The delirium of history will last her for a long time' (*Past*, 1231). As Chesnokov has pointed out, this idea embraced both physiological development, the growth of the actual brain, and cultural, educational progress.[11] In this period he did pay attention to the physiological substructure of thought. His anti-urbanism was at its most intense, and he foresaw 'scarcely any future' for the city workers precisely because 'they are ruined, they are nervous, in their veins the blood is sick, inherited from generations growing up and dying in need, in stuffy air, in dampness' (XIV, 173). But he made no deep study of human biological development; rather he allowed the possibility of such an explanation for the backwardness of the masses, inclined as he was to draw heavily on evolution in nature by way of analogy and illustration. It was on cultural and educational factors that he laid primary emphasis. And this new 'realism' about the downtrodden masses led him to the most gloomy and conservative reflections about the need for political order. He questioned how safe it would be suddenly to free from secular and clerical authority

[11] D. I. Chesnokov, *Mirovozzrenie Gertsena* (Moscow, 1948), pp. 225–42.

the London mob, those outside the educated classes, this 'menagerie' (*Past*, 1224). As the largest urban and industrial centre in the world, London was for Herzen a special case. But in a more general, philosophical vein, he pursued the line of thought to its most bitter conclusion. He asked whether '*rational consciousness and moral independence are compatible with life in a state*' (*Past*, 1225). In a passage written in this period for his memoirs, he gave a striking elaboration of the same reflection.

> Suppose it is proved that this senselessness, this religious mania, is the essential condition of organised society, that for a man to live quietly beside his neighbour they must both be driven out of their wits and scared, that this mania is the one dodge by which history is created? ... I remember a French caricature aimed at some time or other against the Fourierists with their *attraction passionnée*; it represents an ass with a pole fixed upon its back, and a wisp of hay hung on a pole so that it can see it. The donkey, thinking to reach the hay, is obliged to move forward; the hay of course moves too, and the animal follows it. Perhaps the worthy beast might progress in that way, but all the same he would be made a fool of. (*Past*, 796–7)

Herzen was not asserting this possibility as proven. History alone would show the truth. But the distance he had travelled since his halcyon days of believing that 'social life for man is natural and therefore easy' had grown steadily. Certainly he was confident, in contrast to Robert Owen, that 'all guardians and pastors, all pedagogues and wet-nurses may calmly eat and sleep at the expense of the backward child. Whatever rubbish peoples may demand, *in our century* they will not demand the rights of a grown-up. For a long time to come humanity will still be wearing turn-down collars *à l'enfant*' (*Past*, 1227).

Articles such as that on Owen were addressed primarily to Herzen's Russian audience, and the universal, philosophical cast of his reflections indicates that they embraced Russians as well as foreigners, the *muzhik* as well as the western worker. Though he saw the rural population of both the west and Russia, immune from the 'nonsense' of urban life, as the reserve on which the future would be built, he did not exempt them from his perception of the backwardness of the masses (XIV, 173–5). This is borne out by his explicit comments on the state of development of the Russian peasant. In June 1860, registering his disappointment in the Tsar, he spelled out what he saw as the greatest obstacles to progress in

Russia: 'The fatal strength of the contemporary reaction in Russia – a *senseless and unnecessary* reaction – is so difficult to overcome because it rests on two firm granite strongholds – *the stupidity of the government and the immaturity, the undeveloped state of the people*' (XIV, 275). The same point was the premise of the question he posed as vital to Russia's future development: 'Is the absorption of the personality in the commune the *necessary, unavoidable* consequence of communal land-ownership, or does it correspond to the undeveloped condition of the people in general?' (XIV, 189). That he should see the Russian masses as 'poor people doomed to a gloomy life of ignorance and heavy work, with no time to study and think' (XIV, 209), requires emphasis both because of the change that had come over him since the high point of his optimism, and because of the form of nationalist messianism sometimes attributed to him. His sympathy for the masses, which if anything grew in this period as *The Bell* became a casebook of gentry and bureaucratic maltreatment of the peasants, must not be confused with a messianic exception of the Russian people from the fruits of his new 'realism'. This is not at all to deny that he firmly rejected any rigid path of progress, whether economic, political or educational, along which all peoples must pass. He hoped Russia could make rapid strides on the basis of its unique communal structure. On this hope he based his assertion that it is impossible 'to measure Russia by yards and metres', by western measures – their life is different (XIV, 11). But the political implications, in contemporary circumstances, of the backwardness of the masses were as inescapable in Russia as in the west. Russia could not be exempt from the conclusion he drew from France's experience of 1848, that 'Monarchic power in general is a measure of the immaturity of a people, the popular incapacity for self-government' (XIV, 166).

The influence of this conclusion upon the role Herzen adopted in the period of Emancipation was of decisive importance. Since he had no political solution to offer, he could not commit himself to an immediate peasant rising, and he resisted the growing evidence that no satisfactory reform could be achieved without political change. The point was brought out in the winter of 1858–9 when he sought to demonstrate to a Polish critic that his non-revolutionary policy was 'completely in accordance' with 'the chief bases of [his] convictions'. The point of departure was 1848. It was with that catastrophe that emphasis on the *political* solution to society's problems, on schemes for 'direct government', had proved bankrupt. Where monarchy in Britain had fostered free development, democracy in France had been the closest thing to St Petersburg tyranny. 'I well remember how at the one word "republic", the heart raced, but now, after 1849, 1850, 1851, this word arouses as much doubt as hope.' The explanation Herzen offered for this was that only 'where republic and democracy correspond to the development of the people' do they provide more personal freedom and independence. The converse was even more striking – 'Universal suffrage made of France a lunatic asylum.' And although it is in theory much more just, he could see no reason to believe that universal suffrage in France now would lead to a better choice than limited suffrage. 'I am a friend of the republic, of democracy,' said Herzen, 'but far more a friend of *freedom, independence and development*. If people object to me "Yes, but can there be freedom and independence outside a republic and democracy?", I reply that *with them* there cannot be if the people has not *grown up* to them' (XIV, 7–9).

Now, while Herzen's policy of peaceful pressure and exposure of specific crimes seemed to be carrying all before it, the source of his apoliticism was obscured. Until almost the end of the decade he could with conviction dwell on the realism of his stress upon the social question. But the situation in Russia was changing. Even while Herzen enjoyed his greatest influence and fame, the position he had adopted was becoming less and less tenable. He and Ogarev had gradually clarified the minimum that they would accept as genuine emancipation: adequate land for the peasants, no temporary-obligatory phase, no compensation for serf labour, and a system of compensation for the land which did not burden the peasant.[12] At the same time, as the government began to discourage further debate on the question, the evidence was growing that it had resolved upon a very limited form of emancipation involving a reduction in allotments, a temporary-obligatory period and a system of redemption which would leave the initiative in the hands of the landlord and which would involve a contribution from the peasants.[13] If the gulf

[12] B. S. Ginzburg, 'Otnoshenie A. I. Gertsena i N. P. Ogareva k krest'ianskoi reforme v period ee podgotovki (1857–1860gg.)', *Istoricheskie zapiski*, 36 (1951), 187–218. Ginzburg anticipates the date of Herzen's and Ogarev's rejection of peasant contributions to redemption, and of their commitment to an armed rising. This distorts his conclusion, but the article provides useful reference for the development of *The Bell*'s attitude towards emancipation. B. Hollingsworth, 'N. I. Turgenev and *Kolokol*', *Slavonic and East European Review*, XLI (1962–3), 89–100, provides a corrective.
[13] Three important works in English covering the development of the

between the two proposals was not public until Emancipation itself, the government's attitude pointed towards it. Both in foreign policy, with its collaboration with the reactionary powers of Austria and Prussia, and over domestic issues such as the treatment of dissident students and critical gentry like Unkovsky, the government showed it was taking up a deeply entrenched position. Herzen could see what was happening. He could not acquiesce in a liberal compromise which would not, in his eyes, constitute even the first step on the road to total change, and from as early as June 1858 he made increasingly sharp expressions of dissent. At the same time, to the radicals inside Russia headed by Chernyshevskii and Dobroliubov, the stance of conditional patience ceased altogether to be credible. They urged outright revolution. The combination of growing intransigence from the regime and increasing militancy from the left gradually undermined Herzen's policy. But his reaction to this inexorable pincer movement revealed just how deep-seated was his reluctance to accept that nothing could be done without political change.

Because of the respect Herzen commanded among the educated public, the position he adopted was seen to be of considerable political significance, and from 1858 onwards the radicals sought to counteract the liberal pressure placed upon him by Chicherin and others. Through letters to *The Bell* and through the columns of *The Contemporary* they urged him to shed his false hopes in the Tsar and make a clear stand for revolution. Herzen refused – though he expressed his sympathy for their impatience, their motives and their dedication. But radical criticism only became more intense. Dobroliubov launched a biting attack on Herzen's reliance upon the effect of 'exposure', of bringing to light specific outrages committed by the gentry and the government. To Dobroliubov, these abuses were mere symptoms, and to expose them without making concrete demands for the overthrow of the political system which gave rise to them was almost to assist in preserving the regime, in patching it up. But Herzen believed that in Russia's present condition publicity could be a major force for change. The collection and publication of individual cases of injustice and brutality was an important element in his

government's attitude are Emmons, *The Russian Landed Gentry and the Peasant Emancipation*, A. J. Rieber, *The Politics of Autocracy. Letters of Alexander II to Prince A. I. Bariatinskii, 1857–1864*, (Paris, 1966), and D. Field, *The End of Serfdom. Nobility and Bureaucracy in Russia, 1855–1861* (Cambridge, Mass., 1976).

editorial work. He regarded these criticisms from Dobroliubov as purely negative. His first open retort to the strictures of *The Contemporary* appeared in his famous article 'Very Dangerous!!!', published in June 1859. He took exception to Dobroliubov's harsh treatment of the purely literary achievements of the men of the forties, and defended them on the grounds that their activity was limited by the conditions of Nicholas's reign. But his main concern was with the issue of 'exposure' literature. The polemic was slightly complicated by the fact that he was replying at once to this radical attack, and to conservative criticisms of 'exposure' literature in general, based upon the very different argument that it was of no artistic worth.[14] The main thrust of his article, however, was aimed at *The Contemporary*. And the point was taken. Chernyshevskii agreed to travel to London for an *explication* with Herzen.

The encounter between the two outstanding figures of the pre-Marxist revolutionary movement has been the subject of great controversy. Some Soviet scholars, anxious to demonstrate that Herzen was already clearly within *The Contemporary*'s revolutionary camp, have been much exercised over Chernyshevskii's judgement of Herzen following their London meeting. For Chernyshevskii summarised his view when he told Dobroliubov that Herzen was simply 'Kavelin squared'.[15] Since Kavelin was firmly opposed to revolution and a prominent liberal, the conclusion is inescapable that Chernyshevskii saw Herzen's political views in the same light. Yet it has been argued that the phrase implied no political judgement, that Kavelin's liberalism was not yet established, and that Chernyshevskii was only commenting on Herzen's aristocratic personality.[16] Although this specious argument has been summarily dismissed by other Soviet historians, it illustrates the danger that the ideological battle over Herzen's place in Russian history can lead to serious distortion.

For the commentator who attributes slightly less weight to Chernyshevskii's opinion, and who does not share the assumption that

---

[14] See T. I. Usakina, 'Stat'ia Gertsena "Very Dangerous!!!" i polemika vokrug "oblichitel'noi literatury" v zhurnalistike 1857–1859gg.', in M. V. Nechkina *et al.*, eds., *Revoliutsionnaia situatsiia v Rossii v 1859–1861gg.* (Moscow, 1960), pp. 246–70.

[15] N. G. Chernyshevskii, *Polnoe sobranie sochinenii* (16 vols., Moscow, 1939–53), XIV, 379.

[16] A. E. Koshovenko, 'K voprosy o Londonskoi vstreche N. G. Chernyshevskogo c A. I. Gertsenom v 1859g. i formule "Kavelin v kvadrate"', *Revoliutsionnaia situatsiia* (1960), pp. 271–82.

Herzen must have been either a liberal or a revolutionary democrat, the phrase is less disturbing. Of more significance is the debate over the question of what the two men actually discussed in London. Koz'min believed that the main subjects of their talks were precisely those raised in the opposing articles. He denied that they discussed revolution and secret plans for it, since at the time Herzen was opposed to such means.[17] Nechkina, on the other hand, has argued the reverse.[18] She believes that they did indeed discuss the need to build a revolutionary organisation, and even reached broad agreement on steps to be taken to this end. She made great play of the fact that Koz'min had dated incorrectly Ogarev's sketch 'Note on a Secret Society', and she convincingly demonstrated that it had been written as early as 1857 and not in 1860 as he had suggested. Since Herzen annotated the essay, and since the outline of a secret society given there was elaborated by Ogarev in his 'Ideals' written in 1859, she saw in this proof that Herzen and Ogarev were already planning revolution. The fact is, however, that neither of these documents even mentioned the idea of violent revolution. The aim of the projected secret society was to be the spread of propaganda, to help *The Bell's* campaign for enlightenment and for the ferment of pressure for reform. Nechkina either glossed over this distinction or simply implied the reverse, that the envisaged organisation was to be expressly revolutionary. The misconception may have arisen partly because of an error in the dating of other relevant documents. The sketch which does show Ogarev accepting the need for revolution was 'The Aim of the Russian Movement', and according to Nechkina this was written in 1859 or 1860.[19] In fact, as Linkov has demonstrated, it was written *after* Emancipation, probably in the latter part of 1862.[20]

The most important element in the discussions in London, in fact, appears to have been Chernyshevskii's insistence that Herzen, if he was to continue his 'exposure' literature, must combine it with a clear political commitment to the replacement of the regime – whether his alter-

---

[17] B. P. Koz'min, *Iz istorii revoliutsionnoi mysli*, pp. 607–37.
[18] M. Nechkina's view has been reiterated in several of her works. See, for example, her commentary on Ogarev's revolutionary proposals, *Literaturnoe nasledstvo*, 61, (1953), 459–522.
[19] The point is argued out between Sh. M. Levin and Nechkina in *Literaturnoe nasledstvo*, 63 (1956), 867–79. Ogarev's sketch can be found in *Literaturnoe nasledstvo*, 61 (1953), 501–2.
[20] Linkov, *Revoliutsionnaia bor'ba*, pp. 273–4.

native be 'constitutionalist, or republican, or socialist'.[21] And in so far as he needed instruction, Herzen took the point that isolated abuses were mere symptoms of an underlying disease. In the long article he wrote soon after Chernyshevskii's return to Russia, 'Russian Germans and German Russians', he stressed his fundamental opposition to the existing system. His reason for fearing 'our learned friends – western doctrinaires, with their worn-out old robes of political economy, jurisprudence, etc., centralisers like the French and bureaucrats like the Prussians' was that they only 'wish to improve what is bad in itself ... what must be thrown out altogether' (XIV, 185). But the influence of Chernyshevskii and Dobroliubov on their senior at this stage must not be exaggerated. Herzen yielded nothing to their basic criticism that publicity could not in itself be an effective force for change of a fundamental nature. He continued to rely upon it and intensified his efforts to bring to light the crimes of privileged Russia. He opened a new supplement – *Into the Dock!* – specifically devoted to this.[22] Moreover, in spite of Chernyshevskii's urgings, he did not announce a specific programme with regard to the question of the central government. 'Russian Germans and German Russians' was provoked primarily by the dangers he saw in allowing liberal propaganda to go unanswered. And, in denouncing their plans for Russia to develop along the tortuous European path, he did spell out with crystal clarity the central tenets of his Russian Socialism: '(1) The right of each to the land; (2) communal land-ownership; (3) village self-government' (XIV, 183). But, contrary to the dominant Soviet view,[23] this did not constitute an answer to Chernyshevskii's demand that he commit himself to a specific political programme. The 'political' as opposed to the 'social' question remained suspended. The reasons for his silence on this were too deeply rooted simply to be

[21] S. G. Stakevich, 'Sredi politicheskikh prestupnikov' in *N. G. Chernyshevskii* (Moscow, 1928), p. 103, quoted in XIV, 495.

[22] See Z. P. Bazileva, 'Iz istorii izdatel'skoi deiatel'nosti A. I. Gertsena. (Prilozhenie k *Kolokolu* – listy *Pod sud!)*', *Istoricheskie zapiski*, 54 (1955), 436–47.

[23] See, for example, Smirnova, *Sotsial'naia filosofiia*, p. 168, and Usakina, 'Stat'ia Gertsena "Very Dangerous!!!"'. Of course in the long run this decentralised society must imply a change of central government – but such a long-term policy was not new: Herzen at least believed he had been propagating Russian Socialism during 1858 and 1859, before Chernyshevskii's arrival. His subsequent works showed Herzen maintaining his policy of working within the existing political structure. Soviet historians appear to underrate his determination to suspend the 'political' question.

abandoned in the face of Chernyshevskii's solemn admonitions. The next major article he wrote – '1860' – published in January 1860 was another attempt to free the Tsar from the reactionaries surrounding him. He insisted that he still believed the Tsar 'wished to do good' and was inhibited only by irrational fear (XIV, 217). He acknowledged the signs of change, the tightening censorship, the harassment of students. He was not optimistic and recalled reproachfully and nostalgically the hopes raised in 1856. Yet he retained his basic policy of pressure for reform within the existing political framework.

At the end of the following month, February 1860, Herzen published a letter addressed to *The Bell*, known as the 'Letter from the Provinces'. The identity of its author is still not established, but his outlook clearly had much in common with that of Chernyshevskii and Dobroliubov.[24] The letter made an urgent, impassioned plea for immediate preparation for a mass peasant rising, for the violent overthrow of the tsarist regime. In introducing the letter, Herzen made a succinct statement of his complicated attitude. He had hesitated to publish the letter, he said, but in a war 'one cannot tolerate too much disagreement between allies', and he had therefore decided to bring the disagreement into the clear light of day. He firmly placed the correspondent among his allies – *'one extreme* of *our* direction . . . we differ with you *not in ideas* but on means'. The dispute was now explicitly on the revolutionary overthrow of the central government, and Herzen rejected the idea of a wild mass uprising – the political immaturity of the masses made this unacceptable to him. For the first time he did mention the possibility of a revolutionary alternative to a *jacquerie*, a revolution led and organised by an elite. Only now at the end of the fifties, did he see a revolutionary intelligentsia which might conceivably provide such leadership. But as yet he did not give deep consideration to the idea, or to the question of the relationship between the elite and the masses in such a movement – the problem which would be so crucial to his attitude after 1861. Instead, he pointed out that he could not see evidence of any organisation actually taking shape and stressed that it would be premature before the elite itself was united on the question of Russia's future social structure. 1789 had succeeded because of the consensus between Mirabeau and Robespierre, Siéyès and Lafayette; 1848 had failed because of the deep divisions between republicans and socialists. In any case he argued that in all probability it would

---

[24] See XIV, 541–3 for a discussion of the hypotheses on the question of authorship.

be unnecessary to resort 'to the axe'. Illustrating the complexity of his relationship to the Tsar, he insisted that his appeals to the throne should not be taken for veneration, but concluded by posing the question, 'Who in recent times has done anything worthwhile for Russia except the Tsar?' (XIV, 238–44).

Almost in mockery of Herzen's effort to maintain his crumbling policy of reliance upon pressure on the Tsar, the very next month it was confirmed that the late chairman of the Editing Commissions overseeing Emancipation, Ia. I. Rostovtsev, was to be succeeded by V. N. Panin. Panin, the long-serving Minister of Justice, had been one of the chief targets of Herzen's campaign of exposure, a leading member of 'the Black Cabinet'. Herzen reacted with cold fury to this betrayal. He damned the appointment as 'a premeditated humiliation of public opinion and a concession to the planters' party' (XIV, 247).[25] He expressed his feelings in scorn at the absurdity of the choice. He had demanded that the masks be removed, he said, but he had not looked for this! He publicly declared that 'We held on up to the bitter end, to open betrayal, the criminal appointment of Panin', but now the government must be left to its own devices (XIV, 256). His ideological difficulty about acting on any other political premise had forced him to try to believe in the Tsar's radical intentions long after objective conditions had clearly exposed this illusion. And even now with the bulk of his liberal readership still impressed by the sheer fact of emancipation being undertaken at all, and with his own persistent faith in the power of publicity and exposure, in effect he did continue his policy of pressure on the Tsar. But it was by default. He formally recognised his error. In the remaining months before the Emancipation Edict was promulgated, he made a desperate search for an alternative approach to the 'political' problem.

In May he published an extract from the work of Prince P. Dolgorukov, *La Vérité sur la Russe*, in which a constitutional form of government was advocated for Russia. 'The author thinks,' wrote Herzen,

> 'that as socialists we will not agree with his constitutionalist
> endeavours. We think, on the contrary, that there are
> circumstances in which it is impossible to avoid these

[25] Herzen published the news of Panin's appointment in a front page article printed with a black funereal surround. See *'Kolokol': Gazeta A. I. Gertsena i N. P. Ogareva* (Facsimile edition, 11 vols., Moscow, 1962–4), III, 1860, p. 539.

transitional forms ... We thought that the Petersburg Empire
could still perform the one service of destroying the tight knot
of serfdom ... But *it did not know what it wanted* ... Such a
power ought to be taken into wardship.

Citing the exile without trial of Unkovsky as an example of the increasing
arbitrariness of Alexander's rule, Herzen remarked that 'In these circumstances any kind of rail, dam, *gardefous* made by society against the
Winter Palace would be very good' (XIV, 263–4). Thus the crisis of
confidence in his proclaimed policy of working within the absolutist
structure induced by the visibly growing reaction, brought him to savour
the possibility of a constitutional government in Russia. Since 1848 his
castigation of such forms had been absolute. And his scepticism was too
deep for him to develop the idea. He did not enter into the details, into
the possible nature of such a constitutional government. The idea was the
product of uncertainty and a policy vacuum, and not the beginning of a
positive new line of thought. But the very fact that he could even
entertain the possibility was symptomatic of the dilemma he faced over
the 'political' question.

The main line he pursued was expressed in 'After Five Years', published the following month, in June. The movement in which he had
believed with such hope, he declared, had come to a halt. The temptation
was to give in to vexation or despair, but duty demanded that one take the
way out that remained. And he argued that the failure of the government
constituted a signal to the educated public to shoulder the responsibility
itself. He called upon them to withdraw their support, thus weakening
the regime, and to take the initiative themselves for humanising Russia.
Doctrinaires and bureaucrats may remain with it, but the progressive
minority must stand on its own and expect nothing from the government.
The next month he called for the formation among the gentry of a 'Union
for Abstention from Corporal Punishment' (XIV, 287). It is hard to be
sure how literally he intended the idea: a note of irony might have crept in
at the thought that such an effort should be necessary to restrain land-
lords from inflicting physical pain on their serfs. But his tone was serious:
he wanted the enlightened gentry to act independently of the government. He appealed for three or four men in each province, out of a sense
of their own human dignity, to give their word to stop physical punishment on their estates – because 'two active men, moving firmly
towards their goal, are stronger than a whole crowd without an aim'
(XIV, 289). It was only their cursed lack of faith in themselves, in their

own power, which prevented the minority from taking great steps forward. In the same vein, he called upon the officers of the army and navy to unite against corporal punishment of soldiers and sailors. 'The officers can do more than the government, and for this they don't need one tenth the courage they invariably show in such abundance' (XV, 40). At the same time Ogarev, in his 'Letter to a Fellow Compatriot' (August 1860) and 'The New Year' (January 1861) elaborated more far-reaching plans for action without the government. He recommended the foundation of independent banks to provide the credit for a non-government conducted emancipation; he urged enlightened Russia to leave government service and help in educating and developing the country on their own initiative.[26] To inspire in his readers the confidence necessary for independent action, Herzen cited the examples of Wilberforce and Cobden as successful founders of movements for reform deriving their strength from outside the government. 'Man is as weak as a *spark* and as strong as a spark if he believes in his strength and falls *at the right moment* into a prepared milieu' (XIV, 289).

In proposing his own schemes and endorsing those of Ogarev, Herzen was essentially struggling to maintain his separation of the 'social' from the 'political' question on which his non-revolutionary policy for fundamentally revolutionary change was based. Rather than resort to the overthrow of the regime, his first inclination was to attempt to by-pass it. If the Tsar would not act, let progressive Russians act without him. It was with a strong note of approval that at the end of 1860, Herzen described Robert Owen's approach to this problem:

> In a government he saw a superannuated, historical fact
> supported by people who were backward and undeveloped, and
> not a gang of bandits which must be caught unawares. While
> not seeking to overturn the government, he also did not in the
> least seek to *amend it*. If the saintly shopkeepers [Quakers] had
> not put a spoke in his wheel, there would be in England and
> America now hundreds of New Lanarks and New Harmonies;
> into them would have flowed the fresh vigour of the working
> population, and little by little they would have drawn off the
> best vital juices from the States' antiquated tanks. Why should
> he struggle with the moribund? He could let them have a
> natural death. (*Past*, 1240–1)

[26] N. P. Ogarev, *Izbrannye sotsial'no-politicheskie i filosofskie proizvedeniia* (2 vols., Moscow, 1952–6), I, 352–95.

Having lost faith in Alexander, Herzen attempted to found his policy neither on overthrowing nor on reforming the regime, but on *ignoring* it altogether.

But while he was searching for an alternative to his hope in the Tsar, events helped to intensify the pressure upon him for a commitment to immediate revolution. The peasants themselves, the people for whom he felt he was working, were becoming more restive. Herzen reported several disturbances himself, and he could not help but be aware that the threat to the political order had grown. Moreover, as is demonstrated, for example, by his emotional vindication of the murder of a *pomeshchik* by a serf defending his bride's honour, Herzen's sympathy with these outbursts grew as he became more frustrated with the regime (XIV, 233). Lenin believed and many Soviet commentators have followed him in this, that Herzen now came to recognise the 'revolutionary people', and that this was the decisive influence committing him to the movement for outright revolution.[27] The evidence of increasing peasant militancy did, of course, strengthen the case of Chernyshevskii and Dobroliubov. But Herzen's reluctance to join the chorus for revolution was more deeply rooted than a simple failure to believe in the will of the people to rise. In fact, throughout the 1850s he had looked upon a mass uprising as a distinct possibility in Russia, and had warned the establishment about it. It was not their militancy that he doubted, nor the morality of such a rising. It was the political maturity of the masses and their capacity to carry out a revolution that would be *creative* as well as destructive. Thus, although his frustration with the regime and his sympathy with the impatience of the peasantry grew, he continued to resist the pressure of the radicals. He believed they were giving in to a noble-minded impatience which had in the past led men to make the same error. Seeing the light themselves, they could not bear to accept that others were still in the dark. In June 1860, shortly after publishing the revolutionary 'Letter from the Provinces', he explicitly warned that the backwardness of the masses

> yields only to time, a long time. It is just this which turns us to despair, we would rather give up anything – property, freedom – than time. 'Time is money', say the English – in fact it is far

[27] Lenin, *Polnoe sobranie sochinenii*, XXI, 260–1. B. S. Ginzburg, '*Kolokol* A. I. Gertsena i krest'ianskoe dvizhenie v Rossii v gody pervoi revoliutsionnoi situatsii (1859–1861)', *Istoriia SSSR* (1957), no. 5, 173–87. El'sberg, *Gertsen*, pp. 442, 482–7.

more dear, far greater: *time is ourselves* ... [But] it is necessary
to be reconciled with the truth and instead of stubbornness and
waste of strength in the defence of one's path, checked by
reaction, one must go along the path which is open. (XIV, 275)
He was affirming his own willingness to look for alternatives to pressure
upon the regime; but he was also warning against revolution born of
unrealistic haste. The lessons of 1848 continued to restrain him. The
republic of Lamartine and Ledru-Rollin, the ready-made solutions and
artificial formulae, had proved a mirage. They had been irrelevant to
bedrock reality – and that reality was the masses.

Besides this difference on the concrete issue of immediate revolution,
there was another dimension to Herzen's strictures upon the revolutionary circles in Russia. This was brought out in 'The Superfluous and the
Jaundiced', published in October 1860 – Herzen's account of the generation gap between the forties and the sixties, the theme of Turgenev's
famous novel *Fathers and Children*, published two years later. After
reiterating his defence of the literary activity of the 'superfluous' men of
the forties, he launched a fierce counter-attack on their successors, the
Engel'sons and Pecherins and now Dobroliubov and his followers.[28]
They were the 'jaundiced', poisoned at birth by the unhealthy atmosphere of Nicholas's reign, who 'gloomily reproach men for dining
without gnashing their teeth, and for enjoying pictures or music without
remembering the misfortunes of the world' (*Past*, 1579). In Herzen's
reaction there were elements of pique at the criticisms directed at him,
and already he was sensitive to real and imagined sneers at his aristocratic
air, his comfortable life-style, his armchair idealism – a source of friction
which grew in the later 1860s. But there was more to it than that. He
disliked above all 'the vindictive pleasure of their renunciation, and their
terrible ruthlessness ... They went further through the desert of logical
deduction, and easily arrived at those final, abrupt conclusions, which
are alarming in their radical audacity but which, like the spirits of the
dead, are but the essence gone out of life, not life itself.' Beneath his
criticism of their tone – which could 'drive an angel to fighting and a saint
to cursing' – he was reacting against a new brand of revolutionary. The
revolution they proposed was far removed from the heady concept with
which he had matured. This revolution did not pretend to represent a
palingenesis, the birth of a new heaven on a new earth which would meet

[28] Herzen had just republished his own contribution to the literary protest of
the forties, *Who is to Blame?*

the aspirations of the full personality. Herzen's disillusionment had, of course, led him to renounce his most romantic concept of revolution. He knew it to be a dream. Yet remnants of his view of the revolutionary as being himself a full and rounded personality, despite the doomed society around him, lingered on in his approach and made him recoil from this new ethos. His idea of the revolutionary was still too refined for him to accept what he saw as this new self-negating, one-dimensional, ruthless concern for violent upheaval with no guarantee of what lay beyond it. His attack, then, reflected both his resentment at the challenge posed to his leadership, at Dobroliubov's contemptuous dismissal of him and his generation as 'mammoths' of the past, and, at the same time, a deeply felt sense of superiority. For he believed that this 'jaundiced' generation could not last:

> The world, in spite of eighteen centuries of Christian
> contrition, is in a very heathen fashion devoted to epicureanism
> and *à la longue* cannot put up with the depressing faces of these
> Daniels of the Neva ... Their relief is on its way; already we
> have seen men of quite a different stamp, with untried powers
> and stalwart muscles, appearing from remote universities, from
> the sturdy Ukraine, from the sturdy north-east, and perhaps we
> old folk may yet have the luck to hold out a hand across the
> sickly generation to the fresh stock, who will briefly bid us
> farewell and go on their broad road. (*Past*, 1579–81)

Herzen equated Dobroliubov quite explicitly with the 'Daniels of the Neva': it was a new generation, the students of universities such, perhaps, as that of Kharkov, whom he credited with the rounded socialist character he cherished.[29] They were his successors, they would pursue a path to socialism compatible with the principles of his political outlook.

The clash of personality and temperament, and even Herzen's attack on the narrowness of Dobroliubov and his followers, must not distract attention from the substantive issue at stake. This remained the question of immediate revolution. Herzen felt the strength of the 'jaundiced'

---

[29] See E. G. Bushkanets, 'Dobroliubov i Gertsen', *Problemy izucheniia Gertsena*, pp. 280–92, on the controversy over this question. Many Soviet scholars have been inclined to deny or gloss over the fact that Herzen's 'men of quite a different stamp' were precisely in contrast to these 'Daniels' – the revolutionaries around Chernyshevskii and Dobroliubov. See, for example, El'sberg, *Gertsen*, p. 455; Ia. I. Linkov, 'Ideinye i takticheskie raznoglasiia v riadakh revoliutsionnoi demokratii v epoku padeniia krepostnogo prava', *Voprosy istorii*, 6 (1959), 51.

generation's intransigence. In coupling Dobroliubov with such ineffective characters as Engel'son he almost knew he was deceiving himself.
In the course of 'The Superfluous and the Jaundiced' itself, he referred to
The Contemporary as one of the best Russian reviews (*Past*, 1575). He was
struggling to resist the force of their case, their strength on 'logical'
grounds. The possibility of remaining faithful to his demands for change
while rejecting revolution was fast fading. He was abandoning his belief
that the courage and personality of the Tsar were crucial. The following
month he insisted that the growing reaction and the proposed alliance
with Austria depended not on the royal person 'but on the essence of
Tsarism, on the whole system' (XIV, 331). There was no evidence of an
impending independent gentry initiative. The stark choice that the
young radicals held out, between condoning the regime and calling for
revolution against it, became increasingly hard to avoid. Yet Herzen
clung to his policy to the last – and hailed the final Edict as his vindication.

At the beginning of 1861 he heard from Turgenev that the Emancipation Proclamation was imminent. His heart lifted. Although the
details were unknown, and the signs were that they would be less than
ideal, the agitation to which he had devoted so much effort was at last
coming to fruition. He heard St Petersburg was buzzing with excitement:
he longed to be there. 'This is our moment, our last moment – the
epilogue,' he told Turgenev (XXVII, 138). He implored Sasha to take
note of this 'monumental news – it will be talked about for ages' (XXVII,
141). At the end of March he and Ogarev wrote a highly formal letter,
designed to mark the end of a great crusade, of an epoch, to the aged
Decembrist Nikolai Turgenev:

Nikolai Ivanovich!
You were one of the first to begin to talk about the
emancipation of the Russian people; recently, deeply moved,
with tears in your eyes, you celebrated the first day of that
emancipation. Allow us, disciples of your union, to offer you
our greeting, and with a feeling of fraternal or, better, filial
love, to shake you by the hand and warmly embrace you from
an overflowing heart . . .
With deep and tender emotion we have written these lines
and we sign our names with that profound, religious devotion
for the senior figures of Russian freedom which we have felt
throughout our lives. (XXVII, 143)

Where the Decembrists had raised the standard, it had been the task of his generation to achieve this tangible step. Herzen was determined that this was the turning point, that now there could be no going backwards, that he had seen the crowning achievement of his life's work. It was as if half of him knew, just before Emancipation, that all was not well, that too much that was intolerable would remain for him to be able to pronounce his faith in non-revolutionary reform justified. In 'On the Eve', published on 1 March 1861, when he had heard Emancipation was imminent but before it was official, he expressed his misgivings and his regret: 'If only it were possible to say again "You have conquered, O Galilean!", how loudly and with what sincerity we would say it', and defy 'any narrow-minded doctrinaire, immovable upholder of scholastic science' (XV, 33). For he wanted to believe. And when the Edict was finally proclaimed, he organised a great celebration in London to mark the event.[30] In the speech he prepared for the occasion, he welcomed this decisive step forward and reviewed the contribution towards it of his Free Russian Press. Acknowledging that the Tsar was the hero of the day, he forecast that 'Because I give him his due, the revolutionary schematics and rigorists will scold me – they have already scolded me for many of my words' (XV, 218). The seal was to be set on the celebration and on the vindicated policy of *The Bell* by a toast to the Tsar. But on the day the celebration was due, 10 April, news reached London of a massacre by tsarist troops in Warsaw. The feast took place but a gloom hung over the proceedings. The toast was never proposed. Herzen had resisted the 'political' question and the question of revolution as long as he could. He now had to confront the failure of his policy.

[30] Carr draws on contemporary descriptions to evoke the scene, *The Romantic Exiles*, pp. 189–90.

8

The impasse

Herzen was outraged by the repression in Poland. For a moment he allowed the possibility that the crime had been committed without Alexander's permission. But every day that passed confirmed that the repression reflected the Tsar's own policy. The Tsar had already broken the promise implicit in the proclamation of Emancipation. 'Why did *this man* not die on the day of the manifesto to the Russian people on emancipation!' he exclaimed in *The Bell* (XV, 82). And he told Turgenev that 'We will not see Russia for a long time to come yet. The blood in Warsaw has spoiled everything terribly' (XXVII, 150). When the text of the Emancipation Edict arrived in London, it was Ogarev who subjected it to detailed analysis, but Herzen fully shared his conclusion.[1] Like the radicals inside Russia, they found it totally unsatisfactory on the questions of land, of compensation and of the temporary-obligatory period. The Emancipation was essentially a fraud.

In May the government showed its true colours. Herzen received news of the ruthless measures taken against peasant resistance to the obligations imposed by the Edict. The massacre in the village of Bezdna in the Kazan province roused him to a fury of indignation. 'The mind reels, the blood freezes in one's veins reading the naïve, artless account [by the government] of this evil of a kind unknown since Arakcheev,' he wrote in June 1861. 'The tongue-tied illiteracy and duplicity of the government opens the way to murder . . . We don't recognise Russia . . . fresh blood is spilt, corpses lie scattered! . . . Down with the masks,' he concluded, 'it is better to see the savage teeth and the wolf's snout than false humanity . . .

---

[1] Ogarev, *Izbrannye sotsial'no-politicheskie i filosofskie proizvedeniia*, I, 468–526.

and liberalism' (XV, 107–9).[2] His most impassioned plea appeared in
August. The brunt of his attack this time was borne by the Orthodox
hierarchy and their cynical use of peasant superstition to manipulate the
people. 'Not knowing where to turn in painful moments, in moments of
human yearning for rest, for hope, surrounded by a herd of rapacious
enemies, he [the peasant]comes with burning tears to the dumb shrine, to
the dumb relic – and with this relic and this shrine they deceive him, they
console him so that he will not find another kind of consolation' (XV,
134). The church has shown itself criminally indifferent. The people
trusted the Tsar – 'the Tsar ordered them to be killed like dogs' – and
there was no word of protest from the hierarchy. Herzen's indignation
boiled over:

> O if only my words could reach you, toiler and sufferer of the
> Russian land – you whom *that* Russia, the Russia of lackeys
> and hall-porters despises ... if only my voice could reach you,
> how I would teach you to despise your spiritual pastors, placed
> over you by a Petersburg synod and a German Tsar ... you
> hate the *pomeshchik*, you hate the bureaucrat, you fear them –
> and you are quite right; but you still believe in the Tsar and
> the hierarchy ... Don't believe in them. The Tsar is with them
> and they with him. (XV, 135–7)

To Herzen's protest in the name of Poland and the peasantry was
added that in the name of the universities. The measures taken by the
government to intimidate and silence the students were 'a crime against
the spirit, against enlightenment' (XV, 175). The government had
betrayed progress in every sphere; the Tsar could not be exonerated.
Authentic sympathy for the peasantry and disgust with the regime
evoked from Herzen notes of unprecedented militancy. He called the
old-believers to 'faith' and 'deeds' (XV, 108); he made of Anton Petrov,
the leader of the Bezdna resistance, a peasant martyr and urged his
comrades not to pray to him for a miracle, but to draw on his example and
achieve their own true emancipation (XV, 137–8). And in the famous
passage of the leading article of *The Bell* on 1 November 1861, he called
upon the students:

> Listen – since the darkness does not prevent one hearing: from

[2] Herzen expressed his emotion in virulent sarcasm: 'For the massacre of the
unarmed, Count Apraksin received a Vladimir of the third class – and was
offended: he expected a George! How ungrateful, Alexander Nikolaevich –
really, a man puts down two hundred of our Russians, and only a third class
Vladimir!' (XV, 117).

every side of our enormous country, from the Don and from the Urals, from the Volga and from the Dnieper, a moan is growing, a murmur rising – it is the first roar of the ocean waves, which seethe, fraught by storms, after the terrible wearisome calm. *To the people! to the people!* there is your place, exiles of science, show that from you come not petty officials, but soldiers, not homeless mercenaries, but warriors of the Russian people! (XV, 175)[3]

Herzen's attitude provoked the final breach with the liberals. Although Ogarev's plan to demand a *zemskii sobor* (national assembly) from the Tsar was designed to carry moderate opinion into outright rejection of the regime,[4] the government's measures had made it impossible to pursue the policy of uniting the whole body of progressive opinion. The appearance of 'Young Russia' (1862), an extreme and immediate call to arms, and the almost simultaneous outbreak in the capital of fires which had apparently been started deliberately alarmed moderate opinion.[5] In the face of disorder at home and in Poland, society polarised for and against the regime. Memories of personal friendship no longer inhibited Herzen's outright hostility to staunch supporters of the government such as Korsh and Ketscher (XXVII, 214). Kavelin and Turgenev represented a more progressive liberal wing whom Herzen had hitherto seen as allies. But as they rallied to the government, he accepted the existence of the breach.[6] It was the Polish rebellion in January 1863 which most effectively moved liberal opinion behind the government; it was Herzen's support of the Polish cause which precipitated the most

[3] Whereas Soviet scholars interpret this as expressing Herzen's commitment to work for immediate revolution, Venturi sees it as no more than an extension of Ogarev's plan in 1860 for direct efforts to educate the people without reference to the government (*Roots of Revolution*, p. 110). The clearly militant tone of the summons was observed by moderates and raised radical hopes of a revolutionary lead from Herzen. But it was not made in the context of any organisation. It expressed his sympathy with the peasantry, and his exasperation, but it did not reflect a resolution of those factors in his thought which, as will be shown, inhibited him from working for immediate revolution.

[4] See Ia. I. Linkov, 'Ideia krest'ianskoi revoliutsii v dokumentakh *Zemli i voli* 60-kh godov', *Revoliutsionnaia situatsiia* (1962), pp. 263–304. Turgenev's refusal to sign a petition hastened his breach with Herzen.

[5] The public mood engendered by these fires encouraged the government to take action against *The Contemporary* at this point as well.

[6] In 1862 and 1863 Herzen addressed to Turgenev an analysis of their profoundly different views of Russia's future (XVI, 129–98).

drastic fall-off in the circulation of *The Bell*.[7] But the die was already cast in 1861.

Peasant disappointment with the Emancipation measures provoked widespread risings in 1861. These raised the hope among revolutionary circles that their own impatience would now be echoed in a mass rising – if not during 1861, then after the two-year transitional period designated by the government, in 1863. Concentrated in the main cities and provincial universities, these circles began to form links with each other, and leading figures such as Chernyshevskii, Sleptsov and the Serno-Solov'evich brothers began to make plans for a revolutionary society with national pretensions.[8] They represented the socialist wing of the organisation which had taken shape by 1862 under the name of *Land and Liberty*.[9] While the society was being planned, the radicals inside Russia hoped that Herzen would grasp the nettle and place himself at the head of the movement. His enormous prestige would enable him to some extent to set the terms of debate, to make revolution respectable among wavering radicals. Exhorted and inspired by him, so it was believed, many of his admirers would join the revolutionary camp. The large circulation of *The Bell* and the sheer publicity resources of the Free Russian Press made his stance seem of vital importance. Chernyshevskii was deeply depressed when he heard from Sleptsov that Herzen was not likely to give the desired lead.[10] The most striking evidence of the importance attached to Herzen's attitude, and of the invitation to leadership that was being made to him, is provided by V. I. Kel'siev. Kel'siev's recollections took the form of a *Confession* to the police when he gave himself up in 1867: both his judgement and his reliability are in question on certain points.[11] But there is no reason to doubt his description of his visit to St Petersburg in the summer of 1862. He stayed with the Serno-Solov'evich brothers and since he had just come from London, where he was working with

[7] Bazileva, '*Kolokol' Gertsena*, Chapters III and IV charts this decline.

[8] The controversy over the extent of Chernyshevskii's participation in these plans is reviewed by W. F. Woehrlin, *Chernyshevskii: the Man and the Journalist* (Cambridge, Mass., 1971), pp. 263–311.

[9] See Linkov, *Revoliutsionnaia bor'ba*, pp. 151–272 and Vilenskaia, *Revoliutsionnoe podpol'e*, Chapter III. Vilenskaia's view of *Land and Liberty* as an umbrella organisation covering socialists and non-socialists appears to be a valid corrective to Linkov's straightforward identification of the society with the socialists.

[10] See Linkov, *Revoliutsionnaia bor'ba*, p. 164.

[11] V. I. Kel'siev, *Ispoved'* in *Literaturnoe nasledstvo*, 41–2 (1941), 253–470, with a commentary by M. Klevenskii.

Herzen, they were anxious to question him on the great man's attitude to 'the present movement'. Kel'siev's opinion was that Herzen did not wish to fight for 'practical activity' but to remain a propagandist and a leader of public opinion. The brothers were horrified. It seemed to them that Herzen had called forth a vibrant educated minority and now, just when they were looking for direction, he was unable or unwilling to control and steer them. This explained the hopeless fragmentation of opinion among the younger generation. Herzen alone could provide the necessary unity and wisdom. Till now, exclaimed N. Serno-Solov'evich, this chaos had been controlled 'by faith in Herzen and readiness to go through fire and water at his word'.[12]

Assessments of how closely Herzen was involved with the plans of these revolutionary circles differ. Venturi, in his volume on the populist movement, argues that *Land and Liberty* was created by groups of young radicals and officers within Russian in the face of the scepticism of both Chernyshevskii and Herzen. Herzen, he concludes, 'always remained suspicious and hostile to the conspiracy which was coming into being'.[13] That there should be doubt about his involvement is partly explained by Herzen's own account of these years, in which he was disparaging about the society and the movement. But Nechkina has argued that he drew a veil over his true participation, both because he came to regret it and because details could imperil allies in Russia.[14] Linkov, in the most thorough survey, has laid great emphasis on the objectively revolutionary effect of the campaign of *The Bell* throughout these years. There can be little question of this, but he has also suggested that, together with the circle around *The Contemporary*, Herzen and Ogarev were the moving spirits behind and provided the joint leadership of *Land and Liberty*.[15]

Now the evidence that at different moments Herzen was to some extent involved, and even hopeful, is overwhelming. The fact that he coined the name *Land and Liberty* may have less importance than is sometimes attributed to it,[16] but even in the account he himself left,

[12] *Ibid.*, 312–13. See also B. S. Ginzburg, 'Rasprostranenie izdanii vol'noi russkoi tipografii v kontse 1850-kh – nachale 1860-kh godov', *Revoliutsionnaia situatsiia* (1962), pp. 335–60.
[13] Venturi, *Roots of Revolution*, p. 119.
[14] M. V. Nechkina, 'Konspirativnaia tema v *Bylom i dumakh* A. I. Gertsena', *Revoliutsionnaia situatsiia* (1963), pp. 275–97.
[15] Linkov, *Revoliutsionnaia bor'ba, passim.*
[16] See, for example, the weight attached to the fact by I. V. Porokh, *Gertsen i Chernyshevskii* (Saratov, 1963), p. 164.

Herzen admitted that though it was Bakunin who forever thought that revolution was imminent 'to some extent we ourselves believed in it too' (*Past*, 1366). On 1 March 1863, admittedly rather late, when revolutionary hopes were already waning, he publicly identified himself with *Land and Liberty* by announcing its existence in *The Bell* (XVII, 56). It was in fact under the influence of the pressure for revolution in Poland that he expressed the most explicit hopes. Addressing the revolutionary officers of the Russian troops in Poland, he tried to restrain a Polish uprising. It could not succeed, he said, until there was a similar outbreak in Russia itself, and at that moment, late in 1862, there was no such prospect. But, insisting that it would be for the concrete question of the land that the peasants will take up arms, he went on to say that

> It will be impossible to hesitate any longer after the end of the transitional period, that is the spring of next year. The peasant will not yield the land, on the contrary, he will resist; rise then Poland, throw yourselves with your allies and their soldiers into Lithuania and Little Russia in the name of the peasant right to the land – and where will there be any force to resist you? The Volga and the Dnieper, the Don and the Urals will respond to you! (XVI, 251–7)

It was the plight of Poland which, in December, provoked him to ask: 'What are we waiting for? For them to call a Duma? But they never will call one – it will just have to assemble. Minin [an organiser and leader of the people's voluntary militia in 1612] did not wait for the Tsar's order to begin his agitation for the salvation of Russia (XVI, 265).

But a picture of Herzen throwing himself into the revolutionary plans and agitation fundamentally distorts his experience of these years and his basic failure to find a role to replace that which the reaction had foreclosed. This is not to deny the positive attitude of Ogarev and the part played by him, on which Linkov insists. His pamphlet 'What do the people need?' (1862) doubtless was a basic programme for the society, and as early as the summer of 1861 he does appear to have been deeply involved in plans for the society. Ogarev's proposal for a petition to the Tsar for a national assembly, moreover, appears to have represented a deliberate manoeuvre to increase outright rejection of the Tsar rather than a serious hope of extracting concessions from the Tsar.[17] But none of

---

[17] The clearest evidence for this is in Ogarev's sketches, 'The Aim of the Russian Movement', and 'The Foreign Society', *Literaturnoe nasledstvo*, 61 (1953), 500–11.

this illuminates Herzen's attitude. Indeed a striking feature of Linkov's study is just how little evidence there is of Herzen's enthusiasm.[18] His most forthright statements, quoted above, were made in the context of a Polish rebellion which he felt obliged to support in public but which in private he did all he could to restrain (XXVII, 257–8). He approved the petition for a *zemskii sobor*, and intermittently repeated the demand in the later sixties, but the address was in fact never circulated and he certainly did not put his full weight behind it. He did not endorse Ogarev's view of it as a step to an early rising directed at a new political structure.[19] The initiative, the driving force behind the involvement of the Free Russian Press in *Land and Liberty* lay squarely with Ogarev. It was he who conducted the correspondence and negotiations with the revolutionaries inside Russia; it was he who wrote the analyses from which the society drew so much of its inspiration; it was he who filled, with virtually no help from Herzen, the supplement *Obshchee veche*, designed for agitation among the peasants themselves. The close relationship between Herzen and Ogarev makes it necessary to approach with caution the problem of pinpointing their differences. Ogarev himself had his reservations; he warned against an over-centralised organisation, and in 'What do the

[18] Linkov's picture of the role of the London centre and of Herzen's attitude has not stood up well to detailed criticism. See S. D. Lishchiner, 'Sushchestvoval li sovet obshchestva *Zemlia i volia* pri redaktskii *Kolokola?*', *Istoricheskie zapiski*, 79 (1966), 259–72, where Herzen's consistent resistance to participation in *Land and Liberty* is brought out, and U. N. Korotkov, 'U istokov pervoi *Zemli i voli* (neopublikovannaia stranitsa iz tetradi A. A. Sleptsova)', *Istoricheskie zapiski*, 79 (1966), 176–209.

[19] Of course Herzen knew of Ogarev's projects. He made a few notes on the surviving manuscript of 'The Society Abroad'. But, while he did not repudiate Ogarev's approach, his comments were less than enthusiastic. At the crucial point at which Ogarev affirmed that if the government refused a *zemskii sobor*, the aim would be to promote an orchestrated insurrection, Herzen commented: 'But the government can, without refusing or accepting, take *mezzo termine*, concede a part – and that is what it probably will do.' And at the end of Ogarev's long essay, Herzen appended a few brief comments which stressed the limited scope of the society at present and the need to create unity of purpose; he asked what the society had learned from the last Polish revolution, what means it would use to act, and even what it would propagate (*Literaturnoe nasledstvo*, 61 (1953), 509–11). Ogarev shared some of Herzen's underlying reservations – in a letter of May 1862, which Herzen specifically endorsed, he observed that 'The idea of a *zemskii sobor* is still far from the people' (XXVII, 224). See Linkov, *Revoliutsionnaia bor'ba*, Chapters VII and VIII, for an account of the revolutionaries' ideas about the *zemskii sobor*. Linkov elucidates Ogarev's approach with more success than Herzen's.

people need?' he made very moderate political demands and in fact countenanced the continuation of the monarchy.[20] Moderates such as Turgenev and Annenkov misconstrued the difference between the two men, seeing it as basically that between a liberal and a revolutionary.[21] Herzen was no liberal: but the difference in terms of enthusiasm for early revolution was stark. Herzen's own account may be called into question in detail, but the mood he describes rings true. Recalling his refusal to become an 'agent' of *Land and Liberty*, he describes the plenipotentiary sent to him assuring him that the society's membership ran into the hundreds in St Petersburg and numbered three thousand in the provinces:

> 'Do you believe it?' I asked Ogarev afterwards. He did not
> answer. 'Do you believe it?' I asked Bakunin.
> 'Of course, but,' he added, '*well, if there are not as many now
> there soon will be!*' and he burst into a roar of laughter.
> 'That is another matter.'
> 'The essence of it all is giving support to feeble beginnings;
> if they were strong they would not need us,' observed Ogarev,
> who was always dissatisfied with my scepticism on these
> occasions. (*Past*, 1370)

From the first Ogarev had found Herzen reluctant. When Ogarev planned to publish N. Serno-Solov'evich's impatiently revolutionary 'Answer' to the more moderate pamphlet 'The Great Russian', Herzen had written to him that he would not publish it – 'I have an instinct,' he told Ogarev, 'and hitherto every time I have given way it has been a mistake' (XXVII, 177). So far as the objective role of the London centre in the revolutionary plans of these years is concerned, this difference in enthusiasm may be overlooked. But so far as Herzen's intellectual biography is concerned, it is important, and Linkov's assumption of an identity of views between the two exiles is unsatisfactory.

Ogarev was not alone among his contemporaries in noticing Herzen's reluctance. Bakunin judged Herzen to lack 'the stuff of which revolutionary leaders are made'.[22] Kel'siev's view was that 'circumstances *compelled them* [Herzen and Ogarev] *against their will* to become agitators'.[23] Although the Free Russian Press did print the explicitly revolutionary

---

[20] Ogarev, *Izbrannye sotsial'no-politicheskie i filosofskie proizvedeniia*, I, 527–36.
[21] Lampert makes the point that M. Lemke, in his 1920s edition of Herzen's works, shared this misconception (*Studies in Rebellion*, p. 287).
[22] Quoted in Carr, *The Romantic Exiles*, p. 217.
[23] Kel'siev, *Ispoved'*, in *Literaturnoe nasledstvo*, 41–2 (1941), 275.

pamphlet 'To the Young Generation' in 1862, its author, N. V. Shelgunov, recalled that Herzen did not approve it – 'We were still foaming, he had ceased to do so.'[24] However varied their analyses of the cause, the men around Herzen concurred at least on this point, that Herzen's commitment to the revolutionary agitation was half-hearted. He was reluctant, almost grudging. He did not take the helm. In his memoirs, Herzen reflected on his unwilling concession. The case of Bakunin and Poland was the immediate cause of his reflection, but he saw his behaviour then typifying a recurrent character trait:

> How, whence did I come by this readiness to give way, though
> with a murmur, this weak yielding, though after rebellion and
> protest? I had, on the one hand, a conviction that I ought to
> act in one way, and, on the other, a readiness to act quite
> differently. This wavering, this dissonance, *dieses Zögernde*, has
> done me infinite harm in my life, and has not even left me with
> the faint comfort of recognising that my mistake was
> involuntary, unconscious; I have made blunders *à contre-coeur*;
> I had all the arguments on the other side before my eyes. (*Past*,
> 1363)

Although some Soviet authors have tended to play it down, Herzen's ambivalent attitude has nevertheless often been pointed out. Venturi, who has given the most detailed western account of Herzen during the years of *The Bell*, fully recognises his unease about committing himself to revolutionary organisation, but his explanation requires elaboration. 'His experience of 1848,' says Venturi, 'had made him lose enthusiasm for, but not faith, in, violent revolution . . . His ends remained the same, but he no longer believed in the means which had inspired him during the revolution.'[25] While this formula certainly conveys his ambivalence, it does little to illuminate how exactly Herzen himself viewed the choice before him. The pressures on Herzen to commit himself to revolutionary agitation are clearly visible. He saw them in terms of 'love, friendship and indulgence' towards the enthusiasts around him, and of 'false shame', of fear of the jibe that he lacked the courage of his convictions (*Past*, 1264). But what it was that inhibited him, what factors in his own make-up and outlook prevented him from following through the apparently revolutionary summons 'to the people' – it is this that requires explanation.

Several factors have been cited to account for his inhibition. Some

[24] N. V. Shelgunov, *Vospominaniia* (Moscow, 1967), I, 244.
[25] Venturi, *Roots of Revolution*, p. 91.

commentators have seen a rooted resistance to the revolutionary method and violence as such. Before 1861 he had expressed his hope that the Tsar would end 'the bloody era of revolution' (XIII, 296); the aim must be, he said, to protect Russia's development 'from the bloody, terrible convulsions which gave birth to the social idea and brought it to maturity, but which also brought the western people to the edge of the grave' (XIII, 179–80). However, even before Emancipation, Herzen had consistently affirmed the justice of revolution if all else failed. And in the changed circumstances of a manifestly obdurate regime, this recognition of the human cost of revolution would surely induce no more than humane sobriety in calling for upheaval. Between 1861 and 1863 he never explained his reluctance in terms of horror at violence. Herzen himself protested that action must come from within Russia itself, and not from London (XIV, 243). Yet Ogarev's commerce with the young radicals demonstrated that there was an aching need for help and leadership from *The Bell*. Possibly there was in Herzen's attitude an element of *amour-propre*, since those who had been urging revolution on him for several years had been vindicated and his own policy had been destroyed. But to stress this would be to underestimate Herzen's prestige and his self-confidence. More to the point was the simple fact that he questioned the likelihood of success, purely in terms of military strength.[26] The case he made for restraint in .Poland was that a premature rising could not succeed. In Russia too he undoubtedly had a greater sense of reality than Bakunin, and saw through the pretensions of some of the more heady revolutionaries. Yet at times Herzen genuinely believed that the regime might be overthrown, and he admitted that an embryonic organisation did exist for this purpose. His much vaunted realism was not that different from the viewpoint of Ogarev and other revolutionaries. In reply to Ogarev's argument that it was precisely because the revolutionary germ was weak that he should help it, Herzen lamely argued that if this was so, the young revolutionaries should ask him more humbly (*Past*, 1370). Given that he *whole-heartedly wanted* a successful revolution at this moment, Ogarev's argument was impossible to refute. In fact, the source of Herzen's inhibitions lay deeper than doubt in the military strength of the revolutionaries: it lay at the very heart of his political philosophy.

When in 1861 the reaction became blatant, the 'political' question

[26] This is the explanation Linkov offers for those notes of reluctance in Herzen that he does admit (*Revoliutsionnaia bor'ba*, pp. 329–30).

seemed finally unavoidable. The central government was using force to impose a totally unacceptable form of emancipation upon the peasantry. The regime's position was rigid and beyond the reach of peaceful pressure. The justice of peasant violence could not seem more compelling, and Herzen proclaimed this. But this implied the need for primary emphasis upon political change. This was Herzen's problem. For even though at times in the mid-sixties he appeared to recognise quite explicitly that a republic was the necessary condition for progress,[27] at this crucial moment he continued to resist such a shift in emphasis. The new light in which he now saw the Tsar did not correspondingly transform his view of the peasantry. He could not simply abandon the tenets on which his apoliticism had been based. The masses were still politically immature. The total destruction of the government and the immediate devolution of all power to the peasantry, which appealed to Bakunin, was not, therefore, a satisfactory solution to Herzen. As he told Bakunin at the end of the decade in his 'Letters to an Old Comrade', 'What does *denying* the state mean, when the chief condition of its disappearance is the maturity of the masses?' (XX, 591). Nor would he devote himself to a constitutional programme. The logic of the situation might demand that he do so, and as we have seen, he did endorse the idea of a *zemskii sobor* to consider the future. But he consistently and repeatedly refused to concentrate upon the issue of a new form of central government. Even when he was most positive about early revolution, he dwelt upon the overwhelming priority of the question of the land – a priority based, he reiterated late in 1862, 'internally upon the spirit, the genius of the Russian people, and externally upon the insolvency of all political revolutions' (XVI, 256). His lack of warmth for a constitution was based in part upon the same consciousness of the immaturity of the masses – as we have seen it was this that made him believe that ideal political constructs and political revolutions were insolvent. But he was indignant when this point of view was expressed in plainly reactionary terms of the 'people's ignorance, stupidity and brutality'.[28] And in this period he emphasised above all not the masses' incapacity for a

---

[27] 'We are deeply convinced,' he once wrote, 'that social development is possible only in full republican freedom, in full democratic equality' (quoted in Koz'min, *Iz istorii revoliutsionnoi mysli*, p. 598). But Herzen never overcame his reluctance to concentrate upon the political question. For a statement of his basic stance in the later 1860s, see XVIII, 358–65.

[28] Herzen was commenting on two articles on Russia in *The Times* by a British Member of Parliament, Grant Duff (XVIII, 47).

sophisticated political system, but their lack of interest in the entire
question and their overriding concern with the concrete issue of the
land.

Now the solution that other revolutionaries offered to the political
problem, *as Herzen saw it*, was to assume an identity of interests between
the elite and the people which legitimised the exercise of political power
by the elite. The revolution, while resting on the physical might and
democratic sanction of the people, would in fact be controlled and
ultimately governed by a small *avant-garde*. Before 1861, because of his
hopes of peaceful reform, he had not given serious consideration to this
approach. But now, after Emancipation, as *Land and Liberty* began to
take shape and the number of revolutionary pamphlets to multiply, he
faced the prospect directly. His attitude was negative. He detected an
inflated view of the role of the revolutionary elite as the people's leaders,
and a note of disdain for the people themselves. He feared dictatorial
implications behind the assumptions of even the more responsible
revolutionaries. It was this fear, the spectre of an overbearing imperious
elite, which evoked his most authentic, and seemingly paradoxical,
protest against intellectual arrogance in the name of *respect for the people*.
For all his emphasis on the backwardness of the masses in the late fifties,
this respect was no new-found trait in Herzen's thought. Evidence for it
is visible throughout his work in that decade. It embraced the lower
classes of the west as well as those of Russia. Describing at length in his
memoirs the two trials for murder in England of the French working-
class revolutionary Barthélemy, he marvelled at his strength and determination, at how 'this working man . . . had gained his true conception of
beauty and proportion, of tact and grace' (*Past*, 1087). He devoted
another chapter to the vindication of the free press and of political asylum
in England (*Past*, 1111–27). The first was symbolised by the acquittal of
Dr Simon Bernard, accused of publishing seditious material. The second
was achieved by the defeat of the Conspiracy Bill, directed against
foreign exiles. In both cases, according to Herzen, it was the working
class, 'the English people', who saved the country from 'the slur with
which the "conglomerated mediocrity"' would have disgraced it (*Past*,
1114).[29] He was impressed by the French peasants he met in England:
'broad-shouldered, well-grown, with large features, they were an utterly
different breed, not crumpled like the meagre Frenchmen of the towns,
with their thin blood and poor little beards' (*Past*, 1069). In this period of

[29] Herzen delighted in Mill's expression.

intense anti-urbanism, it was the peasant who aroused his greatest enthusiasm. Civilisation had ignored this 'strong-muscled' class 'who work in the pure air, in the sun and rain' (XIV, 173).[30] In so doing, civilisation 'saved him from vulgar half-education and left him in his original and simple poetry of life and dress, in speech and dance'. In the same vein, he refuted the view that aristocratic background and luxury are the source of creativity: 'It is strange that almost all strong people, great poets and thinkers, come not from the rich class, the wine-drinkers, but from the ranks of the workers' (XXVI, 126). If redemption was to come to the west, it was clearly from the people, however backward, that he expected it. But his attention was focused first and foremost on his homeland, and it was Russia which had provided him with the most positive grounds for this respect. For, despite his consciousness of their superstition, illiteracy and backwardness, he saw in the peasants the custodians of an ingredient which could play a crucial part in the solution of Russia's problems: communal ownership of the land. For all his sense of superiority, of 'coming from different volumes in the history of the world' from that of the people, it was their way of life which seemed to offer a way out of the social impasse. As the debate on Russia's future had intensified at the end of the fifties, he made explicit again the theme he had adopted immediately after 1848. The minority 'with amazement' saw some light coming from the illiterate people themselves, he remarked in 1859. Can this 'dumb' victim really 'bring something to the great argument, to the unsolved question, which has halted Europe [and] political economy?' (XIV, 181).

But it was after Emancipation that he gave vent to his full 'populist' protest. As the greatest publicist of socialism based on the peasant commune, and of Russia's freedom to by-pass the path of western bourgeois development, he is justly seen as the father of that broad current of pre-Marxist revolutionary thought which shared these ideas, and which Lenin called 'populist'. But in this period he foreshadowed the defining notion of that narrower 'populist' *movement* of the 1870s. According to the analysis of Pipes, who argues that it is to this movement that the name 'populist' truly belongs, the distinguishing view of the

---

[30] The blind side of Herzen's view of the future was most evident in the passage from which this quotation is drawn. He declared that the need for security had created cities, and that now that this need had passed, it was time to follow simple human instincts and prevent cities such as Moscow growing any further – 'We live in the *city of cities* – in London. Can you really believe that such nonsense has any future?' (XIV, 174).

movement was its belief in the need to subordinate the intelligentsia to
the people, to accept the basic wisdom of the people itself.[31] It was this
idea to which Herzen now gave expression. The same idea had intensified
his humility, his insistence on learning rather than teaching in the early
days of *The Bell*, and had contributed to his criticisms of complacent
liberal enlighteners. It now made him question the assumptions of
revolutionary enthusiasts as well.

Herzen expressed his idea most forthrightly in reply to Chernyshevskii's article, 'Has Not the Change Begun?', published at the end
of 1861.[32] He considered Chernyshevskii had misrepresented the people
in his stress on and approach to their backwardness, and had correspondingly exaggerated the part the elite could play in counteracting
this backwardness. Herzen's response came in 'Emancipation Fodder',
published early in 1862. He would reply, he said, to the persistent radical
attack he felt directed at him: 'From doctrinaires and progressive conservatives, from very young people seeking authority for speed . . . we
have often heard the reproach that instead of criticising the *status quo*, we
should have a programme for the future.' He pointed out that *The Bell*
had published a series of articles by Ogarev on the future of the peasantry, the army, the gentry and so forth; but he maintained his refusal to
issue 'scholastic doctrines' on constitutions and codes of law (XVI,
25–6). For, instead of devising and trying to enforce abstract theories,
the time had come for the intellectuals to be 'more humble'. He echoed the
reproof to hasty action he had given before Emancipation, but now the
emphasis was not on the hopeless backwardness of the people, but on
their right to be respected. The people's concern was for material well-
being. Even when he was most explicitly contemplating an imminent
mass rising, he laboured the point that it would be purely and simply for
the land, for the 'crust of bread', that the people would take up arms.
This revolution will derive 'from the plough, from the allotment of land,

[31] R. Pipes, '*Narodnichestvo*: A Semantic Inquiry', *Slavic Review*, XXIII (1964),
441–58.
[32] Chernyshevskii, *Polnoe sobranie sochinenii*, VII, pp. 855–89. See E. S.
Vilenskaia, 'N. G. Chernyshevskii i A. I. Gertsen o roli narodnykh mass v
osvoboditel'noi bor'be', *Voprosy filosofii*, 8 (1960), pp. 108–19, on Herzen's
reaction to Chernyshevskii's work and on Chernyshevskii's anxiety about the
apoliticism among radicals, which he feared Herzen was encouraging.
Chernyshevskii's actual position, as opposed to the view Herzen took of it,
has been the subject of many studies. See in particular, E. Lampert, *Sons
against Fathers: Studies in Russian Radicalism and Revolution* (Oxford, 1965),
pp. 168–208; Woehrlin, *Chernyshevskii*, pp. 251–7.

and without the land not one step. It will strive towards the combination, on existing popular customs, of *communal self-government* – with full ownership of the land. This approach amazes, confuses, it is unusual, it does not observe the western form, the revolutionary routine, to which revolutionary people are accustomed' (XVI, 256). But elites were always unwilling to accept the people's preoccupation. They were always convinced it is better to teach the people than to learn from it. He made the same point in the long article he wrote in the first half of 1862 on Alexander I and his adviser Karazin. Certainly, he conceded, there is a great deal we can teach the people; but it is also true that we have much to learn from them. Our civilising reformers, however, started from the false premiss that 'we know everything and the people know nothing; as though we had taught the peasant his right to the land, his communal ownership, his system, the *artel* and the *mir*' (*Past*, 1557). But the time had come for the elite to stop issuing 'the will of God' from on high like a latter-day Moses. In a characteristic metaphor, Herzen insisted that 'Manna does not fall from heaven, that is a childish story: it grows from the soil' (XVI, 27).

Herzen demanded not only respect for the wisdom of the people, but deference to their right to make their own revolution, and if necessary to make their own mistakes. 'No kind of experience or wisdom,' he remarked in 'Emancipation Fodder', 'will save a people entering into full life from deviations, set-backs, all sorts of stupidity – but at least let these stupidities *not be exactly the same*; if we are doomed to smash against the rocks, let it not be against the same one which has destroyed a whole series of schooners, boats and ships of the line' (XVI, 27). The people placed land and bread before all: this was the extent of their revolutionary consciousness. To impose the ideas, the constructs of the elite on the people, to continue 'to take the people for clay and ourselves for sculptors', was to repeat the mistakes of history, based on a profound contempt for the people (*Past*, 1557). 'The method of *enlightenment* and *emancipation* invented behind the backs of the people and binding it to *its inalienable* rights and *its* well-being by the axe and the knout, was exhausted by Peter I and the French Terror' (XVI, 27). But he feared it would be revived. When the people do not accept their abstract theories, the elite resort to political power in order to dictate to the people. This was the crime he condemned. Even when he most welcomed a rising, and most militantly expressed his support for the people taking the land, he jibed at those with an answer to the political question. In the

inflammatory summons to immediate revolution, 'Young Russia', he
saw the clearest Jacobin tendencies. He condemned it as 'a variation on
the theme of western socialism, the metaphysics of French revolution, of
political–social dreams' (XVI, 203). 'Terror,' he told the young radicals
who wrote it, 'is easy and quick, far easier than work ... it frees by
despotism, convinces by the guillotine' (XVI, 221). He urged them to
'propagate not Feuerbach, not Babeuf, but *the religion of the land* which
the people can understand' (XVI, 225). 'Young Russia' did not *in fact*
represent the mainstream of revolutionary thought in Russia at the time:
not only was it tactically out of step, but it was unusual in calling for a
dictatorship of the revolutionary minority.[33] But to Herzen it epitomised
precisely the elitism he feared in the whole movement. His protest
against it was only an extension of 'Emancipation Fodder', which, it
should be emphasised, was written *before* 'Young Russia' had appeared.
As he said in that article,

> Propagation is quiet, study is slow, but authority is quick, and
> *avant-garde* people, full of love and faith, *ordered* others to see
> in the darkness, consoling themselves, like our predecessors,
> that 'they will live together – and love one another'. The great
> underlying thought of revolution, in spite of its philosophical
> definition, of the Roman–Spartan ornaments of its decrees,
> quickly turned into police, inquisition, terror. (XVI, 28)

The crime Herzen condemned was resource to force, to the power of
central government, to impose even the most desirable ends – 'radically
altering the civic life while preserving *the powerful authority of the government*' (*Past*, 1236). He rejected the very principle of using authority to
dictate to the people. The prototype of this endeavour he saw in the
approach of Gracchus Babeuf, the revolutionary conspirator executed in
France in 1796. He had sought to seize the state machine and through it
to decree '*the restoration of the natural rights of man which had been forgotten
and lost* ... Babeuf wished by force, that is, by authority, to smash what
had been created by force, to destroy what had been wrongfully

---

[33] See Iu. V. Kulikov, 'Voprosy revoliutsionnoi programmy i taktiki v
proklamatsii "Molodaia Rossiia" (1862g.)', *Revoliutsionnaia situatsiia* (1962),
pp. 241–62, for an attempt to show that Herzen's criticisms of 'Young
Russia' were merely over immediate tactics and not over the basic question of
the relationship between the elite and the masses. But Herzen's attack on its
advocacy of terror that frees by 'despotism', on its Babeufism, was quite
explicit.

acquired.' And had he succeeded, he would have 'forced on the French his *slavery of general prosperity*' (*Past*, 1240).[34]

The fact that Herzen's retort to the revolutionaries, his inhibitions about working for early revolution, should derive both from his consciousness of the backwardness of the people *and* from his respect for them, might suggest a contorted attempt, now that the issue was forced, to conceal a more basic dislike for revolution as such. Some of his contemporaries undoubtedly suspected this. After all, most of the ardent revolutionaries of the period from 1861 to 1863 shared his sense of the backwardness of the people and also made the commune the centre-piece of their programme – and yet managed to opt whole-heartedly for the revolution. But Herzen's 'populism' (in Pipes's sense) was no timely fabrication. It was a mature and calm development of the theme he had taken up in the aftermath of 1848. Then he had foreseen a confrontation between the 'new barbarians' and the old regime which would destroy much that was dear to him as well as much that he detested. 'You are sorry for the old civilisation?' he asked in 1851. 'So am I. But the masses are not' (V, 217). In 1862, the question he asked was 'And you imagine that if one of their children [the children of the brutally oppressed peasantry] has a vibrant spirit, he will not watch with dry eyes as the lunatic asylum of our enlightenment is burned from all four sides?' (XVI, 13). But his attitude to this rejection of the old civilisation had taken on a new realism in the interval. During the 1850s his campaign to unite progressive opinion had not been conducive to elaborating an idea which would alarm the liberals. To some degree the vast difference in value and culture between himself and the peasant had been shrouded in a haze, an agreeable vision of the people becoming fully developed, of synthesising the riches of the western elite with the way of life of the Russian people. But as the government's intransigent position became clear, his campaign gave way to direct polemic with the Westernisers with whom he had worked most closely. Since practical steps acceptable to all progressive opinion could no longer be taken, the alliance was destroyed

[34] Herzen wrote this critique of Babeuf just before Emancipation, in 'Robert Owen'. The article should be compared with Dobroliubov's essay on Owen, published the previous year in *Sobranie sochinenii* (9 vols., Moscow, 1961–4), IV, 7–47. By bringing out the inevitable failure of Owen's efforts, Dobroliubov had implied the need for revolution. Herzen may well have had Dobroliubov's work in mind when he contrasted Owen's peaceful but premature endeavours with the equally premature but oppressive revolutionary method of Babeuf.

and the question of priorities, of the relative importance of civilised, cultured values and the popular way of life could no longer be shelved. And Herzen showed that he was willing to work for a society that would not be peopled by cultured and urbane men of his own stamp. The heady, almost poetic perception of 1851 gave way to a cool recognition that the new Russian socialist society, while undoubtedly fostering more justice, would not retain all that was good in the old society.

His protests against elitist arrogance were not artificially manufactured to rebuff the revolutionary leaders, to justify his inhibitions. It was in fact in formulating his attack on the liberal Westerners that he demonstrated the sincerity of his respect for the Russian peasant. Turgenev in particular made him face some of the realities of his humility before the people. Turgenev's jibe that he had replaced all the idols he denounced with the utterly conservative and blinkered idol of 'the Absolute Sheepskin' of the Russian peasant, brought him to terms with the implications of his populism. He did not simply abuse the heritage of the privileged classes. He argued rather that progression from a less to a more complete condition does not in general happen by the development of the most advanced species. This may be regrettable, but it is Nature's method. Not everything that was young and bright crossed to Rome; not all the grace of the ancient world remained in the Christian epoch; and not all that was grandiose in aristocratic Europe was preserved by the bourgeoisie. 'It is impossible, crossing from town to country, to take with one all the urban comforts – it is enough that in the town, together with them remains the ruined air, the dust and the obnoxious crush' (XVI, 10–11). This realism characterised 'Ends and Beginnings', the series of letters he addressed to Turgenev in 1862 and 1863. 'And so, dear friend,' he began, 'you will positively travel no farther; you want to rest amidst the rich autumn harvest, in shady parks which languidly wave their leaves after the long, sultry summer . . . [You prefer this to] our dreams of a future harvest from which we are separated by storms and hail, by drought and deluge, and all the hard toil that we have not yet done.' Herzen was tolerant of the preference. 'We men of European urban civilisation can, in general, live only a ready-made life. Town life accustoms us from early childhood to the fact that discordant forces are secretly balanced and kept in check behind the scenes.' We are not brought up to like what is new, wild, unformed. But he rejected the assumption that 'the actual forms of Western European life are also the heritage of mankind ... that the manner of life of the European upper classes, as evolved in the historic past, is alone in harmony with the aesthetic needs of human development, that it alone furnishes the condition essential for artistic and intellectual life' (*Past*, 1862–6). This was the introduction to a brilliant assault on the sterility of contemporary bourgeois society – that sterility which was such a strong impulse behind Herzen's populism (in both senses of the word). But the aristocratic and utopian source of his Russian socialism no longer prevented an authentic acceptance of a primitive rural society, however incongruous for an erudite gentleman living in the great metropolis of London. 'The rose,' he accepted, 'is silently fragrant, just as the nightingale sings but certainly does not smell' (XVI, 13).

Herzen's respect for the people, then, was not a function of his taste or distaste for revolution. Indeed he drew from it the conclusion – visible in his polemic with Turgenev – that the people have the right to revolt, to destroy their oppressors. And if they take matters into their own hands, so be it. His sympathies were with them. But his own commitment to revolution, his ability to throw himself into the revolutionary agitation of the Emancipation period, was inhibited by his consciousness of the backwardness of the people and his simultaneous and fundamental protest in the name of their liberty. The apparent paradox reflected the nature of his view of liberty. His commitment to it, which had found its fullest expression in the aftermath of 1848 when he had rejected restrictions on the individual to the point of anarchism, remained primary and overriding. But at the same time, in the disillusion of the fifties, he acknowledged the need for a certain degree of development before freedom could be properly exercised. As he wrote in 1860, 'I value personal freedom so highly that I do not wish to limit it by force in my own son or anyone else. But the first thing I demand for freedom is maturity and masculine strength of character' (XXVII, 25–6). The dilemma to which these two positions, held simultaneously, led him was visible in microcosm in his approach to the problem of the education of his daughters, Tata and Olga. He wanted at once to respect their self-reliance and independence, to give them their liberty, *and* to develop in them full and mature characters. 'Emancipation from the traditional morality, said Goethe, never leads to good unless the mind has grown strong,' he wrote. 'Indeed, only reason is worthy to replace the religion of duty' (*Past*, 976). He was therefore firmly committed to engendering in them this 'strength of character' essential for freedom. But he shrank

from the exercise of authority: even the temporary removal of freedom
and the use of passive obedience to achieve his end were abhorrent. He
shrank from the imposition of the will of one human being over that of
another. 'How can one acquire the necessary influence over a young
person without preaching?' he wondered. 'How can one have authority
without ordering?' In the case of his children he recognised his deficien-
cies, his 'excessive scepticism in the question of education' (XXVII, 96).
But in this case a solution presented itself: he left the painful business of
'ordering' to a governess. He had tried the same solution in Russia. He
had left the tainted use of force, of 'ordering', in the hands of the Tsar,
throwing his own energies into the unsullied work of agitation for the
progressive use of that power. Even now, in the middle of 1862, he spoke
of the possibility of 'The Tsarist power standing at the head of the
people's cause' (XVI, 225). And in the later sixties he intermittently tried
again to work through the Tsar. He would not take on the responsibility
of power, of authority over those to whose freedom he felt himself
dedicated. In his 'Letters to an Old Comrade' at the end of the sixties, his
attitude had not changed. 'One cannot liberate people outwardly more
than they have liberated themselves *inwardly*,' he told Bakunin. Meanwhile he recognised the need for the state, but would not use its power to
shape society. 'What thinking men forgave Attila, the Committee of
Public Safety and even Peter I, will not be forgiven us. We have not heard
voices exhorting us from above to fulfil destiny, nor do we hear sub-
terranean voices from below indicating to us the path to follow' (XX,
588–90).

Herzen later recalled his increasingly difficult position after Emancipation.

> At the same time as the reactionaries lifted their heads and
> called us monsters and incendiaries, some of the young people
> bade farewell, as though we had fallen by the wayside. The
> former we despised, the latter we pitied ... Like knight-errants
> in the stories, who have lost their way, we were hesitating at a
> cross-roads. Go to the right, and you will lose your horse, but
> you will be safe yourself; go to the left and your horse will be
> safe but you will perish; go forward and everyone will abandon
> you; go back – that was impossible. (*Past*, 1309–10)

After 1861 cooperation with the liberals was out of the question. If he was
to find a role, it would be in the vanguard of the revolutionary movement.
The deterioration in his relations with the younger generation during the

sixties has been described in detail by Koz'min.[35] The difference in psychological make-up between the men of the forties and the 'nihilist' generation of the sixties, as well as friction over money matters, exacerbated the estrangement.[36] Herzen's aristocratic air and life-style alienated more humble émigrés. But, as Koz'min pointed out, the central point on which their cooperation foundered was that made in the reproach addressed to Herzen's journal by the authors of 'Young Russia'.

His hopes of a gift from Alexander or some other member of the imperial family; his short-sighted reply to the letter of a man who said that the time had come to begin to sound the alarm and summons the people to rise, and not to play the liberal; his complete failure to understand the contemporary situation in Russia, his hope of peaceful revolution; his aversion for bloody deeds, for extreme measures, the only way by which anything can be achieved – has finally discredited the journal in the eyes of the republican party.[37]

It was Herzen's failure to grasp the nettle of revolution which cost him the respect of the younger generation. Once lost, it was never regained. His works were read with less and less respect, his contributions to the debates at the end of the decade were made from a position of increasing and self-conscious isolation. The circulation of *The Bell* dwindled. Attempts to resuscitate it on the Continent were unsuccessful. The final attempt to transform it into a French journal failed. It would be a long time before Herzen's inhibition at the moment of crisis would be forgiven by the revolutionary movement. When many of the ideas he had put

[35] B. P. Koz'min, 'Gertsen, Ogarev i "molodaia emigratsiia"', *Literaturnoe nasledstvo*, 41–2 (1941), 1–177.

[36] For further discussion of Herzen's relationship with the younger generation, see Carr, *The Romantic Exiles*, pp. 227–34; Lampert, *Studies in Rebellion*, pp. 253–9; I. Berlin, *Fathers and Children* (Oxford, 1973), *passim*. See also Walicki, *The Controversy over Capitalism*, pp. 10–13. Walicki explains the rift between Herzen and the younger generation in terms of the difference between their criticisms of capitalism: where Herzen's was aristocratic, that of the democratic *raznochintsy* of the sixties reflected the class standpoint of small producers endangered by the development of capitalism. As has been pointed out, Herzen was initially attracted to the commune in part precisely because of the protection it offered against 'proletarianisation of artisans and peasants'. In any case, Herzen's critique of capitalism did not inherently inhibit his revolutionary commitment – and it was his inhibition which cost him the respect of the younger generation.

[37] B. P. Koz'min, ed., *Politicheskie protsessy 60-kh gg. Materialy po istorii revoliutsionnogo dvizheniia v Rossii* (Moscow, 1923), p. 264.

forward were elaborated and propagated by Lavrov and others in the seventies, Herzen himself was forgotten. His death in 1870 went almost unnoticed; he left no party, no band of followers, and in the last decades of the nineteenth century his fame rapidly faded.

But what to the younger generation appeared an aristocratic lack of stomach for the ultimate commitment may be seen to have derived in fact from a more complex apoliticism rooted in his understanding of the state of development of nineteenth-century Russia. The regime was obdurate. But since the people were politically immature, he would not incite a wild *jacquerie*. The alternative revolutionary path, as he saw it, rightly or wrongly, involved grasping authority in the name of liberty. This he refused to do. As a result he was rendered politically ineffective. 'Who will be to blame if we don't carry anyone with us,' complained Ogarev in 1868, 'when we don't propagate in essence either revolution, or submission, or a constitution? ... I ask you seriously what we deny, and where we are going, for I cease to understand.'[38] Herzen's conclusion at the end of his life that 'we need apostles who will preach not only to their disciples but to their adversaries', in the face of regimes he knew to be antithetical in nature to his aspirations, evoked no political response (XX, 593). His role had been written out of the revolutionary drama.

[38] Quoted in Linkov, *Revoliutsionnaia bor'ba*, pp. 457–8. For Ogarev's letters to Herzen in this final period, when Ogarev increasingly found himself in greater sympathy with Bakunin than with Herzen, see the collection in *Literaturnoe nasledstvo*, 39–40 (1941), 363–573, with an introduction by Iu. Krasovskii.

SELECTED BIBLIOGRAPHY

Primary sources

Gertsen, A. I., *Sobranie sochinenii*. 30 vols. Moscow, 1954–65.

Gertsen, A. I., *Polnoe sobranie sochinenii i pisem*, ed. M. K. Lemke. 22 vols. Petrograd, 1919–25.

Gertsen, A. I., *Kto vinovat?*, introduction by S. Rozanova. Moscow, 1969.

Gertsen, A. I., *O razvitii revoliutsionnykh idei v Rossii*, commentary by E. S. Vilenskaia and V. E. Illeritskii. Moscow, 1958.

Gertsen, A. I., *My Past and Thoughts. The Memoirs of Alexander Herzen*, translated by Constance Garnett, revised by Humphrey Higgens, with an introduction by Isaiah Berlin. 4 vols. New York, 1968.

Gertsen, A. I., *From the Other Shore*, translated by M. Budberg, and *The Russian People and Socialism*, translated by R. Wollheim, with an introduction by Isaiah Berlin. London, 1956.

Gertsen, A. I., *Selected Philosophical Works*, translated by L. Navrozov. Moscow, 1956.

For letters published since the completion of the new Soviet edition of Herzen's works, see:

Mervaud, M., 'Herzen et Proudhon', *Cahiers du Monde Russe et Soviétique*, XII (1971), nos. 1–2, 110–88.

Mervaud, M., 'Six lettres de Herzen à Proudhon', *Cahiers du Monde Russe et Soviétique*, XII (1971), no. 3, 307–15.

Mervaud, M., 'À propos du conflit Herzen–Herwegh: un inédit de Proudhon', *Cahiers du Monde Russe et Soviétique*, XIV (1973), no. 3, 333–48.

Vuilleumier, M. *et. al.* eds., *Autour d'Alexandre Herzen: documents inédits*. Geneva, 1973.

Zviguilsky, A., *Alexandre Herzen. Lettres inédites à sa fille Olga*. Paris, 1970.

Chernyshevskii, N. G., *Polnoe sobranie sochinenii*, 16 vols. Moscow, 1939–53.

Confino, M., ed., *Daughter of a Revolutionary. Natalie Herzen and the Bakunin-Nechaev Circle*, translated by Hilary Sternberg and Lydia Bott. London, 1974.

Dobroliubov, N. A., *Sobranie sochinenii*. 9 vols. Moscow, 1961–4.

Dragomanov, M. P., *Pis'ma K. D. Kavelina i I. S. Turgeneva k A. I. Gertsenu*. Geneva, 1892.

Literaturnoe nasledstvo, 39–40, *A. I. Gertsen I*. Moscow, 1941.

Literaturnoe nasledstvo, 41–42, *A. I. Gertsen II*. Moscow, 1941.

Literaturnoe nasledstvo, 61, *Gertsen i Ogarev I*. Moscow, 1953.

Literaturnoe nasledstvo, 62, *Gertsen i Ogarev II*. Moscow, 1955.

Literaturnoe nasledstvo, 63, *Gertsen i Ogarev III*. Moscow, 1956.

Literaturnoe nasledstvo, 64, *Gertsen v zagranichnykh kollektsiakh*. Moscow, 1958.

Nechkina, N. V. *et. al.*, eds., *'Kolokol': Gazeta A. I. Gertsena i N. P. Ogareva*. Facsimile edition. 11 vols. Moscow, 1962–4.

Nechkina, N. V. *et. al.*, eds., *'Poliarnaia Zvezda'. Zhurnal A. I. Gertsena i N. P. Ogareva, 1855—1869*. Facsimile edition. Moscow, 1966–8.

Ogarev, N. P., *Izbrannye sotsial'no-politicheskie i filosofskie proizvedeniia*. 2 vols. Moscow, 1952–6.

Secondary sources

Annenkov, P. V., *The Extraordinary Decade. Literary Memoirs*, translated by I. R. Titunik, ed. A. P. Mendel. Michigan, 1968.

Annenkov, P. V., *P. V. Annenkov i ego druz'ia. Literaturnyia vospominaniia i perepiska 1835—1885 godov*. St Petersburg, 1892.

Barghoorn, F. C., 'Russian Radicals and the West European Revolutions of 1848', *Review of Politics*, 11 (July 1949), 338–54.

Barghoorn, F. C., 'The Russian Radicals of the 1860's and the Problem of the Industrial Proletariat', *Slavonic and East European Review*, XXI (1943), 57–69.

Bazileva, Z. P., 'Iz istorii izdatel'skoi deiatel'nosti A. I. Gertsena. (Prilozhenie k *Kolokolu* — listy *Pod Sud!*)', *Istoricheskie zapiski*, 54 (1955), 436–47.

Bazileva, Z. P., *'Kolokol' Gertsena*. Moscow, 1949.

Beliavskaia, I. M., *A. I. Gertsen i pol'skoe natsional'no-osvoboditel'noe dvizhenie 60-kh godov XIX veka*. Moscow, 1954.

Berdyaev, N., *The Russian Idea*, translated by R. D. French. London, 1947.

Berlin, Isaiah, *Fathers and Children*, Oxford, 1973.

Berlin, Isaiah, 'Herzen and Bakunin on Individual Liberty', *Continuity and Change in Russian and Soviet Thought*, ed. E. J. Simmons. Cambridge, Mass., 1955.

Berlin, Isaiah, 'A Marvellous Decade, 1838–1848: The Birth of the Russian Intelligentsia', *Encounter* (June 1955), 27–39; (Nov. 1955), 21–9; (Dec. 1955), 22–43; (May 1956), 20–34.

Berlin, Isaiah, 'Russia and 1848', *Slavonic and East European Review*, XXVI (1948), 341–60.

Blum, J., *Lord and Peasant in Russia from the Ninth to the Nineteenth Centuries.* Princeton, 1961.

Bowman, H. E., 'Revolutionary Elitism in Chernyshevskii', *American Slavic and East European Review*, XIII (1954), 185–99.

Bowman, H. E., *Vissarion Belinsky, 1811–1848: A Study on the Origins of Social Criticism in Russia.* Cambridge, Mass., 1954.

Brower, D. R., 'The Problem of the Russian Intelligentsia', *Slavic Review*, XXVI (1967), 638–47.

Brower, D. R., *Training the Nihilists. Education and Radicalism in Tsarist Russia.* Ithaca and London, 1975.

Brown, E. J., *Stankevich and his Moscow Circle, 1830–1840.* Stanford, California, 1966.

Bushkanets, E. G., 'Dobroliubov i Gertsen', *Problemy izucheniia Gertsena*, ed. V. P. Volgin *et al.* Moscow, 1963, pp. 280–92.

Cadot, M., *La Russie dans la vie intellectuelle française (1839–1856)*, Paris, 1967.

Carr, E. H., *Michael Bakunin.* London, 1937.

Carr, E. H., *The Romantic Exiles. A Nineteenth-century Portrait Gallery.* London, 1968.

Carr, E. H., '"Russia and Europe" as a Theme of Russian History', *Essays presented to Sir Lewis Namier*, ed. R. Pares and A. J. P. Taylor. New York, 1956, pp. 357–93.

Carr, E. H., 'Some Unpublished Letters of Alexander Herzen' *Oxford Slavonic Papers*, II (1951), 80–124.

Carr, E. H., *Studies in Revolution.* London, 1962.

Chesnokov, D. I., *Mirovozzrenie Gertsena.* Moscow, 1948.

Chizhevskii, D. I., *Gegel'v Rossii.* Paris, 1939.

Christoff, P. K., *An Introduction to Nineteenth-century Russian Slavophilism. Vol. I: A. S. Xomjakov.* The Hague, 1961.

Christoff, P. K., *The Third Heart. Some Intellectual—Ideological Currents and Cross-currents in Russia, 1800–1830.* The Hague, 1970.

Confino, M., 'On Intellectuals and Intellectual Traditions in Eighteenth- and Nineteenth-century Russia', *Daedalus*, 101 (Spring 1972), 117–49.

Corbet, C., 'Dobroljubov et Herzen', *Revue des Études Slaves*, 27 (1951), 70–7.

Custine, Marquis de, *Journey for Our Time: The Journals of the Marquis de Custine*, translated and edited by P. P. Kohler. London, 1953.

Davison, R. M., 'Herzen and Kierkegaard', *Slavic Review*, XXV (1966), 191–209.

Dement'ev, A. G., *Ocherki po istorii russkoi zhurnalistiki 1840–1850gg.* Moscow, 1951.

Dmitrieva, S. S., 'Protest protiv "Obvinitel'nogo akta" Chicherina', *Literaturnoe nasledstvo*, 63 (1956), 209–19.

Eidel'man, N. Ia., *Gertsenovskii 'Kolokol'*. Moscow, 1963.

El'sberg, Ia. E., *Gertsen: zhiz n' i tvorchestvo*. Moscow, 1956.

El'sberg, Ia. E., 'Ideinaia bor'ba vokrug naslediia Gertsena v nashe vremia', *Problemy izucheniia Gertsena*, ed. V. P. Volgin. Moscow, 1963, pp. 432–48.

Emmons, T., 'The Peasant and the Emancipation', *The Peasant in Nineteenth-century Russia*, ed. W. S. Vucinich. Stanford, California, 1968, pp. 41–71.

Emmons, T., *The Russian Landed Gentry and the Peasant Emancipation of 1861*. Cambridge, 1968.

Fedosov, I. A., *Revoliutsionnoe dvizhenie v Rossii vo vtoroi chetverti XIX v. (Revoliutsionnye organizatsii i kruzhki)*. Moscow, 1958.

Field, D., *The End of Serfdom. Nobility and Bureaucracy, 1855–1861*. Cambridge, Mass., 1976.

Field, D., 'Kavelin and Russian Liberalism', *Slavic Review*, XXXII (1973), 59–78.

Florinsky, M., 'Russian Social and Political Thought, 1825–1855', *Russian Review*, 6 (1947), no. 2, 77–85.

Frank, V., 'U istokov istorii russkoi intelligentsii', in *Izbrannye stat'i*. Moscow, 1974.

Gerschenkron, A., 'The Problem of Economic Development in Russian Intellectual History of the Nineteenth Century', *Continuity and Change in Russian and Soviet Thought*, ed. E. J. Simmons. Cambridge, Mass., 1955, pp. 37–88.

Gershenzon, M. O., *Istoriia Molodoi Rossii*. Moscow, 1923.

Gershenzon, M. O., *Obrazy proshlago*. Moscow, 1912.

Ginzburg, B. S., *'Kolokol* A. I. Gertsena i krest'ianskoe dvizhenie v Rossii v gody pervoi revoliutsionnoi situatsii (1859–61)', *Istoriia SSSR* (1957), no. 5, 173–87.

Ginzburg, B. S., 'Otnoshenie A. I. Gertsena i N. P. Ogareva k krest'ianskoi reforme v period ee podgotovki (1857–1860gg.)', *Istoricheskie zapiski*, 36 (1951), 187–218.

Ginzburg, B. S., 'Rasprostranenie izdanii vol'noi russkoi tipografii v kontse 1850-kh-nachale 1860-kh godov', *Revoliutsionnaia situatsiia v Rossii v 1859–1861gg.* Moscow, 1962, pp. 335–60.

Ginzburg, L. Ia., *'Byloe i dumy' Gertsena*. Leningrad, 1957.

Ginzburg, L. Ia., 'C togo berega Gertsena', Izvestiia Akademii Nauk SSSR. Otdelenie literatury i iazyka, XXI (1962), 112–24.

Gleason, A., European and Muscovite. Ivan Kireevsky and the Origins of Slavophilism. Cambridge, Mass., 1972.

Hare, Richard, Pioneers of Russian Social Thought. Oxford, 1951.

von Haxthausen, August, Studies in the Interior of Russia. Chicago, 1972.

Hollingsworth, B., 'N. I. Turgenev and Kolokol', Slavonic and East European Review, XLI (1962–3), 89–100.

Ivanov-Razumnik, R. V., Istoriia russkoi obshchestvennoi mysli. St Petersburg, 1911.

Kaplan, F. I., 'Russian Fourierism of the 1840s: A Contrast to Herzen's Westernism', American Slavic and East European Review, XVII (1958), 161–72.

Karpovich, M. M., 'Chernyshevski between Socialism and Liberalism', Cahiers du Monde Russe et Soviétique. I (1960), 571–83.

Kel'siev, V. I., Ispoved', with commentary by M. Klevenskii, Literaturnoe nasledstvo, 41–2 (1941), 253–470.

Kohn, H., ed., The Mind of Modern Russia: Historical and Political Thought of Russia's Great Age. New Jersey, 1955.

Korotkov, Iu. N., 'U istokov pervoi Zemli i voli (neopublikovannaia stranitsa iz tetradi A. A. Sleptsova)', Istoricheskie zapiski, 79 (1966), 176–209.

Koshovenko, A. E., 'K voprosu o Londonskoi vstreche N. G. Chernyshevskogo c A. I. Gertsenom v 1859g. i formule "Kavelin v kvadrate"', Revoliutsionnaia situatsiia v Rossii v 1859—1861gg. Moscow, 1960, pp. 271–82.

Koyré, A., Études sur l'histoire de la pensée philosophique en Russie. Paris, 1950.

Koz'min, B. P., 'Gertsen, Ogarev i "molodaia emigratsiia"', Literaturnoe nasledstvo, 41–2 (1941), 1–177.

Koz'min, B. P., Iz istorii revoliutsionnoi mysli v Rossii: izbrannye trudy, eds., V. P. Volgin et al. Moscow, 1961.

Koz'min, B. P., 'K voprosu ob otnoshenii A. I. Gertsena k I Internatsionalu', Istoricheskie zapiski, 54 (1955), 430–35.

Koz'min, B. P., Politicheskie protsessy 60-kh gg. Materialy po istorii revoliutsionnogo dvizheniia v Rossii. Moscow, 1923.

Krasovskii, Iu., 'Ranniaia redaktsiia povesti Dolg prezhde vsego', Literaturnoe nasledstvo, 61 (1953), 27–88.

Kucherov, A., 'Alexander Herzen's Parallel between the U.S. and Russia', Essays in Russian and Soviet History in Honour of Geroid Tanquary Robinson, ed. J. S. Curtiss. Leiden, 1963.

Kulikov, Iu. V., 'Voprosy revoliutsionnoi programmy i taktiki v proklamatsii "Molodaia Rossiia" (1862g.)', *Revoliutsionnaia situatsiia v Rossii v 1859–1861gg.* Moscow, 1962, pp. 241–62.

Labry, R., *Alexandre Ivanovic Herzen, 1812—1870: Essai sur la formation et le développement de ses idées.* Paris, 1928.

Labry, R., *Herzen et Proudhon.* Paris, 1928.

Lampert, E., *Sons Against Fathers: Studies in Russian Radicalism and Revolution.* Oxford, 1965.

Lampert, E., *Studies in Rebellion.* London, 1957.

Lenin, V. I., *Polnoe sobranie sochinenii.* 55 vols. Moscow, 1958–65.

Levin, Sh. M., 'Gertsen i krymskaia voina', *Istoricheskie zapiski*, 29 (1949), 164–99.

Levin, Sh. M., 'K datirovke novykh ogarevskikh dokumentov', *Literaturnoe nasledstvo*, 63 (1956), pp. 867–71.

Levin, Sh. M., 'K voprosu ob istoricheskikh osobennostiakh russkogo utopicheskogo sotsializma', *Istoricheskie zapiski*, 26 (1948), 217–57.

Lichtheim, G., *Marxism.* London, 1971.

Lichtheim, G., *The Origins of Socialism.* London, 1969.

Lichtheim, G., *A Short History of Socialism.* London, 1970.

Linkov, Ia. I., 'Ideia krest'ianskoi revoliutsii v dokumentakh *Zemli i voli* 60-kh godov', *Revoliutsionnaia situatsiia v Rossii v 1859–1861gg.* Moscow, 1962, pp. 263–304.

Linkov, Ia. I., 'Ideinye i takticheskie raznoglasiia v riadakh revoliutsionnoi demokratii v epoku padeniia krepostnogo prava', *Voprosy istorii*, 6 (1959), 47–68.

Linkov, Ia. I., 'Nachalo revoliutsionnoi agitatsii A. I. Gertsena obrashchennoi k narodnym massam', *Istoricheskie zapiski*, 66 (1960), 301–11.

Linkov, Ia. I., 'Osnovnye etapy istorii revoliutsionnogo obshchestva *Zemlia i volia* 1860-kh godov', *Voprosy istorii*, 9 (1958). 33–57.

Linkov, Ia. I., *Revoliutsionnaia bor'ba A. I. Gertsena i N. P. Ogareva i tainoe obshchestvo 'Zemlia i volia' 1860-kh godov.* Moscow, 1964.

Lishchiner, S. D., 'Sushchestvoval li sovet obshchestva *Zemlia i volia* pri redaktsii *Kolokola?' Istoricheskie zapiski*, 79 (1966), 259–72.

Lukashevich, S. M., *Ivan Aksakov, 1823–1886. A Study in Russian Thought and Politics.* Cambridge, Mass., 1965.

Lunacharskii, A. V., *Sobranie sochinenii.* 8 vols. Moscow, 1963–7.

Malia, M., *Alexander Herzen and the Birth of Russian Socialism, 1812–1855.* Cambridge, Mass., 1961.

Malia, M., 'Herzen and the Peasant Commune', *Continuity and Change in Russian and Soviet Thought*, ed. E. J. Simmons. Cambridge, Mass., 1958, pp. 197–217.

Malia, M., 'Schiller and the Early Russian Left', *Russian Thought and*

Politics, eds. H. McLean, M. Malia, G. Fischer. The Hague, 1957, pp. 169–200.

Malia, M., 'What is the Intelligentsia?', *Daedalus*, 89 (1960), no. 3, 441–58.

Masaryk, T. G., *The Spirit of Russia: Studies in History, Literature and Philosophy*, translated by E. and C. Paul. London, 1955–7.

Mazour, A., *The First Russian Revolution, 1825: The Decembrist Movement, Its Origins, Development and Significance*. Berkeley, California, 1937.

McConnell, A., 'Against all Idols: Alexander Herzen and the Revolutions of 1848. A Chapter in the History of Tragic Liberalism'. Ph.D. Dissertation, Columbia University, 1954.

Mervaud, M., 'Herzen et la Pensée Allemande', *Cahiers du Monde Russe et Soviétique*, V (1964), 32–73.

Meysenbug, Malwida von, *Mémoires d'une idéaliste*, translated extract in *Gertsen v vospominaniiakh sovremennikov*, ed. V. A. Putintsev. Moscow, 1956, pp. 325–74.

Miller, I. S., '"Slushny chas" i taktika russkoi revoliutsionnoi partii v 1861–1863', *Revoliutsionnaia situatsiia v Rossii v 1859–1861gg*. Moscow, 1963, pp. 147–64.

Monas, S., *The Third Section. Police and Society in Russia under Nicholas I*. Cambridge, Mass., 1961.

Nahirny, V., 'The Russian Intelligentsia: from Men of Ideas to Men of Convictions', *Comparative Studies in Society and History*, IV (1962), no. 4, 403–35.

Nechkina, M. V., 'Eshche raz o datirovke konspirativnykh dokumentov Ogareva iz "Prazhskoi kollektsii"', *Literaturnoe nasledstvo*, 63 (1956), 872–79.

Nechkina, M. V., 'Konspirativnaia tema v *Bylom i dumakh* A. I. Gertsena', *Revoliutsionnaia situatsiia v Rossii v 1859–1861gg*. Moscow, 1963, pp. 275–97.

Nechkina, M. V., 'Novye materialy o revoliutsionnoi situatsii v Rossii (1859–1861gg,)', *Literaturnoe nasledstvo*, 61 (1953), 459–522.

Nechkina, M. V., 'Vozniknovenie pervoi *Zemli i voli*', *Revoliutsionnaia situatsiia v Rossii v 1859–1861gg*. Moscow, 1960, pp. 283–98.

Nechkina, M. V., *et al.* eds., *Revoliutsionnaia situatsiia v Rossii v 1859–1861gg*. 5 vols. Moscow, 1960, 1962, 1963, 1965, 1970.

Partridge, M., 'Aleksandr Gertsen i ego angliiskie sviazi', *Problemy izucheniia Gertsena*, ed. V. P. Volgin *et al*. Moscow, 1963, pp. 348–369.

Partridge, M., 'Alexander Herzen and the English Press', *Slavonic and East European Review*, XXXVI (1957–8), 452–70.

Partridge, M., 'Alexander Herzen and the Younger Joseph Cowen, M.P. Some Unpublished Material', *Slavonic and East European Review*, XLI (1962), 50–64.

Partridge, M., 'Herzen's Changing Concept of Reality and its Reflection in his Literary Works', *Slavonic and East European Review*, XLVI (1968), 397–422.

Partridge, M., 'The Young Herzen: a Contribution to the Russian Period of the Biography of Alexander Herzen', *Renaissance and Modern Studies*, I (1957), 154–79.

Pereira, N. G. O., *The Thought and Teachings of N. G. Chernyshevskij*. The Hague and Paris, 1975.

Perkal', M., *Gertsen v Peterburge*. Leningrad, 1971.

Pipes, R., *Karamzin's Memoir on Ancient and Modern Russia. A translation and analysis by R. Pipes*. Cambridge, Mass., 1959.

Pipes, R., '*Narodnichestvo*: A Semantic Inquiry', *Slavic Review*, XXIII (1964), 441–58.

Plamenatz, J., *German Marxism and Russian Communism*. London, 1966.

Plekhanov, G. V., *Sochineniia*. 24 vols. Moscow, 1923–7.

Pokrovskii, S. A., 'O roli Chernyshevskogo i Gertsena v sozdanii revoliutsionnoi organizatsii', *Voprosy istorii*, 9 (1954), 81–8.

Porokh, I. V., *Gertsen i Chernyshevskii*. Saratov, 1963.

Putintsev, V. A., *Gertsen — pisatel'*. Moscow, 1963.

Putintsev, V. A., ed., *Gertsen v vospominaniiakh sovremennikov*. Moscow, 1956.

Raeff, M., *Origins of the Russian Intelligentsia. The Eighteenth-century Nobility*. New York, 1966.

Randall, F. B., 'Herzen's *From the Other Shore*', *Slavic Review*, XXVII (1968), 91–101.

Reeve, H. S., 'Utopian Socialism in Russian Literature: 1840s–1860s', *American Slavic and East European Review*, XVIII (1959), 374–93.

Riasanovsky, N. V., 'Fourierism in Russia: An Estimate of the Petrashevcy', *American Slavic and East European Review*, XII (1953), 289–302.

Riasanovsky, N. V., *Nicholas I and Official Nationality in Russia, 1825–1855*. Berkeley, California, 1959.

Riasanovsky, N. V., *A Parting of Ways. Government and the Educated Public in Russia 1801—1855*. Oxford, 1976.

Riasanovsky, N. V., *Russia and the West in the Teaching of the Slavophiles. A Study of Romantic Ideology*. Cambridge, Mass., 1952.

Rieber, A. J., *The Politics of Autocracy. Letters of Alexander II to Prince A. I. Bariatinskii, 1857–1864*, ed. with an historical essay by A. J. Rieber. Paris, 1966.

Ritter, A., *The Political Thought of Pierre-Joseph Proudhon*. Princeton, 1969.

Rozanova, S., *Tolstoi i Gertsen*. Moscow, 1972.

Schapiro, L., 'The Prerevolutionary Intelligentsia and the Legal Order',
    Daedalus, 89 (1960), no. 3, 459–71.
Schapiro, L., *Rationalism and Nationalism in Russian Nineteenth-century
    Political Thought*. New Haven, 1967.
Scherer, J. L., 'The Myth of the "Alienated" Russian Intellectuals: Michael
    Bakunin, Aleksei Khomyakov, Vissarion Belinsky, Nikolai Stankevich,
    Alexander Herzen'. Ph.D. Dissertation, Indiana University, 1968.
Seeley, F. F., 'Herzen's "Dantean" Period', *Slavonic and East European
    Review*, XXXIII (1954), 44–74.
Seton-Watson, H., 'The Intellectuals: Russia', *Encounter*, 24, (1955), 43–53.
Seton-Watson, H., *The Russian Empire, 1801-1917*. Oxford, 1967.
Shashko, P., 'Unity and Dissent among the Russian Westerners'. Ph.D.
    Dissertation, University of Michigan, 1969.
Shelgunov, N. V., *Vospominaniia*, in *N. V. Shelgunov, L. P. Shelgunova, M.
    L. Mikhailov vospominaniia*. Moscow, 1967, vol. I.
Shpet, G., *Filosofskoe mirovozzrenie Gertsena*. Petrograd, 1921.
Simmons, E. J., ed., *Continuity and Change in Russian and Soviet Thought*.
    Cambridge, Mass., 1955.
Skerpan, A. A., 'The Russian National Economy and Emancipation'. *Essays
    in Russian History*, eds. A. D. Ferguson and A. Levin. Hamden,
    Connecticut, 1964, pp. 161–230.
Smirnova, Z. V., *Sotsial'naia filosofiia A. I. Gertsena*. Moscow, 1973.
Squire, P. S., *The Third Department: The Establishment and Practices of the
    Political Police in the Russia of Nicholas I*. Cambridge, 1968.
Stakevich, S. G., 'Sredi politicheskikh prestupnikov' in *N. G. Chernyshevskii*
    (Moscow, 1928), p. 103.
Swart, K. W., *The Sense of Decadence in Nineteenth-century France*. The
    Hague, 1964.
Teriaev, G. V., *A. I. Gertsen – velikii myslitel', predshestvennik russkoi
    sotsial-demokratii*. Moscow, 1962.
Thaden, E. C., 'The Beginnings of Romantic Nationalism in Russia',
    American Slavic and East European Review, XIII (1954), 500–21.
Tocqueville, Alexis de, *Recollections*, translated by G. Lawrence, ed. J. P.
    Mayer and A. P. Kerr. London, 1970.
Tregenza, J. M., 'C. H. Pearson in Russia and his Correspondence with
    Herzen, Ogarev and Others, 1858–1863', *Oxford Slavonic Papers*, XI
    (1964), 69–82.
Tuchkova-Ogareva, N. A., *Vospominaniia*. Moscow, 1959.
Usakina, T. I., 'Stat'ia Gertsena "Very Dangerous!!!" i polemika vokrug
    "oblichitel'noi literatury" v zhurnalistike 1857–1859gg.', *Revoliutsionnaia
    situatsiia v Rossii v 1859–1861gg*. Moscow, 1960, pp. 246–70.
Utechin, S. V., *Russian Political Thought. A Concise History*. London, 1964.

Venturi, F., *Roots of Revolution: a History of the Populist and Socialist Movements in Nineteenth-century Russia*, translated by F. Haskell, introduction by I. Berlin. London, 1960.

Vilenskaia, E. S., 'N. G. Chernyshevskii i A. I. Gertsen o roli narodnykh mass v osvoboditel'noi bor'be', *Voprosy filosofii*, 8 (1960), 108–19.

Vilenskaia, E. S., *Revoliutsionnoe podpol'e v Rossii (60-e gody XIX v.)*. Moscow, 1965.

Volgin, V. P., *et al.* eds., *Problemy izucheniid Gertsena*, Moscow, 1963.

Volgin, V. P., 'Sotsializm Gertsena', *Problemy izucheniia Gertsena*, ed. V. P. Volgin *et al*. Moscow, 1963, pp. 43–81.

Volodin, A. I., *Gertsen*. Moscow, 1970.

Volodin, A. I., 'Iubilei Gertsena 1912g. i stat'ia V. I. Lenina "Pamiati Gertsena"', *Istoricheskie zapiski*, 67 (1960), 77–102.

Volodin, A. I., *V poiskakh revoliutsionnoi teorii (A. I. Gertsen)*. Moscow, 1962.

Vucinich, A., *Social Thought in Tsarist Russia. The Quest for a General Science of Society, 1861–1917*. Chicago and London, 1976.

Vucinich, W. S., ed., *The Peasant in Nineteenth-century Russia*. Stanford, California, 1968.

Walicki, A., *The Controversy over Capitalism: Studies in the Social Philosophy of the Russian Populists*. Oxford, 1969.

Walicki, A., 'Russia', *'Populism': its meaning and national characteristics*, eds. G. Ionescu and E. Gellner. London, 1969.

Walicki, A., *The Slavophile Controversy*, translated by H. Andrews-Rusiecka. Oxford, 1975.

Walters, F. M., 'The Peasant and the Village Commune', *The Peasant in Nineteenth-century Russia*, ed. W. S. Vucinich. Stanford, California, 1968, pp. 133–57.

Westwood, J. N., *Endurance and Endeavour. Russian History, 1812–1971*. Oxford, 1973.

Woehrlin, W. F., *Chernyshevskii: the Man and the Journalist*. Cambridge, Mass., 1971.

Zapadov, A., *Istoriia russkoi zhurnalistiki XVIII–XIX vekov*. Moscow, 1963.

Zenkovsky, V. V., *A History of Russian Philosophy*, translated by G. L. Kline. London, 1953.

Zenkovsky, V. V., *Russian Thinkers and Europe*, translated by G. S. Bodde. Michigan, 1953.

INDEX